D1526326

Bibliography and the Book Trades

MATERIAL TEXTS

Bibliography and the Book Trades

Studies in the Print Culture of Early New England

HUGH AMORY

Edited by

DAVID D. HALL

PENN

University of Pennsylvania Press

Philadelphia

10   9   8   7   6   5   4   3   2   1

Published by
University of Pennsylvania Press
Philadelphia, Pennsylvania 19104-4011

Library of Congress Cataloging-in-Publication Data

Amory, Hugh
    Bibliography and the book trades : studies in the print culture of early
New England / Hugh Amory ; edited by David D. Hall.
        p.   cm. (Material texts)
    ISBN 0-8122-3837-0 (acid-free paper)
    Includes bibliographical references and index.
    1. Book industries and trade—New England—History—17th century. 2. Book industries
and trade—New England—History—18th century. 3. Printing industry—New England—
History—17th century. 4. Printing industry—New England—History—18th century.
I. Hall, David D. II. Title. III. Series
Z473 .A548   2004   2004054962

Contents

Short Title List

Amory, *First Impressions*	Hugh Amory, *First Impressions: Printing in Cambridge, 1639–1989* (Cambridge, Mass.: Harvard University, 1989).
Bailyn, *Merchants*	Bernard Bailyn, *The New England Merchants in the Seventeenth Century* (Cambridge, Mass.: Harvard University Press, 1955).
Bond and Amory, *Harvard Catalogues*	W. H. Bond and Hugh Amory, eds., *The Printed Catalogues of the Harvard College Library, 1723–1790, Pubs. CSM* 68 (1996).
Bristol	Roger P. Bristol, *Supplement to Charles Evans's American Bibliography* (Charlottesville: University Press of Virginia, 1970).
Coll. MHS	*Collections of the Massachusetts Historical Society*
DAB	*Dictionary of American Biography*, ed. Dumas Malone (New York: Scribners, 1937).
Duniway, *Freedom of the Press*	Clyde A. Duniway, *The Development of Freedom of the Press in Massachusetts* (New York: Longmans Green, and Co., 1906).
Evans	Charles Evans, *American Bibliography*, 14 vols. (Chicago, 1903–34; Worcester, Mass.: American Antiquarian Society, 1955–59).
Fairbanks and Trent, *New England Begins*	Jonathan L. Fairbanks and Robert F. Trent, eds., *New England Begins: the Seventeenth Century* 3 vols. (Boston: Museum of Fine Arts, 1982).
Ford, *Boston Book Market*	Worthington C. Ford, *The Boston Book Market, 1679–1700* (Boston: Club of Odd Volumes, 1917).

Ford, *Mass. Broadsides*	Worthington C. Ford, *Broadsides, Ballads, &c. Printed in Massachusetts, 1639–1800* (Boston: Massachusetts Historical Society, 1922).
Hall, *Worlds*	David D. Hall, *Worlds of Wonder, Days of Judgment: Popular Religious Belief in Early New England* (New York: Knopf, 1989).
HLB	*Harvard Library Bulletin*
Holmes, *Cotton Mather*	Thomas J. Holmes, *Cotton Mather: A Bibliography of His Works*, 3 vols. (Cambridge, Mass.: Harvard University Press, 1940).
Littlefield, *Boston Booksellers*	George E. Littlefield, *Early Boston Booksellers, 1642–1711*, 2 vols. (Boston: Club of Odd Volumes, 1900).
Littlefield, *Boston Printers*	George E. Littlefield, *The Early Massachusetts Press, 1638–1711*, 2 vols. (Boston: Club of Odd Volumes, 1907).
Mass. Records	*Records of the Governor and Company of the Massachusetts Bay in New England*, ed. N. B. Shurtleff, 6 vols. (Boston, 1853–54).
Mather, *Diary*	*The Diary of Cotton Mather*, ed. Worthington C. Ford, 2 vols. (New York: Frederick Ungar, 1957).
Morison, *Harv. Coll.*	Samuel Eliot Morison, *Harvard College in the Seventeenth Century*, 2 vols. (Cambridge, Mass.: Harvard University Press, 1936).
Morison, *Intellectual Life*	Samuel Eliot Morison, *The Intellectual Life of Colonial New England* (Ithaca, N.Y.: Cornell University Press, 1956), first published in 1936 under the title of *The Puritan Pronaos*.
NAIP	North American Imprints Project of the American Antiquarian Society (a machine-readable catalogue; linked with ESTC).
NEHGR	*New England Historic Genealogical Register*
Pollard and Redgrave	*A Short-Title Catalogue of Books Printed in England . . . and of English Books Printed Abroad, 1475–1640*, 3 vols., 2d ed., rev. and enl. (London: Bibliographical Society, 1976, 1986, 1991).

PBSA — *Papers of the Bibliographical Society of America*

Procs. AAS — *Proceedings of the American Antiquarian Society*

Procs. MHS — *Proceedings of the Massachusetts Historical Society*

Pubs. CSM — *Publications of the Colonial Society of Massachusetts*

SB — *Studies in Bibliography*

Sewall, *Diary* — *The Diary of Samuel Sewall, 1674–1729*, ed. M. Halsey Thomas, 2 vols. (New York, Farrar, Straus, and Giroux, 1973).

Shipton and Mooney, *National Index* — Clifford K. Shipton and James E. Mooney, *National Index of American Imprints* (Worcester, Mass.: American Antiquarian Society, 1969).

Shipton and Sibley, *Harvard Graduates* — Clifford K. Shipton and John L. Sibley, *Biographical Sketches of the Graduates of Harvard College*, 17 vols. (Cambridge, Mass.: Harvard University Press, 1873–1975).

STC — (see Pollard and Redgrave)

Thomas, *Hist. Printing* — Isaiah Thomas, *The History of Printing in America*, ed. Marcus McCorison (1874; repr., New York: Weathervane Books, 1975).

WMQ — *William and Mary Quarterly*

Wing — Donald G. Wing, *Short-title Catalogue of Books . . . 1641–1700*, 2nd rev. ed., 4 vols. (New York: MLA, 1972–1994).

Winship, *Cambridge Press* — George Parker Winship, *The Cambridge Press, 1638–1692* (Philadelphia: University of Pennsylvania Press, 1945).

Winthrop Papers — *Winthrop Papers* (Boston: Massachusetts Historical Society, 1929–).

Wroth, *Col. Printer* — Lawrence C. Wroth, *The Colonial Printer*, 2nd ed. (Portland, Me.: Southworth-Anthoesen Press, 1938).

Introduction

The essays that are gathered together in *Bibliography and the Book Trades* describe the book culture of early New England and especially the artisans, merchants, and patrons who animated this culture, be it by arranging for books to be printed, imported, and distributed or by transforming copy into printed and (sometimes) bound books, broadsides, and ephemera. The first person to tell the story of this culture in any systematic manner was Isaiah Thomas, a Worcester, Massachusetts printer and bookseller who, late in life, published *The History of Printing in America* (1810). Many others have added to or corrected Thomas's telling of the tale, but none have done so with more exactness than Hugh Amory (1930–2001).[1] Thus it was fitting that the American Printing History Society at its annual meeting in January 2002 awarded him posthumously (the first person to be so acknowledged) an Individual Laureate Award "in grateful recognition of his services in advancing our understanding of the history of printing and its allied arts."

This was an honor he deserved. Beginning with essays he published in the late 1980s, and extending to the three chapters he wrote for *The Colonial Book in the Atlantic World* (2000), Hugh made himself the best informed and most interesting historian of printing and book-selling in early America of his generation. Although he greatly admired and drew on such predecessors as Rollo Silver, Thomas J. Holmes, and George Parker Winship, he surpassed everyone before him in his close attention to the material aspects of printed texts (physical bibliography), his ability to transform these details into a fresh understanding of printing and book-selling, and his awareness of wider economic, social, and political contexts, whether in colonial America or in Europe. An iconoclast by temperament, he excelled as well in his scrutiny of much-repeated truisms, some of them dating back to Thomas's *Printing in America*.

No less remarkable was his capacity to collaborate with scholars trained in other disciplines and marching to quite different drummers. Rarely do bibliographers and cataloguers command the attention of a broad academic audience. As Hugh remarked in a paper he delivered in May 2001, literary historians have seemed "not so much critical of as oblivious to the traditions of American bibliography," noting that the bibliographic entries in the first volume of the *Cambridge History of American Literature* (1994) omitted "a staggering number of basic references" and pointing out that, because two literary historians writing on Susanna Rowson's *Charlotte Temple* ignored the history of editions on both sides of the Atlantic[2] in favor of "an ideal, utopian text," neither was able to explain the success of the book in early nineteenth-century America.[3] Here we encounter the voice of someone who was using the tools of bibliography to rethink the field of "American literature," a voice we hear again in the essay in this collection on the Bay Psalm Book. But where collaboration blossomed in Hugh's life was in the happy setting of the "History of the Book in American Culture," a project sponsored by the American Antiquarian Society that afforded him the space and opportunity to write at greater length, and with far more attention to political and social history, than he could do in exhibition catalogues, keepsakes, talks, and festschriften. Energized by the challenges of this project, he was able to establish a point of view that drew together in a single narrative the materialities of the printed book and the practices of the book trades.

The voice of these essays is also, however, that of a bibliographer writing at a distinctive moment in the evolution of his discipline. Inheriting the assumptions and methods of the New Bibliography, Hugh was deeply affected by D. F. McKenzie's critique of those assumptions and his effort to fashion an alternative "sociology of texts." The opening essay in this collection reflects the influence on Hugh of McKenzie's analysis of writing, orality, and print as these figured in the interaction between the Maori and the English missionaries in early nineteenth-century New Zealand. "The Trout and the Milk" is charged with frustration about the definition of bibliographical "fact" that W. W. Greg and others had articulated. No less important in defining this historical moment was the emergence of "the history of the book," first in French and German and subsequently in Anglo-American scholarship. Suddenly, cultural and social historians were incorporating aspects of the book trades, together with information on authorship, literacy, and reading practices, into studies of high and low culture, the impact of the Protestant Reformation and the fashioning of the Enlightenment, the rise of commercial or "mass" culture, and the evolution of authorship and intellectual property. Was this a party to which bibliographers were invited? For Hugh the answer proved to be yes, and although certain expressions of discomfort with the history of the book float to the surface in the essays that follow, readers will also discover that his scholarship is perhaps the best sustained demonstration of how a bibliographer's attention to the materialities of a text and the specifics of book trade practices can open out into arguments that affect our understanding of authorship, reading, and writing.

That someone who began as a scholar of Henry Fielding turned his attention to the imprints of early New England and, from these imprints, to book history, was a matter of circumstances. One such circumstance was the 350th anniversary of the founding of the first printing office in North America

(1639/40) on the grounds of newly founded Harvard College, an event that Harvard's principal rare book library, the Houghton, commemorated in an exhibition for which Hugh wrote the catalogue.[4] Another was the project, to which reference has already been made, to prepare a five-volume "History of the Book in America." In December 1990 Hugh was invited to join the editorial board charged with supervising the series. A short while later he agreed to share with me the responsibility of editing and writing for the volume that would cover the colonial and Revolutionary periods, *The Colonial Book in the Atlantic World*.[5] *Bibliography and the Book Trades* contains the chapter he wrote on the New England book trades in the seventeenth century, together with four essays that have been previously published and two that are published here for the first time.

It bears reemphasizing that Hugh's point of view was grounded in physical bibliography as it was being rethought in the 1970s and 1980s. In keeping with D. F. McKenzie, to whom he dedicated "The Trout and the Milk," Hugh rejected the "quite unexamined and unjustified distinction between the 'bibliographical facts' constituted by the discipline and other kinds of facts." He insisted, on the contrary, that "collateral" or "external" evidence such as "trade records, ex-libris, rubrication dates, law suits, and literary allusions . . . have always eked out and sometimes corrected the data of the books themselves." Deploring the "hermetic tendency of bibliographical literature" and its "impervious[ness] to the social and linguistic contexts" that "generate" the "facts," he also decried the "Anglo-American obsession (not to put too fine a point on it) with authorial intention." In the same review essay from which I have been quoting, he professed his own admiration for that "host of scholars who have . . . explored the public arena of books —theatrum libri."[6]

Yet he was equally uncomfortable with historians, and especially historians of literature, who did not heed the details of physical bibliography or the practices of the book trades. He warned in 1984 that book historians were inclined to slight "the careful description . . . of material objects," and, when he came upon the term "print culture" that I was brandishing in the early eighties, derided it as meaningless. Long before we undertook our collaboration, he also singled out for derision certain statements of mine to the effect that (in his paraphrase) "physical bibliography is a thing of the past." (It is modestly comforting to note that in the same review essay he also dismissed Robert Darnton's comments on bibliography.) When Hugh ventured forth to slay such dragons, he armed himself with a relatively narrow definition of bibliography. In a review of McKenzie's manifesto of 1986, *Bibliography and the Sociology of Texts*, he worried that it "turns bibliography into a game without rules," by which he meant that McKenzie's interest in "mis-readings" and variants would leave the textual editor at sea, forever postponing the task—in Hugh's opinion, the necessary task—of deciding which variant readings to prefer.[7]

Even so, we must take seriously his admiration of McKenzie and his complaint of a hermetic narrowness. In the context of early American imprints, one object of his ire was the practice of defining the American book in strictly national (i.e., post 1776) terms. Hugh pointed to the criteria employed by Charles Evans for his *American Bibliography* (1903–55) as a key example of this tendency. Such bibliographies told us next to nothing about what was in bookstores and libraries, or what the more educated colonists preferred to read. Nor did he like Evans's practice of giving each colonial newspaper a single entry for all of the issues published in the course of a year, insisting, rather, that each should be counted as a separate item. Like others before him, he regretted that Evans did not specify the kinds of collateral evidence, such as advertisements, on which he relied for some of his titles. Not surprisingly, Hugh was able to find titles or editions that Evans had overlooked or misidentified.[8]

But the central motif of his revisionist perspective was a historically informed suspicion of bibliographies organized on national or regional grounds. Among his countering arguments was the observation that "national boundaries change and national identity is far from stable." He expressed himself somewhat fiercely on this point in a paragraph that was transposed in the course of our editorial work from the opening chapter of *The Colonial Book* to the Introduction, where it is credited to me. These, however, are his words:

Imprint bibliography . . . defines an American imprint as a book printed in the area that would one day become the continental United States. A very different picture (and a different form of bibliography) would emerge if we considered . . . the predominance of English books in the catalogues of colonial libraries, in the advertisements and sales catalogues of booksellers, and in the rather more loosely described contents of probate inventories. As another bibliographer [Thomas Tanselle] has sadly observed, Evans and [Roger P.] Bristol "[do] not tell one very much about what was being read in America, or even what was available in bookshops." Their continuation by Clifford K. Shipton and James E. Mooney tell us even less. Indeed, the *Short-Title Evans*, unlike its equivalents for England, theoretically excludes even titles that were printed abroad for sale in the national area.[9]

That he felt a larger issue was at stake was also apparent in his review of Paul Gutjahr's *An American Bible: A History of the Good Book in the United States* (1999). Here again, as in his comments on the literary historians who overlooked the bibliographical evidence for understanding *Charlotte Temple*, he remarked on the near-willful ignorance among Americanists of the British and continental book trade, noting that "there was little that textually or physically distinguished" the "national origins" of Bibles printed "on both sides of the Atlantic for publication in both" Britain and the United States and noting, as well, the inadequacies of the bibliography on which Gutjahr had principally depended.[10]

Some of the implications of Hugh's transatlantic perspective would become clear in his chapters for *The Colonial Book* and in the essays, all included in *Bibliography and the Book Trades*, that he wrote about early New England. In these he began by setting aside the made in America/made elsewhere distinction and the literary historian's preoccupation with an ideal text. Doing so enabled him to recover the rich histories and complicated materialities of practices and texts and, in doing so, to rethink a host of truisms. His analysis of the Bay Psalm Book, which follows in this book, is a notable case in point, as is the skepticism he brought to bear on the famous statement by the seventeenth-century poet-minister Michael Wigglesworth that his narrative poem *The Day of Doom* (1662) had "greater accepta[n]ce then I could have expected: so that of 1800 copies there were scarce any unsold (or but few) at the yeers end."[11]

When he turned to analyzing the stock of the Boston bookseller Michael Perry, who died in 1700, Hugh was able to address a question of considerable importance to historians of religion and culture in early New England, whether the colonial reader relied on locally printed books or on imports from England. He was willing to concede that, during the early decades of settlement, the colonists depended on the stock of books they brought with them, an observation borne out by a separate analysis of books recorded in the Essex County, Massachusetts, inventories. But the inventory of Perry's shop suggested that, by the end of the century, the situation had changed. The argument depends on calculating the annual rate of sales of locally printed books, a figure he then compared with his estimates of the number of copies of certain titles being imported from overseas. Subsequently, he extended this analysis, adding to James Raven's description in *The Colonial Book* of the importation of books in the eighteenth century "A Note on Imports and Domestic Production." For this note he figured out a method of translating weight, the unit of measure used by the English customs office, into numbers of actual books, a calculation repeated in the essay on Perry. To his satisfaction he was then able to demonstrate that during the colonial period imported books outnumbered local imprints, provided that the latter category omitted newspapers, almanacs, and the like—perhaps not the fairest basis for comparison. But the point of the exercise was really to underscore the inadequacy of imprint bibliographies limited to American production, and of the nationalism that underlay such projects.

Another aspect of this argument was the very limited market for books until nearly the end of the seventeenth century, as evidenced in books and broadsides that remained unsold and "in print" long after they were issued, or in the "old" Bibles on which the colonists relied for much of their stock of this book. I can remember my surprise when Hugh first alluded to the trade in second-hand books as an important aspect of book culture in the colonies, for I had allowed my fascination with what was being printed to obscure this aspect of the situation. Nor had I ever stopped to consider the formats of the books that people owned or how this information was pertinent to the history of reading. Anyone who uses probate inventories made after death to discern patterns of ownership and reading will find that Hugh transformed this genre of scholarship by turning his bibliographer's eye on the stock of books in seventeenth-century Essex County.

Always Hugh was attentive to the material aspects of books and manuscripts: figuring out fonts of type as these were employed by the Cambridge printers, identifying the Bible from which a tiny scrap of paper in an Indian grave site had been taken, and scrutinizing the signatures and annotations in the books collected by Thomas Prince as a means, among others, of getting at the second-hand book trade in New England. "Marks" in and on books were, for him, signs of larger structures or circumstances; they were evidence he sought to place in social and cultural context. Always, too, he protested any efforts of rare book librarians, literary scholars, and antiquarians to erase the messiness of the past by turning books into "icons."

Hugh understood printed books and broadsides as existing in sheets — that is, the printed sheets of paper that eventually were folded into various formats. Given the chance, he defined the book trade as consisting of the exchange of sheets. Quite rightly, he regarded the production of printed sheets as the most accurate measure of a printer's output. Moreover, only by counting sheets and attending, inter alia, to the differing sizes of these sheets, could the historian determine the kinds of business — the "demand" for their work — that printers were undertaking. A count based on titles or on the number of pages in books or, no less misleadingly, on the entries in a catalogue such as the North American Imprints Project, would distort in one direction or another the production of colonial printers. He demonstrated the significance of this critique by noting the large disparities between a count he made of Boston printing based on sheets with figures compiled by Thomas Tanselle and Mary Ann Yodelis using other methods. Hugh conceded that NAIP, a machine-readable revision of Evans that the American

Antiquarian Society undertook in the 1970s and 1980s, was "fuller, more accurate, and much more accessible than any of its predecessors." Nonetheless he regarded "union catalogues . . . designed as a tool for locating copies [as] of little worth" to the historian of printing, citing, among their limitations, the impossibility of measuring the extent of job printing (the ephemera that, by and large, Evans and his successors did not record) but, more fundamentally, voicing a judgment that "entries (i.e., records) cannot be equated with books, since a single book may have more than one record, and a single record may cover more than one book."[12]

Deeper feelings were at work in Hugh when he argued in "The Trout and the Milk" that Native Americans used the Bible for purposes at odds with those of the missionaries who wanted to convert them to Christianity. He was quietly uneasy with my chapter in *The Colonial Book* on readers and writers in seventeenth-century New England, feeling I had made too much of homogeneity and religion. (The difference between him and me as scholars, he remarked after he became ill, was that I was a believer and he was not.) Distant as he was in the nineties to religion, he was no less skeptical of assertions that printing was a "divine art and mystery." Nor was he sympathetic to the kindred statement, voiced by some modern scholars, that printing had a singular "logic" or was somehow linked with the rise of democracy. "Print," he declared in the penultimate paragraph of *The Colonial Book*, "represented *both* authority *and* nonconformity, the imperial center *and* the colonial periphery, the voice of the clergy *and* that of the laity . . . : how could it not, when all these different interests used it?" The final sentence of the Afterword sums up his point of view: "the uses of print are far too complexly and deeply embedded in their time and culture for such technological (or even cultural) reductionism, as we have tried to show in this volume."[13]

Still, he himself had a thesis to argue about books and book culture in early America. In his introductory chapter in *The Colonial Book*, "Reinventing the Colonial Book," he remarked on the "nexus" between language, religion, and canonicity (or "literature") in certain parts of early modern Europe. Here too, he recalled the differences between the London and "provincial" trades in England. These observations led him to note the singularities of printing and book-selling in early America: unlike the provincial trade in England, the colonists were not bound by rights to copy and had no literature or canon of their own creation. Lacking a metropolis or center, writers and printers worked in curiously "private" ways. Given these aspects of the colonial situation, he thought it more fruitful to compare the colonial trade with Irish and Scottish practices, a point, however, he made too briefly for it to be effective. We would misread his model if we thought of it as a means of reasserting American uniqueness, for he insisted throughout this chapter that he intended "colonial" to signify the constant, enclosing presence of an imperial system.

I would not pretend that the meaning of every sentence in the essays that follow is transparently self-evident. To aid those who come fresh to his work I have added headnotes to each essay indicating arguments and contexts, and made occasional (bracketed) interpolations in the notes. That Hugh sometimes became cryptic or allusive has much to do with his near-instinctive combativeness as well as the immense amount of information he took for granted. There were many battles to fight: against nationalistic imprint bibliographers, lackadaisical literary historians, the more extreme versions of the "new bibliography," and banalities emerging within the history of the book. Hence the shifts in tone that occur within a given essay and chapter, though irony was usually his weapon of choice. His independence of mind bore great fruit, for it was matched with a formidable intelligence and a fantastic knowledge of books. Such independence also came at a price, as some of his friends in the library world could testify. But in the multiple collaborations that led to *The Colonial Book*—principally his and mine, for he shared his thinking freely with me during the years we worked closely together—he found an alternative to independence that enabled him to expand his knowledge of books into something larger. I like to think that it was an alternative in which he found a pleasure equal to my own.

These essays appear here as they were published or read, save that I have filled out or added a number of citations, employed short titles and otherwise regularized punctuation, capitalization, and citations in the notes, provided endnotes for "The Trout and the Milk," and, either silently or via notes of my own, commented on or corrected any errors of fact or issues of interpretation I was able to detect. Hugh was meticulous to the nth degree in how he cited imprints and page numbers, employing brackets for dates, publishers, and pages if this information was not explicitly provided on title pages or the body of a text. Here as in *The Colonial Book in the Atlantic World*, a more commonsense approach prevails. The more challenging task has been to ensure that certain allusions are intelligible to the general reader. Thus I have sometimes provided first names or amplified a reference—for example, the allusion to "Captain Dornithorne" in "'A Bible and Other Books.'" Unaware, myself, of this Captain, I have (silently) added the words, "in *Adam Bede*."

I am grateful to the owners of copyright for agreeing to allow these essays to be reprinted; to Judy Amory for her strong support of this project; to Kenneth Carpenter, David McKitterick, and Roger Thompson for their comments on an earlier draft of this introduction, and to Alan Degutis, James N. Green, Paul Sternberg, Roger Stoddard, and an anonymous reader for the press, for assistance of other kinds. Eric Unverzagt aided greatly in preparing the texts for republication.

Notes

1. Born July 1, 1930, in Massachusetts, he earned a B.A. magna cum laude with highest honors at Harvard College in 1952, served for two years in the U.S. army, earned an LL.B. (1958) at Harvard Law School and a Ph.D. in English (1964) at Columbia University, taught at Columbia and Case Western Reserve University before moving in 1973 to the Houghton Library as Rare Book Cataloguer, retiring from this position in 1995. He regarded himself as a scholar of Henry Fielding, on whom he undertook a dissertation in English literature at Columbia University and on whom he was working up until the time of his death in Brookline, Massachusetts, on November 21, 2001. He pursued his interests in Fielding as a Munby fellow in bibliography at Cambridge University Library in 1980–81, and again as textual editor of the Wesleyan edition of the Works of Henry Fielding, in which capacity he edited two volumes of Fielding's *Miscellanies* (1993–1997).

2. Nowhere citing, for example, R. W. G. Vail, *Susanna Haswell Rowson, the Author of Charlotte Temple; A Bibliographical Study* (Worcester, Mass.: American Antiquarian Society, 1933).

3. These statements are taken from Hugh Amory, "Remarks Delivered at the Roundtable on *The Colonial Book in the Atlantic World*," American Literature Association, May 25, 2001, printed in *The Book*, 54, 55 (American Antiquarian Society, 2001).

4. Amory, *First Impressions.*

5. Ours was truly a collaborative project, so his editorial pen and voice affected the shape of every chapter.

6. Hugh Amory, "Physical Bibliography, Cultural History, and the Disappearance of the Book," *PBSA* 87 (1984): 41–47; Amory, "The Trout and the Milk: An Ethnobibliographical Talk," *HLB* 7 (1996): 50; Amory, "'Not in Amory' Either: Evans and Advertisements," in *Roger Eliot Stoddard at Sixty-Five: A Celebration* (New York: Thornwillow Press, 2000), 65. "Extraneous" appears in W. W. Greg's manifesto of 1912, "What Is Bibliography . . .?"

7. *Book Collector* 36 (1987): 413, a reference I owe to *Making Meaning: "Printers of the Mind" and Other Essays of D. F. McKenzie*, ed. Peter D. McDonald and Michael F. Suarez, S.J. (Amherst: University of Massachusetts Press, 2002).

8. See, e.g., "'Not in Amory,'" passim.

9. Hugh Amory and David D. Hall., eds., *The Colonial Book in the Atlantic World* (New York: Cambridge University Press, 2000), 7–8; further comments to this effect appear in chap. 1.

10. *WMQ* 3rd ser. 57 (2000): 450–53. He also administered another cuff at "print culture," an explanatory term for Gutjahr, but not for Hugh.

11. Amory and Hall, *The Colonial Book*, 106–8, at 107.

12. Ibid., 515; and see below, "A Note on Statistics."

13. Ibid., 484, 485.

1. The Trout and the Milk:
An Ethnobibliographical Essay

"I subjoin a few sentences taken from his unpublished manuscripts," Ralph Waldo Emerson remarked in his homage to Henry David Thoreau, "not only as records of his thought and feeling, but for their power of description and literary excellence." The very first of these sentences is the source of the metaphors of the trout and the milk that Hugh appropriated for the essay that follows: "Some circumstantial evidence is very strong, as when you find a trout in the milk."[1] A tour de force of bibliographical detection, this essay opens out into a speculative inquiry about the meaning of the Bible, be it in English or in John Eliot's translation of 1661–63 into Algonquian, to the Indians in New England, the broader issue being the relationship between the English colonists and the Native Americans they attempted to subdue and convert. In tone and substance the essay reflects the influence of D. F. McKenzie's exposure of missionary assumptions about the "literacy" of the Maori in New Zealand and the political consequences of those assumptions. And, in emphasizing the failure of the New England colonists' campaign to evangelize the Indians, the essay relies on scholarship of the 1970s and 1980s by Francis Jennings and James Axtell, especially. Readers interested in a response to these scholars should consult Richard W. Cogley, *John Eliot's Mission to the Indians Before King Philip's War* (Cambridge, Mass.: Harvard University Press, 1999), with footnotes that provide an excellent review of the literature on Indian-colonist relations.

SOURCE: *Harvard Library Bulletin* n.s. 7 (1996): 50–65. Permission to republish has been granted by the President and Fellows of Harvard College.

The title of this essay has two *bêtes noires* in view. It refers, mockingly of course, to *The Raw and the Cooked*, a book by a French Academician who, pursuing an enterprise founded by Bishop Wilkins, Leibniz, and Rousseau, holds that the knowledge to be derived from the oppositions between things is more fundamental than the knowledge founded on structures of words. Writing, which distinguishes "civilized" from "primitive" logic, may thus be seen as a colonialist instrument of enslavement, together with the falsely impressive heaps of books "entassés dans nos bibliothèques," as Lévi-Strauss invidiously describes them in *Tristes tropiques*. This position cannot fail to enrage librarians like myself.

On the other hand, my title invokes Henry David Thoreau's proof of the occasional value of circumstantial evidence: the material origins of the trout and the milk are such that their conjunction should, on mere inspection, expose the human agency that brought them together. This *mot* I take to be paradigmatic of a certain view of bibliography as a discipline dedicated to the accumulation of "facts," but impervious to the social and linguistic contexts that generated them. I am thinking here, of course, of Sir Walter Wilson Greg, who famously described our subject as "pieces of paper or parchment covered with certain written or printed signs," adding, "with these signs [the bibliographer] is concerned merely as arbitrary marks; their meaning is no business of his." Henry Bradshaw had a similar formula: "arrange your facts vigorously and set them plainly before you, and *let them speak for themselves*, which they will always do."[2] Unlike Thoreau, who correctly assumes that such conjunctions are only rarely telling, the "New Bibliography" championed by Greg, R. B. McKerrow, and Fredson Bowers places them at the center of their methodology.[3] And they posit a firm, but quite unexamined and unjustified distinction between the "bibliographical facts" constituted by the discipline itself, and other kinds of fact, for which the non-bibliographical world is more or less responsible—often less, in the dim view that these bibliographers take of their neighbors.

Not surprisingly, practitioners of neighboring disciplines in their turn have questioned, rejected, or more commonly ignored the findings of these bibliographers: even in library cataloguing, the "New Bibliography" has yet to win general acceptance after some seventy years, and its eminence within the study of literature is under challenge from a "newer" and more broadly conceived bibliography, the history of the book. I should add, to prevent misunderstanding, that I would in no way deprecate the careful description of the material objects to which I have devoted much of my life, only insisting that the "contents" of a book extend far beyond "certain written or printed signs," and that the collection and arrangement of facts is not as value-neutral as Bradshaw supposes. Raw data must be "cooked," as it were, before it can ever "speak."

Ultimately, I propose to pursue what I have called "ethnobibliography," an attempt to align my ideal with the "ethnohistory" of James Axtell and others, and to distance it slightly from what D. F. McKenzie has called a "sociology of texts." A "text," particularly the mental kind favored by French theorists, has no real location, crossing readily from one culture to another, as when Roland Barthes "reads" the *absence* of street signs in Tokyo.[4] Books, on the other hand, are almost always individual or tribal objects and as such are far more amenable to cultural or social definition. The few books that have achieved iconic status, such as the First Folio edition of Shakespeare's plays, the Gutenberg Bible, and the Bay Psalm Book, are, of course, another matter. Perhaps my profession is showing, but as a librarian I am conscious that perhaps the majority of the books ever printed have rarely been read: libraries have much in common with grandmother's attic, and a good thing too, but this fact, which forbids us to think of books as texts, in no way exhausts their cultural significance.

The occasion of this essay is a medicine bundle about the size of the bowl of a tablespoon, excavated from the grave of an eleven-year-old girl in a seventeenth-century Mashantucket Pequot cemetery in Ledyard, Connecticut. The bundle, which was associated with a bear's paw, consisted of a piece of fine woolen cloth and a page from a Bible, folded and rolled together. It was preserved by contact with an iron ladle, which converted the cloth and paper to a lump of iron salt known as a pseudomorph, because it exactly reproduces the form and structure of the original in a different material. This is my trout. The milk is the seventeenth-century culture or cultures represented by the object and the grave, which was a pagan burial. The child was laid in a flexed, fetal position, facing southwest, in the direction from which the Algonquian creator Cautantowwit or Kiehtan sent the first corn and beans, and in which he rules the underworld. What is a page from the Bible doing in this pagan site?

Bibliography, as Greg defines it, to be sure, would have no difficulty with this question: the collocation would be as meaningless as the discovery of a Bible in a trash basket, or its use as a doorstop. In much the same spirit, such bibliography has often devoted itself to erasing the obvious differences created by the provenance of the books "entassés dans nos bibliothèques" in favor of the more or less invisible similarities imbued by their original manufacture. Interest might, perhaps, center on the fact that I have been able to identify only one other copy of the Bible, at Pennsylvania State University, so that volume one of the revised *Short-Title Catalogue* could, if it had wished, have listed two locations, one copy at University Park, Pennsylvania, and the other, imperfect, in private hands, at Ledyard, Connecticut, where the pseudomorph has been reburied. These "solutions," I submit, tell us a good deal about the limitations of Greg's definition; but little else.

Beyond such responses or evasions, one might point out that the object is, or was, after all, a medicine bundle, not a Bible, and as such is not a bit out of place in a Pequot grave. The Indians, indeed, rather favored European objects for their grave goods. Just as the Iroquois might cut and forge an Iroquois breastplate from a European brass kettle, so the Pequot might use a Bible as the raw material for a Pequot object; so, in his turn, the Englishman placed the Koh-i-noor diamond in his crown jewels and the Frank attached Roman cameos to the covers of his gospel book. From the European viewpoint, the Koh-i-noor and the Roman cameos are imperial objects whose associations fit them for their new uses; the Moguls and the Romans, on the other hand, might well analogize their reuse to the top hat sported by a stereotypical cannibal king in a European cartoon. Such "entangled objects," as Nicholas Thomas calls them, have separate functions from either cultural perspective; but there is also a shared perception of the special value of the object.[5]

The Pequots' reuse of the Bible for "medicine," indeed, has a certain eerie appropriateness. "The most common native perception of arriving Europeans," James W. Bradley observes, summarizing the work of George R. Hamell, "was that of returning culture heroes, supernatural man-beings originating from beyond the world's rim and offering the substances of 'power' from the Under(water) World."[6] In particular, the natives were aware of and impressed by the power of print. In Rhode Island, among the Narragansetts, Roger Williams reported their awe: "when they talke amongst themselves of the *English* ships, and great buildings, of the plowing of their Fields, and especially of Bookes and Letters, they will end thus: *Manittôwock* They are Gods."[7] "We who take literacy and printing so much for granted," adds James Axtell, "may have difficulty recapturing the sense of wonder, the almost totemic reverence, engendered by a tribal, exclusively oral person's first encounter with a book"; and he cites Father Sagard, reporting how the Hurons lingered over the Jesuits' books: "they were satisfied with counting the leaves of our books and admiring the pictures in them, and that with such close attention that they paid no heed to anything else, and would have passed whole days and nights over them if we had allowed them to do so."[8] Father Sagard might almost be describing an Anglo-American bibliographer. Don McKenzie notes reports of similar cases from among the Maori: "Many people who know not a letter wish to possess themselves of a copy of the translated Scriptures because they consider it possesses a peculiar virtue of protecting them from the power of evil spirits."[9] Few seventeenth-century persons, whether European or Indian, indulged the view, so popular in the nineteenth century, that the invention of printing promoted the diffusion of useful knowledge and innocent pleasure. For most of them, as for our present-day literary theorists, print was about power: God invented writing, says Father Sagard, when he handed down the law. A New Englander who believed that the possession of a Bible made him invulnerable to Indian attack was unwise, as it proved, but not, I think, unrepresentative.

We need not doubt, then, that the makers of the Pequot medicine bundle might attribute a sort of talismanic power to the printed or written word. Here I am irresistibly reminded of Lévi-Strauss's little "leçon d'écriture" in *Tristes tropiques*, adduced to prove his belief that writing is an instrument for enslaving helpless illiterates, to which I have already alluded. Here he tells of a Nambikwara chief who intuited this truth and seized on it to enhance his power. First the chief drew a series of squiggly lines on a piece of paper, anxiously testing their effect on the anthropologue, who "innocently" pretended to understand. Thus primed, the chief proceeded to "read" his document to the tribe, as a record of a series of gifts that he had elicited from Lévi-Strauss, who, of course, then failed to deliver. Jacques Derrida has demolished this anthropological man of straw in his *De la grammatologie*, and there is no need to repeat his criticisms here; but surprisingly, neither he nor Lévi-Strauss notice that the chief was trying to enslave the colonialist. The anthropologue's perfidious refusal to honor the power of the squiggly lines is a piece of Eurocentric arrogance: the Nambikwara chief actually lost status by his little fraud when his colonialist "friend" failed to play the game.

In short, and obviously enough, one would have thought, the power of writing rests on a social pact: it is not inherent in technology. The Indian perceives writing as "medicine" or pure, undifferentiated power because he does not grasp the European pact that creates it, but to exercise power over the Indians requires another, separate pact that is invisible to Europeans in their turn. The European and Indian cultures are intricately entangled, and to make sense of them would require more than the Musée de l'Homme in Paris, where Lévi-Strauss deposited his loot. One would need a museum with separate entrances and exits for every culture in it, connected by a maze of exhibitions whose only clue was an ever-changing concept of cultural authenticity: something akin to a library, I believe. Such I cannot provide, but it is time to take a closer look both at the materials represented by the pseudomorph, and at the cultures that produced them.

1. The Milk

The history of the Pequots is an astonishing tale of genocide and reintegration. They are often remembered today as the earliest of the New England tribes that the Europeans extirpated. In reprisal for the mysterious death of a wampum trader, the Europeans attacked in 1637, slaying some four hundred women, old men, and children when the warriors were away. Such captives as they took were sold into slavery in Bermuda, or to the more cooperative tribes of the Narragansetts and the Mohegans. The Treaty of Hartford in 1638 officially ended the "war," imposing a heavy tribute of wampum on the remaining Pequots and suppressing the very name of the tribe, who would henceforth be known as the Mashantucket or "Western" Indians. As a people who were legally as extinct as the ancient Medes, their suppressed identity would later provide Herman Melville with a splendidly poignant name for the doomed vessel of Captain Ahab.[10]

In 1666, Governor John Winthrop of Connecticut settled the remaining Mashantuckets on a reservation of about 2,000 acres near New London, in what is now Ledyard, Connecticut. There they have remained ever since, in dwindling numbers, at first producing wampum for the colony, and later farming. The size of the reservation steadily diminished until 1856, when the State of Connecticut sold off 600 acres for a trust fund, leaving only 204 acres for the Pequots to live on. By the twentieth century, the numbers of the tribe were reported as between twenty-six and forty, and their trust capital amounted to only a few thousand dollars, but they hung on, led by two determined half-sisters, until 1970, when the victory of the Penobscots against the State of Maine finally changed the odds. The reservation then had only nine full-time inhabitants. Since that time, they have vindicated their tribal status in the federal courts, which renders the sale of their land illegal and exempts them from the jurisdiction of the State of Connecticut. The main advantage of this ruling is that Connecticut law forbids gambling, which thus becomes an Indian monopoly: in the first twenty-eight months of its operation, Foxwoods, the Pequot casino, grossed over thirty million dollars. With $900,000 compensation for the land that Connecticut illegally sold in 1856, the tribe have now enlarged the reservation to its original size, their numbers have grown to over 150 persons, and they have reassumed their original name. More important for my talk, they have launched a project to recover their history and archaeology under the direction of Professor Kevin McBride of the University of Connecticut, who turned up the pseudomorph that I am hoping to explain.

Apart from some half-hearted attempts by the Mayhews from Martha's Vineyard, no one evangelized the Pequots before about 1720. Sarah Kemble Knight, traveling from Boston to New York in 1704, reported that they were "the most salvage of all the salvages of that kind that I had ever Seen: little or no care taken (as I heard upon enquiry) to make them otherwise."[11] Like the "praying Indians" of Massachusetts Bay, New Plymouth, and Martha's Vineyard—variously known as Massachusetts, Nipmucks, Pokanokets, and Wampanoags—the Pequots spoke a dialect of Algonquian, and in theory, at least, John Eliot's translation of the Bible was accessible to any of them who could read or hear it read. The savage repression they had recently experienced may have been reflected in the wealth of grave goods the Pequots laid in their graves, but it was a practice that continued among the "praying Indians" as well.

Their so-called savagery was not the product of any real isolation from the Europeans, however; on the contrary, the Pequots and other tribes along Long Island Sound were the principal manufacturers of wampum, which served both the English and the Dutch as a local currency. Originally an item of ceremonial or ritual exchange, wampum gradually enabled a triangular trade between the colonists, the Pequots who made it, and the Iroquois, who controlled access to the beaver skins that were North America's most profitable export. The trade was partly driven by ecological change, as the beaver along the Merrimac and in Maine were hunted out, and the free-range cattle and swine introduced by the colonists replaced the deer that had once provided the Pequots with clothing; but the Indians also actively sought European products: iron tools and weapons, copper pots, glass beads, and cloth. Not all the wampum, moreover, was an article of trade. Under the Treaty of Hartford, and by other forms of extortion, the tribe paid over 21,000 fathoms of wampum in tribute and fines between 1661 and 1664: that is almost seven million beads, worth £5,000, for which the Pequots received nothing in exchange.

The presence of woolen cloth, iron ladles, and other such European trade goods in a pagan Indian grave should therefore come as no surprise, unless it be that the exploited people were able to afford them: the ritual animal hide that had formerly covered the deceased had become a woven blanket. The Bible fragment, however, is highly unusual: the only New England parallels I know of are a fragment of an engraved "Ecce Homo" (Figure 1) and some leather book covers, both from Narragansett graves. The image, about the size of a quarter, had probably been cut from a larger engraving, and was bound between two pieces of mica, apparently for use as a locket; it was found in the grave of a Narragansett child in North Kingston, Rhode Island. Versions of the scene were engraved after Lutherans like Matthaeus Merian as well as Catholics like Josse Andries during the seventeenth century, but New England's iconoclasts would have had no truck with either. Like the so-called "Jesuit rings" found in the same sites, the image probably came from Catholic missions in Maine, New York, or Canada.

Though scanty almost to vanishing, the evidence enforces the connection between print and religion that has been a constant in European contact with exotic cultures, and which is largely "overwritten" by the more abundant, muter evidence of cloth, beads, and pots—objects that do not "speak" to us, though they may have been equally vocal to the Indians. Wooden horses of all kinds there have always been, such as the clocks and astronomy that the Jesuits dangled before the Chinese in the seventeenth century, but the earliest wholly sincere attempt to interest an alien in secular western intellectual culture is probably the musical offerings dispatched aboard the space probes Voyager I and II (1977). Our two examples are additionally important because, for once (or twice), they bear on how the Indians appropriated the

Figure 1. "Humilitas," by Matthaeus Merian; detail of the title page of *Nouitestamenti D. N. Iesu Christi . . . historiæ* (Franckfurt, 1627). Courtesy of the Department of Printing and Graphic Arts, Houghton Library, Harvard University. The approximate extent of the Narragansett fragment is indicated by the superimposed oval, but the original was cut from a different engraving of the same subject, which I am unable to identify. "Christ is invariably represented wearing the emblems of kingship with which the mocking soldiers had earlier invested him: the crown of thorns and a purple or red cloak; he may also hold a reed scepter. His wrists, often crossed, are usually tied with a cord or chain and he may have a rope knotted round his neck"— James Hall, *Dictionary of Subjects and Symbols in Art*, rev. ed. (New York: Harper and Row, 1979), "Ecce Homo." The similar iconography of "The Man of Sorrows" adds stigmata; the bucket at Christ's feet, containing the instruments of his torturers (the "arma Christi"), is Merian's embellishment of the tradition.

Bible, not on the more familiar tale of how the missionaries imposed it on their alien subjects. The finely woven cloth and the printed fragment of the Pequot girl's medicine bundle have Indian as well as European "powers," though their Indian "power" is less obvious to us than that of the bear's paw buried with them. But it is time to examine the pseudomorph itself: we have some idea of the milk; let us catch our trout.

2. The Trout

On the back of the pseudomorph we may distinguish some four layers of the original bundle, the bands of light and dark, corresponding, I suppose, to the dark cloth and white paper that were folded together. The manner of folding remains obscure—whether quarto, accordion, or some other pattern—but certainly the bundle was not just crumpled together. The original investigator, Dr. Linda Welters, an authority on textiles at the University of Rhode Island, was examining the bundle under a microscope when a piece of the "cloth"-layer broke away, revealing about six partly legible words. These she drew and sent this remarkably faithful drawing (Figure 2) with a murky microphotograph to the American Antiquarian Society, which referred the problem to me (I had recently given a talk there on American copies of the Bible). Responding to the syllable "sal-," which she correctly guessed was the first syllable of "salvation," Dr. Welters proposed that the text was Biblical, but she was unable to identify it further. Luckily, I happened to read the first two words as "new song," and this directed my attention immediately to the Psalms, where, with a concordance, I fairly soon identified the text as the opening of Psalm 98. In the Authorized Version, as here, it reads "O sing unto the Lord a new song, for he hath done marvellous things." After Dr. Welters announced her discovery at a Winterthur conference, the assembled congregation rose and chanted the entire text. This response may be prematurely Eurocentric in its assumption that the significance of the discovery lies in its textual contents. More important than the text, at least to a bibliographer, is the edition; Greg got that much right, at least, though he strangely ignores the inquirer's ordinary point of departure.

The apparent size of the type is nonpareil, i.e., 20 lines of it, if we had them, would measure about 41 mm. This size normally appears in Bibles of octavo or under, which we may call "small-format Bibles" for short. The text of such Bibles has been regularly laid out in two columns since the twelfth century, and in seventeenth-century English Bibles these columns are usually separated by a rule. Part of such a rule appears to the right of the text, facing the last two lines (the upper half being hidden by a deposit of calcite). Two line-endings are visible, and one may be confidently inferred. My initial assumption, then, which turned out to be false, was that we had a fragment from the left-hand column of a page; I was uncertain of the "rule" at first, which I supposed might equally well be the two-line initial "I" at the beginning of Psalm 101, in the second column. On that assumption, one could readily infer the layout of the whole page. The size of the type was also doubtful, since it seemed to me that the paper might well have expanded or stretched in the presence of moisture and its metamorphosis into iron oxide. 20 lines of

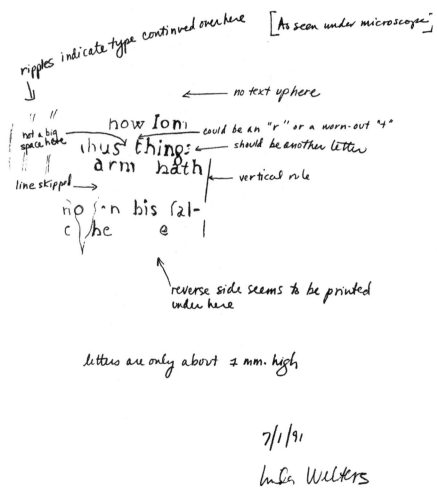

Figure 2. Transcript of the pseudomorph's text, by Linda Welters. American Antiquarian Society.

pearl, the next size smaller type, measure about 32 mm., and the difference over the few lines preserved by the pseudomorph would only amount to 2 mm. With these misgivings, I prepared a reconstruction of the text, indicating missing or obscured letters (Figure 3), and circulated it to the hapless librarians of the principal Bible collections: Ms. Katharine Kominis, of the Zion Research Collection, at Boston University; Dr. Peter J. Wosh, of the American Bible Society, in New York; and the Rev. Alan F. Jesson, of the British and Foreign Bible Society, whose collections are now housed in Cambridge University Library. I also dunned Dr. Brian McMullin of Monash University (Victoria), who was then at work at Cambridge University Library on a bibliography of early English Bibles.

Ex ungue leonem, says the proverb. It is an article of faith among bibliographers that you can identify even a fragment of an edition during the hand-press period (ca. 1450-b. 1820) by its "setting," i.e., the position of the words and letters relative to one another and to the page. The severest test of this dogma comes in frequently printed books like the Bible, where whole editions may be line-for-line the same, and individual copies often intermix the sheets of different editions. Such *zwitterdrucke* or "hybrid editions," as they are known, come about when the original publisher adds fresh stock to the solera of sheets in his warehouse, or when some later second-hand bookseller "perfects" an imperfect copy (Francis Fry, whose collection came to the British and Foreign Bible Society, was famous for this). When a fragment consists of only six words, one may well be diffident of one's trade. Furthermore,

Reconstructed text

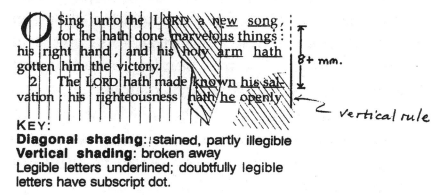

KEY:
Diagonal shading: stained, partly illegible
Vertical shading: broken away
Legible letters underlined; doubtfully legible
letters have subscript dot.

Figure 3. Reconstruction of the Bible fragment, identifying the text (Ps. 98:1–2), by Hugh Amory.

as Brian McMullin informed me, Bibles were already being printed by a stereotype process in the seventeenth century. If my Bible had been so produced, I could only hope to identify the plates, with some chance of knowing the period of their use; a very chancy proposition, since the plating of the text often meant that the imprint date itself remained unchanged.

I accordingly launched my plea without much hope of success, and spent the interim examining Bibles at Harvard, the Boston Public, and the New York Public libraries. My colleagues nobly reported back, confirming my pessimism: they had examined a total of some hundred small-format editions printed between 1660 and 1720, none of which matched my reconstruction. I am particularly grateful for the assistance of Dr. McMullin and the Rev. Alan Jesson, who had the heaviest burden. In fact, these findings proved more material than any of us suspected. Our *sondage* into the ocean of print represented by these libraries established, I believe, that Bibles with the line-endings represented by my reconstruction were surprisingly rare. In fact, my own research initially encountered only two such Bibles: one, whose time and columniation did not match my reconstruction; and another, at the New York Public where Psalm 98 was set in the right-hand column, so that there was no rule to the right. The New York Public edition is not in the revised edition of Wing, but the pre-1956 edition *National Union Catalogue* reported another copy at Pennsylvania State University (Nbi 0002965). On the off-chance that the second copy might be wanting leaf X3, I wrote off to Penn State, and the librarian, Charles W. Mann, reported that it was, in fact, another edition, with a border of rules around the pages. This was the only exact match I have found to date (Figure 4).

The text of the two editions seems to have been printed from the same setting of type, apart from the border of rules, but their title pages are entirely reset, within different woodcut borders. The New York Public edition has an illustrated title-page signed "Ioh. Pistorius" (a Dutch engraver), showing Moses, Aaron, and a view of London fallaciously designed to support the truth of the imprint; the Penn State edition has an architectural title-border, with the engraved motto "Cor mundum crea in me Deus Ps 51." Both editions were ostensibly printed in London by Christopher Barker in 1669 and 1679–80, respectively, but since Barker had died in 1599, these imprints are transparently false; both were probably printed in Holland. The signature of "Adam Ouldam 1679" on the front flyleaf of the Penn State edition presumably represents his date of purchase, in 1679 or early 1680 (Old Style). I have not been able to identify either Adam Oldham or the next possessors of the Bible, the Ferrer family.

Piratical Dutch editions were common in the English trade before the *this* generation, and said, It is a people that do erre in their heart, and they have not known my wayes.

11 Unto whom I sware in my wrath, that they should not enter into my rest.

PSAL. XCVI.

1. *An exhortation to praise God,* 4 *for his greatnesse,* 8 *for his kingdome,* 11 *for his generall judgement.*

O Sing unto the LORD a new song: sing unto the LORD all the earth.

2 Sing unto the LORD, blesse his name: shew forth his salvation from day to day.

3 Declare his glorie among the heathen, his wonders among all people.

4 For the LORD is great, and greatly to be praised: he is to be feared above all gods.

5 For all the gods of the nations are idols: but the LORD made the heavens.

6 Honour and majestie are before him: strength and beauty are in his sanctuary.

7 Give unto the LORD (O ye kindreds of the people) give unto the LORD glorie and strength.

8 Give unto the LORD the glory due unto his name: bring an offering and come into his courts.

9 O worship the LORD in the beautie of holinesse: fear before him all the earth.

10 Say among the heathen, that the LORD reigneth: the world also shall be established that it shall not be mooved: he shall judge the people righteously.

11 Let the heavens rejoyce, and let the earth be glad, let the sea roar, and the fulnesse thereof.

12 Let the field be joyfull, and all that is therein: then shall all the trees of the wood rejoyce.

13 Before the LORD, for he cometh, for he cometh to judge the earth: he shall judge the world with righteousnesse, and the people with his truth.

PSAL. XCVII.

1 *The majestie of Gods kingdome.* 7 *The church rejoyceth at Gods judgements upon idolatrie.* 10 *An exhortation to godlinesse and gladnesse.*

THe LORD reigneth, let the earth rejoyce: let the multitude of isles be glad thereof.

2 Clouds and darknesse are round about him: righteousnesse and judgement are the habitation of his throne.

3 A fire goeth before him, and burneth up his enemies round about.

4 His lightnings enlightned the world: the earth saw and trembled.

5 The hils melted like wax at the presence of the LORD: at the presence of the Lord of the whole earth.

6 The heavens declare his righteousnesse: and all the people see his glorie.

7 Confounded be all they that serve graven images, that boast themselves of idols: worship him all ye gods.

8 Sion heard, and was glad, and the daughters of Judah rejoyced: because of thy judgements, O LORD.

9 For thou LORD, art high above all the earth: thou art exalted far above all gods.

10 Ye that love the LORD, hate evill, he preserveth the soul of his saints, he delivereth them out of the hand of the wicked.

11 Light is sown for the righteous, and gladnesse for the upright in heart.

12 Rejoyce in the LORD, ye righteous: and give thanks at the remembrance of his holinesse.

PSAL. XCVIII.

1 *The Psalmist exhorteth the Jews,* 4 *the Gentiles,* 7 *and all the creatures to praise God.*

¶ A Psalme.

O Sing unto the LORD a new song, for he hath done marvellous things: his right hand, and his holy arm hath gotten him the victorie.

2 The LORD hath made known his salvation: his righteousnesse hath he openly shewed in the sight of the heathen.

3 He hath remembred his mercie and his truth toward the house of Israel: all the ends of the earth have seen the salvation of our God.

4 Make a joyfull noise unto the LORD, all the earth: make a loud noise, and rejoyce, and sing praise.

5 Sing unto the LORD with the harp: with the harp, and the voice of a psalme.

6 With trumpets and sound of cornets make a joyfull noise before the LORD, the King.

7 Let the sea roar, and the fulnesse thereof: the world, & they that dwell therein.

8 Let the flouds clap their hands: let the hills be joyfull together.

9 Before the LORD, for he cometh to judge the earth: with righteousnesse shall he judge the world, and the people with equity.

PSAL. XCIX.

1 *The Prophet setting forth the kingdome of God in Zion,* 5 *exhorteth all, by the example of forefathers, to worship God at his holy hill.*

THe LORD reigneth, let the people tremble: he sitteth between ý cherubims, let the earth be mooved.

2 The LORD is great in Zion, and he is high above all people.

3 Let them praise thy great and terrible Name; for it is holy.

X 3   4 The

Figure 4. The Holy Bible (1669–80), O.T. sig. X3r, showing the setting of Ps. 98:1–2; in this state, it is enclosed in rules. Reproduced with the permission of Rare Books and Manuscripts, the Pennsylvania State University Libraries.

emergence of the Oxford Bible Press in the 1680s, and a date around 1680 corresponds well with the date of burial, which at present is estimated between 1660 and 1720. Mercy Bruyning (or Browning), one of the main Dutch distributors of these editions, had a son selling books in Boston. We know that the Boston merchant John Usher was importing Dutch editions of the English Bible ca. 1675–80, including some stereotyped 18mos with an engraved imprint "Cambridge 1648," but printed by Joachim Nosche of Amsterdam in the 1670s. Copies are found bound with editions of the Bay Psalm Book printed "for Hezekiah Usher of Boston [or 'Bostoo']," evidently a false imprint, since Hezekiah, John's father, had left off trade in 1669. The importation of these editions into New England, then, is certain, though how the Pequot fragment came into their hands can only be conjectured, and the rest of my talk must be largely, as is now the fashion, historical fiction.

3. Ethnobibliography

Small-format Bibles have a well-established pattern of use and possession that bears significantly on the meaning of our fragment. The Bible is one of the few seventeenth-century texts available in multiple formats and sold at a wide range of prices, which makes the format an expressive index of the text's reception. In general, folios were designed for liturgical use, on a lectern. Since New England Congregationalists did not read Biblical "lessons," however, such folios tended to be used for study and annotation, for which the ampler margins suited them. Their expense restricted this application to the wealthy and powerful, typically ministers, who were among New England's elite. Quartos were the format of choice for family Bibles: they were large enough to be visible to the neighbors in the downstairs parlor, as proof of the family's godly status; their glosses and illustrations (particularly in the Geneva version) benefited the uninstructed paterfamilias; and they were regularly used to record the success of the husband and wife's sexual activity. By 1640, the modern, authoritative text of the King James Version was available in all formats, whereas the older (and thus more familiar and beloved) Geneva Version was restricted to quarto.

Small-format Bibles, on the other hand, are typically personal possessions. They rarely have the marginal apparatus found in the larger formats, and the text usually omits the Apocrypha, which Calvinist theologians had rejected. How much these Bibles were actually read is certainly a question: pearl and even nonpareil type is wearisome in quantity; spectacles were primitive; and candlelight was dim. Their cheapness, portability, and small print were better suited to the junior members of society, whose eyes were good, or to "preachers' Bibles" for the brief citation of the minister's text. A well-known

Figure 5. Richard Mather, by John Foster, c. 1670–75. Courtesy of the Houghton
Library, Harvard University.

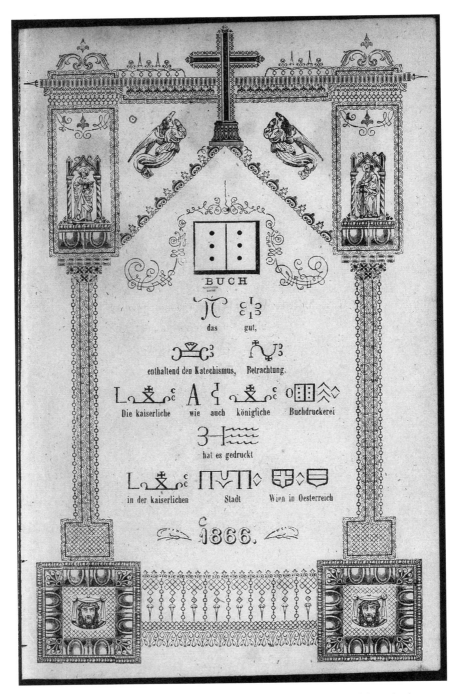

Figure 6. *Buch das gut* (Wien, 1866); a printed version of Micmac hieroglyphs devised for the Franciscan Recollect mission in the seventeenth century. Courtesy of the Houghton Library, Harvard University.

seventeenth-century portrait of Richard Mather shows him holding a small-format Bible in one hand and grasping a pair of spectacles in the other, having just announced his text to the congregation (Figure 5). Incidentally, the portrait also demonstrates how easily one may recognize a Bible, even if the text (here represented by cross-hatchings) is quite illegible. The Bible is one of the few small books in the seventeenth century that is regularly printed in two columns; not that anyone has ever doubted what Richard Mather was holding, but it is nice to be able to show that even pre-literates could be certain of what they had. They might even have distinguished a Protestant Bible, in two columns, from a Catholic Bible, in one, as portrayed in a Micmac hieroglyph (Figure 6).

The bindings of small-format Bibles also reflect their use. Particularly on the smallest, in 18mo and 24mo, we find red or black morocco, gilt, with silver clasps and gilt or gilt-and-gauffered edges. Such splendid objects are obviously meant for show, as part of Sunday go-to-meeting dress; indeed the binding is more valuable than the book. The owner may dutifully open them to the preacher's text, but then, having read or heard read the verses to be expounded, he or she will close and clasp the volume until the next Sunday. So, one imagines, will the preacher, who has probably recited his text from memory in any case. As we would expect, multiple copies of the Bible are often recorded in seventeenth-century New England inventories, because the various formats serve for different occasions. The family Bible is really too cumbersome to take to church, the red morocco binding may be too painfully gaudy for poor Aunt Hester, and Mr. Chillingworth seems to have misplaced his, dear. For literate and preliterate alike, then, small-format Bibles serve as tokens of Biblical knowledge, acquired for the most part in the larger formats or orally.

Such considerations are our only guide in conjecturing how an English Bible came into Indian hands. Bibles were certainly not ordinary items of trade, and it is hard to imagine the motives for a gift: the object was personal to its European owner, and the language, script, and ideology were all potential obstacles to Indian interest. The cloth with which the leaf is folded, moreover, is not the coarse duffle that the Europeans ordinarily sold to Indians; it is the finest bit of web in the cemetery. Its color can no longer be determined, but it is dark, and the Indians preferred to trade for bright colors, usually red or blue. The association of the cloth and the leaf, then, rather tells against a commercial origin.

If we can rule out gift or purchase, the initial transfer of these goods to Indian hands was probably hostile. By 1660, the Pequots were "pacified" and no longer raided their European neighbors or counted coup by taking their possessions, apart, perhaps, from the odd stray damage-feasant cow or hog that invaded the Pequot crops (of which, indeed, they complained to the Connecticut authorities). One rather suspects that the materials were looted by Mohawk war parties or bands of Wampanoags during King Philip's War. A Narragansett Indian, for example, supplied Mary Rowlandson with a Bible he had taken in a raid on Medfield, "a wonderful mercy of God" to her in her captivity. I like to think that the cloth originally belonged to the sleek black pelt of a beast like Richard Mather, who urged Saul's slaughter of Amalek as justification for the Pequot "war."[12] You may remember that the Lord, or rather his prophet Samuel, commanded Saul to "slay both man and woman, infant and suckling, ox and sheep, camel and ass" (1 Sam. 15:3); and when Saul temporarily demurred at this senseless destruction, the Lord repented that he had ever made him king of Israel. Well! Not that the Pequots were necessarily aware that the Bible was so intimately connected with their destiny, but the cloth is as central a feature of Mather's portrait as the Bible: not for nothing were the English clergy commonly designated as "the cloth" or the Jesuits as the "black robes." Black had long been the color of high-status clothing.

However the Indians may have acquired their copy, they proceeded to incorporate it into their culture by sharing it about. Unlike the Europeans, who could share the Bible by reading it aloud, the Indians—excluded by the double barrier of language and script—could only pass the leaves around; so today, some European bibliophile may fondle an illegible leaf from an Eliot Indian Bible, acquiring its mana. Don McKenzie cites examples of Maoris who rolled up leaves of the Bible and stuck them in their ears or used them for wadding in muskets, as an extra bit of power behind the shot.[13] The merely personal religious token becomes a communal possession: the insulation is stripped from the religious wires so that a number of individuals are empowered.

Part of the cultural baggage we inherit from the Reformation is the assumption that one must be literate to "know the Bible," which can be true, at best, only at the level of an individual. A culture is not "literate" or "illiterate" as such: though we are accustomed to speak of "print culture" and "book culture," these compounds are best understood (like "printing press" or "bookshop") as summarizing the effect of the culture on its own creations. The "uses of literacy," in Richard Hoggart's phrase,[14] are various and unevenly distributed among Europeans and Indians alike according to their own cultural norms. Mary Rowlandson's captors included some who quoted the Bible in English (the only language she understood) and one who had printed it in Indian; others, perhaps, knew only what it was for or what it looked like.[15] In these respects, Nov-Anglia and Algonquia differed only in degree. We need not understand a technology in order to "make it work," as our experience of an "electronic revolution" should remind us: the mere possession of a Bible or a part of a Bible "worked" for Christian and pagan alike, even if the Christians demanded literacy and the pagans did not.

More is involved here than a contrast between Puritan *gesellschaft* and Pequot *gemeinschaft*. Private property, indeed, never had much meaning for the Indians (hence the proverbial "Indian givers"), and we should not even assume that the medicine bundle belonged to the Indian girl during her life. On the contrary, it was probably given after her death, but grave goods, which are permanently withdrawn from social exchange, are about as personal as property can get. The Pequots, I think, knew what a Bible was: pieces of paper printed in two columns, folded and bundled together for durable bulk in a valuable covering. This is a perfectly adequate description of our medicine bundle which, like a small-format Bible, was also a personal possession. Both cultures recognized its decorative, talismanic function: the Europeans by wrapping it in morocco and clasping it in silver, the Pequots by covering it up tight in the best cloth they had. On some level, it matters little whether we describe small-format Bibles as European medicine bundles, or this medicine bundle as an Indian Bible. The two are culturally congruent, in their respective cultures.

Roger Stoddard has propounded the paradox that "authors do *not* write books," which I would take one step further, "nor do printers print them."[16] Properly speaking, books are made by folding and binding sheets that may or may not contain printing; our medicine bundle, with its interleaved binding or doublures, is an extreme example. As such, books need not be uniquely associated with literacy or a text, nor should codicology be restricted to manuscripts. Formats have expressive functions that bibliography, as conceived by Greg, ignores to its cost; English books circulated and communicated in ways that the Stationers' Company never cared to imagine. I regret that such truisms have been considered a threat to "bibliography": indeed, Fredson Bowers in his 1957–58 Sandars Lectures[17] might well be seen to have argued for a wider cultural role for the discipline, but unfortunately he made such excessive and exclusive claims that he alarmed esoterics like Alice Walker, offended exoterics like Edmund Wilson, and in the end probably persuaded no one but his own coterie.

Over and above these considerations, I would ask, quite practically, how anyone could determine the source of the Pequot fragment without recourse to "meaning"? In theory, one might run the typeface against the entire corpus of nonpareil type printed down to 1720, and this patient investigation would in time—no little time—produce more reliable, impartial, and scientific results than any I can boast of. But has any bibliographer ever proceeded in this blinkered fashion? As G. Thomas Tanselle rightly points out, Greg often violated his own dictum, as did other eminent practitioners of the "New Bibliography." When Charlton Hinman moved from the identification of type to the examination of spelling preferences, for example, he abandoned physical for socio-cultural evidence. Such, however, was never the pretense. When McKenzie tested Hinman's assumptions from the evidence of printers' records and found them wanting,[18] he was only pursuing Hinman's inquiry by other means, and it is literally preposterous of Thomas Tanselle to object that McKenzie was therefore "denigrating analytical bibliography." Nor is it much of a recommendation for the discipline. There are plenty good fish as ever came out of the sea, says the proverb, and the same is equally true of milk.

For Further Reading

This essay originated as a talk delivered for the amusement of my colleagues in Houghton Library on 12 December 1991: though I have substantially revised and updated it, I have tried to preserve its informal character, and offer these references only as an acknowledgment of my debts. The illustration of the text of the medicine bundle was drawn by Dr. Linda Welters, of the University of Rhode Island, and I am grateful for her permission to use it here; for information on the image of *Ecce Homo*, I am indebted to Dr. Paul Robinson of the Rhode Island Historical Preservation Commission, to Marjorie B. Cohen of the Harvard University Art Museums, who identified the subject, and to Terry Dzilenski, of the Mashantucket Pequot Museum, who brought it to my attention. Regrettably, the original fragments may not be reproduced here.

   1. Sociology and Anthropology: Roland Barthes, *Empire des signes* (1970; English trans., 1982); William Cronon, *Changes in the Land* (New York, 1983); Jacques Derrida, *De la grammatologie* (1967; English trans., 1976); Claude Lévi-Strauss, *Tristes tropiques* (1955; English trans., 1961); Nicholas Thomas, *Entangled Objects* (Cambridge, Mass., 1991); V. Neal et al., *Spaceflight: A Smithsonian Guide* (Washington, D.C., 1995), 175–79, describes attempts to communicate by space probes with trans-solar skrælings. John Harvey, *Men in Black* (London, 1995) gives a useful account of the social history of black cloth.

   2. Indian History and Culture: for regional overviews, see Bruce G. Trigger, ed., *Handbook of North American Indians*, vol. 15: *Northeast* (Washington, D.C., 1978), and James Axtell, *The Invasion Within: The Contest of*

Cultures in Colonial North America (New York, 1985); for archaeology, see Susan G. Gibson, ed., *Burr's Hill* (Providence, 1980) describing the finds (with many illustrations) in seventeenth-century Wampanoag graves at Warren, Rhode Island, including a "Jesuit's ring" and some leather book covers; Stuart John Tuma, Jr., "Contact Period (1500–1675) Burials in Southeast New England" (Master's thesis, University of Massachusetts, Boston, 1985) has a cumulated catalogue of finds to date. On the Pequots, see the classic, but highly polemical work of Francis Jennings, *The Invasion of America: Indians, Colonialism, and the Cant of Conquest* (Chapel Hill, N.C., 1975) and *The Pequots in Southern New England*, ed. Laurence M. Hauptman and James D. Wherry (Norman, Okla., 1990), which also includes a preliminary analysis of the archaeology by Kevin McBride. Nathan Cobb, "Betting on the Future," *Boston Globe Magazine* (1 March 1992) is a useful journalistic account of recent developments. Paul A. Robinson et al. give a preliminary report on the Narragansett graves at North Kingston, Rhode Island in *Cultures in Contact*, ed. William W. Fitzhugh (Washington, D.C., 1985); and I have also profited from James W. Bradley, *Evolution of the Onondaga Iroquois: Accommodating Change, 1500–1655* (Syracuse, N.Y., 1987). Lynn Ceci, *The Effects of European Contact and Trade on the Settlement Pattern of Indians in Coastal New York, 1524–1665* (New York, 1990), is the standard account of wampum.

3. Bibliography: on the general controversy mentioned at the beginning of my talk, see D. F. McKenzie, *Bibliography and the Sociology of Texts* (London, 1986); Jerome J. McGann, *A Critique of Modern Textual Criticism* (Chicago, 1983); and the characteristically lengthy response of G. Thomas Tanselle, "Textual Criticism and Literary Sociology," *Studies in Bibliography* 44 (1991): 83–143. The ultimate casus belli is D. F. McKenzie, "Printers of the Mind: Some Notes on Bibliographical Theories and Printing-House Practices," *Studies in Bibliography* (1969): 1–75; see also Roger E. Stoddard, "Morphology and the Book from an American Perspective," *Printing History* 17 (1987): 2–14. On the bibliography of the Bible, see Christopher De Hamel, *A History of Illuminated Manuscripts* (Boston, 1986), chap. 4; M. H. Black, "The Printed Bible," in *The Cambridge History of the Bible*, vol. 3, ed. S. L. Greenslade (Cambridge, 1963), chap. 12; Worthington C. Ford, *The Boston Book Market, 1679–1700* (Boston, 1917); Paul G. Hoftijzer, *Engelse boekverkopers by de Beurs* (Amsterdam & Maarssen, 1989); and two articles by Brian J. McMullin, "The Bible and Continuous Reprinting in the Early Seventeenth Century," *The Library* 6th ser. 5 (1983): 256–63, and "Joseph Athias and The Early History of Stereotyping," *Quaerendo* 23 (1993): 184–207. On print and illiteracy, see James Axtell, "The Power of Print in the Eastern Woodlands," in his *After Columbus* (New York, 1988), 88–99, summarized in his *Invasion*

Within, above, and D. F. McKenzie, *Oral Culture, Literacy, and Print in Early New Zealand* (Wellington, N.Z., 1985).

Appendix

[The edition of the Bible that matches the pseudomorph is more fully described as follows:]

The Old Testament only, without Apocrypha: within an architectural woodcut border, showing, in ascending order, King David praying, a heart burning on an altar, and the Tetragrammaton in glory; inscribed "Cor mundum crea in me Deus Ps.51";

THE HOLY | BIBLE, | Containing the Old | Testament and the New: |¶ *Newly translated out of the Ori- | ginall Tongues : and with the former | translations diligently compared | and revised by his Majesties | speciall Commandement.* | Appointed to be read in Churches. | [rule] | London | Printed by *Christopher Barker*, | Printer to the Kings most | Excellent Majestie, | [rule] *Anno Dom*. 1680. 12.mo: A-GgI2 = 360 leaves.

Second title page, within the same border:

THE NEW | TESTAMENT | of our LORD and SAVIOUR | JESUS CHRIST. |¶ *Newly translated out of the Ori- | ginall Greek : and with the former | translations diligently compared | and revised by his Majesties | speciall Commandement.* | [rule] | LONDON, | Printed by *Christopher Barker*, | Printer to the Kings most | Excellent Majestie, | [rule] | *Anno Dom*. 1669. 12.mo: (A)-(I)I2. (K)6 = 114 leaves.

Locations: Pennsylvania State University University Park, Pa.: bound in original (?) black morocco, traces of ties; with a 1638 edition of Sternhold and Hopkins' Metrical Psalms (STC 2.680.6). Imperfect: leaves Z2.11 wanting; V12 slightly mutilated; imprint date on first title page barely legible, altered in manuscript to 1669 (but cf. Herbert 7S4, dated 1680 and 1669). (John) Ferrer family birth records, 1693–1710, on verso of N.T. title page.

Notes

1. "Thoreau," in *Lectures and Biographical Sketches*, in *Emerson's Complete Works*, 6 vols. (Boston: Houghton Mifflin, 1921), 4, second pagination: 482.

2. W. W. Greg, "Bibliography—An Apologia" (1932), repr. in *Sir Walter Wilson Greg A Collection of His Writings*, ed. Joseph Rosenblum, Great Bibliographers Series 11 (Lanham, Md.: Scarecrow Press, 1998), 141; Tony Stokes, *Henry Bradshaw 1831–1866*, Great Bibliographers Series 6 (Metuchen, N.J.: Scarecrow Press, 1984), 30–31.

3. R. B. McKerrow, *An Introduction to Bibliography for Literary Students* (Oxford: Clarendon Press, 1927; rev. ed., 1928); Fredson Bowers, *Principles of Bibliographical Description* (Princeton N.J.: Princeton University Press, 1949). For an excellent account of the emergence of the "New Bibliography," see David McKitterick's "Introduction" to McKerrow's *Introduction* (repr., Winchester, UK: St. Paul's Bibliographies, 1994).

4. Roland Barthes, *Empire of Signs*, trans. Richard Howard (New York: Hill and Wang, 1982), 33–36.

5. Nicholas Thomas, *Entangled Objects: Exchange, Material Culture, and Colonialism in the Pacific* (Cambridge, Mass.: Harvard University Press, 1991).

6. James W. Bradley, *Evolution of the Onondaga Iroquois: Accommodating Change, 1500–1655* (Syracuse, N.Y.: Syracuse University Press, 1987); [exact source of quotation not located].

7. Roger Williams, *A Key to the Language of America* (1643), quoted in James Axtell, "The Power of Print in the Eastern Woodlands," *WMQ* 3rd ser. 44 (1987): 302.

8. Quoted in James Axtell, *The Invasion Within* (New York: Oxford University Press, 1985), 102–3.

9. D. F. McKenzie, *Bibliography and the Sociology of Texts* (1986; repr., Cambridge: Cambridge University Press, 1999), 107.

10. [In late May 1637 a force of colonists attacked and eventually set on fire the wigwams in a Pequot "fort" near the present-day site of Mystic, Connecticut. This battle resulted in the death of almost everyone in the fort, a group that included warriors as well as women and children. Retreating to the west, most of the remaining members of the tribe were surrounded by the colonists in late June near present-day Southport, Connecticut. On this occasion the trader and translator Thomas Stanton negotiated the surrender of the women, children, and older men, some of whom were subsequently employed as servants or slaves among the colonists, and others sold outside the colony. See Alfred A. Cave, *The Pequot War* (Amherst: University of Massachusetts Press, 1996).]

11. *The Journal of Madam Knight* (New York: Peter Smith, 1935), 39. [Contrary to Amory's account, the context suggests that Madame Knight was not referring specifically to the Pequots.]

12. [Mary Rowlandson], *The Sovereignty & Goodness of God* (Cambridge, Mass., 1682), 14. [In *New Englands First Fruits* (London, 1643), alluding to the Pequot War, the unknown author, most likely Henry Dunster, declared (p. 21) "that the name of the Pequits (as of *Amaleck.*) is blotted out from under heaven, there being not one that is, or, (at least) dare call himselfe a Pequit." I have not been able to find any evidence of Richard Mather making such a statement.]

13. McKenzie, *Bibliography*, 108.

14. Richard Hoggart, *The Uses of Literacy: Changing Patterns in English Mass Culture* (Boston: Beacon Press, 1961).

15. [An allusion to the Indian known as James Printer or James the Printer, who may possibly have set type for the Cambridge 1682 edition of Rowlandson's captivity narrative. See Amory, *First Impressions*, 41.]

16. Roger Stoddard, "Morphology and the Book," in *A Library-Keeper's Business*, ed. Carol Z. Rothkopf (Newark, Del.: Oak Knoll, 2002), 33.

17. *Textual & Literary Criticism* (Cambridge: Cambridge University Press, 1959).

18. "Printers of the Mind: Some Notes on Bibliographical Theories and Printing-House Practices," *SB* 22 (1969): 1–75.

2. "Gods Altar Needs Not Our Pollishings": Revisiting the Bay Psalm Book

Like the "The Trout and the Milk," this essay on the Bay Psalm Book is animated by Amory's unhappiness with some of the implications of the New Bibliography. Aiming his fire at the notion of an ideal or "iconic" text, he used the variations among six surviving first editions of the Bay Psalm Book to demonstrate that changes were constantly being introduced during (and because of) the process of printing and assembling sheets into bound books. The details of this painstaking collation appear in three appendices, all of them stemming from Amory's efforts to identify the fonts being used by the Cambridge press, a matter that is visually demonstrated in Figure 7. Running titles are indicated in Figure 8, here transposed from the appendix in which it originally appeared. That the technology of the hand press lent itself to such consequences was old news,[1] but Amory was the first to demonstrate so carefully its consequences for the Bay Psalm Book. Moreover, he detected signs of intentional rewriting that occurred as the book was being printed. Ten years later, in 1650/51, Henry Dunster redid much of the translation and it was his version, together with further variants, that was subsequently reprinted. Not until the middle of the nineteenth century, and in the context of the emergence of a group of rare book collectors—George Brinley, Edward Crowninshield, and others—was the first edition of 1640 suddenly thrust into the status of "the Icon."[2]

SOURCE: *Printing History* 12 (1990): 2–14, which has granted permission to republish the essay.

The "Bay Psalm Book" can mean three very different things: a book, surviving in eleven of the original run of 1,700 copies printed at the Cambridge press; a nineteenth-century institution, enforced through facsimiles of the first edition, whose contents scarcely matter; and a text, revised in 1651 and reprinted down to the late eighteenth century. These are the proper subjects of physical bibliography, critical theory, and textual criticism, respectively. I shall revisit all of these, starting in physical bibliography, with the type. How many fonts did the Cambridge press have? Where did they come from? When and how were they first employed?

There have not been many studies of the Bay Psalm Book of late, except by musicologists. I return to issues that have been neglected for over thirty years. Their neglect is an unconscious tribute to three works of scholarship: George Parker Winship's 1945 Rosenbach lectures; Lawrence Starkey's Ph.D. thesis, written under the direction of Fredson Bowers in 1949; and Zoltán Haraszti's 1956 facsimile edition and commentary. Of these, Starkey, the first to apply the methods of Greg and McKerrow to American printing, concentrates on physical bibliography, that is, the book; Haraszti is the first and nearly the last scholar to study the text; and Winship antici-pates the current vogue for book trade history.[3] Winship's vision of New England culture seems somewhat blinkered today, even by comparison to the earlier work of Samuel Eliot Morison, yet his collection of primary mate-rials was nearly exhaustive and, despite inaccuracies of transcription, remains indispensable.

The chief characters in my tale are the Cambridge press's proprietor, Elizabeth Glover, relict of the wealthy minister Jose Glover, who assembled the printing shop but died on the voyage from England; Henry Dunster, her sec-ond husband and president of Harvard College until 1654, when he resigned on charges of antipaedobaptism; and three printers, Stephen Day,[4] inden-tured servant of the Glovers, his son Matthew, and their successor Samuel Green, from whose loins sprang most of the early colonial printers. The press was originally located in the Dunster house (now the site of the Cambridge Savings Bank in Harvard Square), but in 1659 it was moved to the Indian College, a brick building erected on the adjacent corner of Harvard Yard and torn down in 1692. Thanks to a lawsuit between President Dunster and the Glover heirs, we can account for every sheet of paper the Glovers brought over and can work out the press runs for most of the productions of the press from its arrival in 1638 down to 1654, the date of the lawsuit.

I have divided my material into three sections, which I will call the Type, the Icon, and the "Text," the quotation marks around the last to be presently explained.

1. The Type

In a recent excavation at the site of the Indian College, a Peabody Museum (Harvard) team unearthed twelve pieces of seventeenth-century type. Sur-prisingly, this tiny sample of Samuel Green and Marmaduke Johnson's stock exhibited five different heights to paper.[5] A foundry normally had a set of molds of matching heights, so that the seventeenth-century printer Joseph Moxon could speak of "a Fount . . . of Letter of all Bodies" (Oxford English Dictionary, meaning 1), as though the defining characteristic of a font was its height to paper. During its occupancy of the Indian College from 1659 to 1692, then, the Cambridge press required a fresh supply of type on at least five occasions. We know of only three supplies delivered in this period, for which our records are exceptionally full; but the testimony of the spade speaks for a history that is rich in accidents. With patient make-ready, a skilled workman might get these different fonts to work together on a wooden press,[6] but, as we shall see, seventeenth-century workmen were rarely care-ful, and sometimes woefully untrained.

Lawrence Starkey, who first studied and classified the types of the Cambridge press, distinguished only five fonts in its productions down to 1663. Designating their bodies by the measurement of twenty lines in millimeters, there were a 95 english, an 83 pica, a 68 long primer, and two breviers measuring 53 and 52 mm. respectively.[7] To these may be added a sprinkling of exotics: a 115 great primer greek, probably the so-called "Fell greeks" designed by Haultin; and an unpointed 95 two-line english hebrew. Some striking 160 double-pica lunar phases, first found in a title border of the almanac for 1647 (Evans 21), may also have belonged to the original stock; at any rate, they are never used for their ostensible purpose in the surviving products of the press. The long primer, forming a total of only thirteen lines in the Bay Psalm Book, never appears again; it is apparently replaced by the 53 brevier, first found in the 1646 almanac. In Starkey's view, there were no new supplies of type before 1659, when the 52 brevier arrived for the Indian Bible. Of all these sorts, only the 52 brevier survived to be dug up in Harvard Yard.

I can add at least two new fonts to Starkey's list[8] (Figure 7). The Bay Psalm Book displays nine lines of pica, distributed in groups of three and six; but this is not the same as Starkey's pica, which is first used in 1645 for the text of the *Narragansett Declaration*. In the Bay Psalm Book, the "s" tilts to the right, the eye of the "d" is smaller than that of the "b," and the capital and minuscule "w"s cross near the top. In the *Narragansett Declaration*, however, the "s" is upright, the "d" and "b" have the same size eye, and the "w"s cross in the middle. The Bay Psalm Book pica has a wider set: the word "Churches" on the title-page is a full letter longer than the same word in the *Platform of Discipline* (1649). Starkey declares that the English type in John Wilson's elegy on Joseph Brisco (1657) is the same as that of the Bay Psalm Book. On the contrary, the minuscule "o" of the elegy is the same height as the minuscule "n," and the eye of the "o" tilts correctly to the left; whereas the Bay Psalm Book's "o" is taller than the "n," and the eye tilts to the right. The elegy uses a true apostrophe, where the Bay Psalm Book regularly uses an inverted comma.

Winship supposed that the first types came from Amsterdam, an inveterate error he inherited from Isaiah Thomas. Starkey first exposed the error, but did not pursue the historical implications of his correction.[9] Glover's types are almost certainly of English origin. The "sh" ligature is so rare in continental printing that its absence can be used to localize anonymous imprints, and the intrusive "w" is a characteristic supplement added by English founders to continental matrices.[10] All the Bay Psalm types, moreover, including the exotics, were actually in use in England; that is, the matrices were English, though I have yet to find an identically damaged piece of type

Brisco Elegy (1657): 95 english

THere is no *Job* but cries to God and hopes,
And God his ear in Chrift; to cries he opes,
Out of the deeps to him I cry'd and hop'd,
And unto me his gracious ear is op'd :
Doubt not of this ye that my death bewail,
What if it did fo ftrangely me affail :

Bay Psalm Book (1640), Ps. 18: 95 english

40 And my foes necks thou gaveft mee,
    that I might waft mine enemyes.
41 They cryde but there was none to fave,
    to God, yet with no anfwer meet.
42 I beat them then as duft i'th winde
    and caft them out as dirt i'th ftreet.

Bay Psalm Book (1640), title-page: 83 pica

Whereunto is prefixed a difcourfe de -
claring not only the lawfullnes, but alfo
the neceffity of the heavenly Ordinance
of finging Scripture Pfalmes in
the Churches of
God.

Narragansett Declaration (1645), p. 6: 83 pica

ing & expreffing much diftemper in their counteuance & carriage . The
Englifh meffengers not hoping for better fucceffe at that time, departed;
telling Pefficus that if he would returne any other anfwer , he fhould fend it
to the Englifh trading-houfe, where they intended to lodge that night . In
the morning he invited them to returne, and promifed them a Guide to Un-
cas, but would grant no ceffation of Armes . When they came to Providence they underftood that in their abfence a Narrowganfet Indian had bin
there , and faining himfelfe to be of Connecticot, fpake in that dialect , but

Figure 7. Four fonts used by Massachusetts printers, 1640–1657.

in printed texts from either side of the Atlantic. The exotics, which are quite uncommon, appear in the printing of William Jones, a well-known Puritan whom the Star Chamber drove out of business in 1637. The romans and italics appear in books printed by John Norton the younger and perhaps others. Norton, too, was in trouble with the Star Chamber, though his religious sympathies are not as clear as Jones's.[11] I would conjecture, then, that Glover surreptitiously obtained his type from the stock of a sympathetic printer like Jones, and not directly from one of the four licensed English founders, who were much more strictly supervised.[12]

After 1643, the press abandons all its original romans and italics, as well as its ornaments and two-line initials. Only the exotics continue in use, or at any rate, the hebrews. Two Greek words in the 1643 *Theses may* be in the same great primer found in the *Platform of Discipline* and later, but the total evidence is ludicrously small. The disuse of the older stock after 1643 demands an explanation: either the earlier font's height to paper made it inconvenient to work with later material or, owing to Stephen Day's incompetence, it was ruined in printing only 140 reams. By 1669, the colonists were once more writing to their benefactors in England, whining that all their type, including the brevier that had arrived in 1659, was "much worn, and unfit to be used for printing."[13] They had printed perhaps 600 reams, some with a fourth typestock imported by Marmaduke Johnson.

However we explain this impressive history of waste, we need not doubt the arrival of a new font around 1643. It is confirmed by two memoranda in College Book III, which are undated but apparently arranged in chronological order. Isaiah Thomas, who first noted these in 1810, unfortunately confounded them with a memorandum by President Leonard Hoar in College Book I, and this error descended to Winship. Starkey disentangled most of the confusion, but lingered under the illusion that Hoar had written all three memoranda during his brief presidency from 1672 to 1675. In fact, the list in College Book III was copied out by Thomas Danforth in 1654 or 1655, apparently from earlier records now lost.[14] The first entry records that "Mr Joss: Glover gave to the Colledge a ffont of printing Letters"; this must refer to the types that arrived in 1638. The second entry states that "Some Gentlemen of Amsterdam gave towards the furnishing of a Printing-Press with Letters . . . fourty nine pound & somthing more"; this can only refer to the printing press that was already in Cambridge. Following the second entry is a benefaction to the library made by Hugh Peter and others in 1643.[15]

The early history of the Cambridge press, then, divides into three periods, according to its principal stocks of type: an english period, attested only by the Bay Psalm Book and the 1643 *Theses*; a pica period, beginning with the *Narragansett Declaration* (1645); and a brevier period, beginning with the Indian Bible in 1659. This scheme emphasizes the *ad hoc* character of the press's operations, but not, I think, inappropriately. George Brinley's unique run of almanacs for 1646 through 1650 survived, I suppose, because they were bound in a single volume.[16] Starkey intriguingly suggests that no almanacs were printed between 1640 and 1645, but we might also explain the lacuna on the hypothesis that the earlier almanacs were sheet format, which could not be bound up with the octavos of 1646 and later. Certainly, a sheet format was the only practicable solution to the problem of printing twelve panels of 31 lines each in english, illustrated with double pica lunar phases, on pot paper. Indeed, since sheet almanacs were conventionally printed on one side only, Captain Pierce's almanac for 1640 (Evans 2) may have occupied two sheets.

The only regular Cambridge publications at this time, the annual almanac and the Harvard *Theses* and *Quaestiones*, were probably all published together for the August commencement at the college. They consumed on average half a ream of paper a year during the first fifteen years of the press's history, amounting to only half of one percent of its output. I estimate that only 180 almanacs a year were dispersed among the assembled notables, clergy, and students.[17] No doubt the potential market was larger, but as Bernard Bailyn has shown, the colonists had difficulty exploiting it. They attempted the manufacture of cast-iron kettles, cloth, graphite, glass, and even salt—all much more necessary commodities than almanacs—and failed miserably.[18] Print and liquor were among their few going concerns, and even print, where everything but labor was already paid for, prospered indifferently well. The *Capitall Lawes* of 1642, a text that every child was required to learn, was still "in print" in 1674.[19] The treasurer of the Bay Colony, Richard Russell, unwisely invested in a stock of the 1648 *Laws*, which did not sell, and the General Court had to bail him out in 1651.[20] We can make a pretty good guess at his market. The General Court demanded fifty free copies for local notables in Boston, and the *Laws* themselves required one copy for every township. This accounts for approximately eighty copies in all, and the market could hardly have been twice as large. Six hundred were printed, of which substantial numbers remained unsold and unsalable in 1651. The Cambridge printers ran off one Bay Psalm Book for every eight persons in the colony in 1640, and again in 1651. Is it conceivable that the first edition had actually sold out before 1651? Not to me. The almanac, surely, provides a more reliable measure of the colonial market, which was roughly the size of the one or two hundred persons attending Harvard commencement.[21]

A man who prints half a ream a year and may otherwise be idle for up to three years at a time is still, I suppose, a "printer," but he had better be other things as well if he wants to eat. Stephen Day was a locksmith, hired as such, and, to judge by his letters, barely literate; he absented himself from Cambridge for considerable periods after 1642, prospecting for iron and graphite and promoting the "Nashaway Plantation" in the Nipmuck country southwest of Boston. G. E. Littlefield first doubted that Day could ever have been a printer, and nominated Day's son Matthew for the prototypographer of British North America. The doubt has gradually hardened into certainty on the part of most later authorities.[22] I see no escape from Stephen's own testimony, however, that he managed "the Printing Presse and the utensils and appurtenances thereof," which is confirmed by a grant from the General Court in December 1641 and again in 1657, declaring that Stephen was "the first that set upon printing."[23] Samuel Eliot Morison concludes, I think correctly, that, "As a locksmith, [Stephen] undoubtedly set up the press, and managed it for Mrs. Glover." Morison further suggests that Stephen left off around the time of her death in 1643.[24] It may have been a year or two earlier, but probably was no later.

Stephen may have negotiated new terms after his arrival. At any rate, there is no mention of the £51 plus interest he should have owed Glover's estate when his indenture expired; on the contrary, he claims a substantial reward from the General Court and £100 from Henry Dunster. The press never provided Stephen or his successors with steady work, so it is not surprising if they moonlighted. Matthew Day, who was probably a locksmith like his father, was the first college steward. Sergeant Samuel Green of the Cambridge militia was clerk of the writs for Middlesex County, while also serving as college printer, barber, and stationer. Stephen's personal resentment against Dunster, so strongly expressed that the President prayed for his soul in open court, may suggest that he felt himself betrayed into an idle and unprofitable calling. Interestingly, his resignation—or dismissal—coincides with the arrival of a fresh supply of type; but before addressing the reasons why, let us consider what his book became.

2. The Icon

The actual title of the Bay Psalm Book is *The Whole Booke of Psalmes, faithfully translated into English metre*. Very nearly the same title and exactly the same biblical epigraphs adorn the title-page of the Church of England's official metrical version by Sternhold and Hopkins, which the Bay Psalm Book was designed to replace. For distinction's sake, the new version came to be known in the eighteenth century as the "New-English version" or the "New England Psalter," but it has served for Scottish and English as well as for American worship. Its nondescript title and contents camouflaged the first edition so well that Isaiah Thomas in 1810 confessed he was unable to find more than a single copy, then in the private possession of the Reverend William Bentley of Salem.

The nineteenth century kissed this ugly liturgical frog, with the usual result. In 1847, the catalogue of the Prince Library, as Old South Church now chose to call its accumulation of old American books, disclosed no fewer than five copies of the Bay Psalm Book in the Society's possession. The eyes of collectors like Edward Crowninshield and George Livermore narrowed, and in a few years, four of the duplicates had flown the coop, one in exchange for a superior copy.[25] Luther Farnham's carefully qualified 1855 comment on the Crowninshield copy suggests the overheated atmosphere of acquisition at this moment: it was "perhaps the only [perfect copy] owned by a private individual in New England."[26] As he may have known, there were already two imperfect copies owned by private individuals in New England, one of which would soon be perfected and sold to a private individual in New York.

The crowning touch to the collectors' feast came from Nathaniel Bradstreet Shurtleff, sometime mayor of Boston and the same fine filiopietistic hand who compiled or caused to be compiled the standard editions of the early Bay Colony and Plymouth Colony records. He had acquired (or, according to the librarian, borrowed) the Mather copy from Old South Church in 1860 and proceeded to use it for what he called *A Literal Reprint of the Bay Psalm Book* in 1862. This type facsimile was only marginally more common than the original: Shurtleff printed fifty copies on ordinary paper, fifteen on large paper, and one on vellum, all but the ordinary paper *hors commerce*. Thus begins a tradition from which we are still unable to shake free: the only form of republication that our stifling reverence for the original permits is in facsimile; four such editions have so far appeared.

Shurtleff established the name by which the book is now known, which was current, he said, among "antiquaries." In his 1885 bibliography, Wilberforce Eames extended it to cover any edition of the New England version, a usage that is now generally accepted.[27] Shurtleff, on the contrary, implied that there was only one Bay Psalm Book, the first edition; furthermore, that there was only one official copy of the first edition—*his* copy, formerly Richard Mather's, whom Shurtleff mistakenly believed to have been the editor. The religious sympathies of the Old Planters[28] and the Pilgrims to the north and south of Boston, of course, had long since ceased to be distinct from those of the Puritans; but in Shurtleff's ear, the unregenerate North Shore still sang Sternhold and Hopkins, and the sectarian South Shore,

Henry Ainsworth's version.[29] Here, in his hands, he held the unwobbling pivot of the Puritan Middle Kingdom, neither a book nor a text, but an institution.[30] So sang or seemed to sing the sometime mayor of Boston. He edited his copy like a notary, ignoring the translators' intentions, and paying scrupulous attention to the compositor's warts.

The most recent echo of his fantasies that I have noted is in the meticulously researched catalogue of the Boston Museum of Fine Arts 1982 exhibition, *New England Begins*. Even there, the imperturbable authority of a successful nickname has affixed its sly imprimatur. The Bay Psalm Book, writes the dazzled cataloguer, "is an icon of American civilization, documenting the colonists' need for their own press a mere ten years after settlement, and more important, their need for a singular interpretation of a rite that changed the nature of religious worship—the congregational singing of the psalms."[31] One would hardly imagine that other Protestants, including members of the Church of England, sang psalms, and to the same tunes; that no New England synod had resolved on this version or formally expressed any need for it; and that any Bay Colony congregation was free to reject it. "Singular interpretations" of religious rites were common enough—for these, one might turn to the Baptists or Quakers, and be hanged. Here was the Hebrew verity, and the translators were not the only ones, they thought, in need of it. John Cotton dedicated it, quite generally, "to God and his Churches" (**2v). One copy, indeed, found its way to heterodox Rhode Island before 1687.[32]

Plans for the new psalm book seem to postdate the arrival of the press in October 1638.[33] Hugh Peter, writing to a Bermudian correspondent on 10 December 1638, knows of no definite commitments, and invites his friend to send along a manuscript: "Wee haue a printery here and thinke to goe to worke with some speciall things, and if you have any thing, you may send it safely by these."[34] It all rather sounds as though the colonists were wondering what to do about the new arrival. I doubt that this was in any way exceptional: it was some years before Australia discovered a use for the so-called Howe press, which arrived with the First Fleet. Graham Shaw points out that the first press in Calcutta was equally superfluous.[35]

Certainly, Glover's materials were ill-suited to printing the metrical psalms. Only 35 of the 544 editions of the metrical psalms described in the second edition of the *Short-Title Catalogue of Books Printed in England . . . and of English Books Printed Abroad, 1475–1640* are in a one-column english, quarto format. All of these were printed in black letter between 1561 and 1614; by 1639, both the face and the format were beginning to look obsolete. The format was notably wasteful of paper, moreover: one-column pica, octavo would have saved about seventy-one reams, but it seems that the printer did not have a sufficient stock of smaller type. The result was an oddity, the only one-column roman, quarto edition of the metrical psalms yet printed. Even music type was wanting.

To be sure, there was more involved than the colonists' religious needs. Legally, the Star Chamber decree of 1637 forbade the sale or importation of type without a license, and we may doubt that Archbishop William Laud would have sanctioned a new Puritan press, even in far-off Cambridge, Massachusetts. The Stationers' Company jealously guarded its monopoly over the metrical psalms, particularly defending the canonicity of the Sternhold and Hopkins version.[36] The London licenser might have challenged the translators' orthodoxy. These obstacles were largely removed by 1643, when the College ordered the pica used in the *Narragansett Declaration*. The Star Chamber had been abolished on 5 July 1641, and the political and religious climate of England now very greatly favored the colonists. In 1638, Glover had a more difficult game to play.

"It is doubtful whether the seventeenth-century American felt strongly the need of his community for a printing press," Lawrence Wroth long ago remarked. Manuscript, proclamation, and word-of-mouth could easily handle the task of distributing information in a small community, Wroth notes; in exceptional cases, the text could always be printed in England or Holland. He continues: "The spread of the art to other American towns occurred in the same generation that saw it penetrate the life of the English provinces . . . [so that] the demand for the press in seventeenth-century America did not arise from a sense of deprivation on the part of the people."[37] The extensive early literature encouraging emigration to New England frequently called for carpenters, blacksmiths, locksmiths, and other skilled artisans, but never for printers.[38] The press, so far as we can tell, was an unexpected windfall for the colonists, but their consumption of its products was limited. In short, the evidence localizes the need for a printing press in the individual psyche of Jose Glover, not in his community. Here I must appeal from bibliography to a higher science. The man who proposed to carry a printing shop 3,000 miles, present the type to Harvard College, and retain the press and paper for himself seems slightly unbalanced—a recognizable type of Harvard benefactor, but hardly representative of the colony and its needs.

Over two hundred years would pass before Glover's neuroses were institutionalized in an "icon of American civilization." The eleven surviving copies are notoriously "rare," as the 1,700 seventeenth-century copies were not; and the rules of their institutional owners only allow a comparison of their state of perfection, in which they differ as little as angelic orders. At a point of origin around 1850, we may distinguish the four originally perfect *rarissimi* from the seven originally imperfect *rariores*. A facsimile is a device for maintaining such a hierarchy, and all four of the originally perfect copies have now been reproduced. Any textual collation is forbidden by filiopietistic pact, for it would reduce all copies to a rough equality and emphasize their continuity with later, revised editions. The last person to attempt it was Thomas Prince in 1758, but his collation, entered in the margins of a "perfect" copy, is whited out in the 1956 facsimile edition. The ostensible reason for the deletion is to return us to 1640; the real reason is to return us to 1850, when the Bay Psalm Book was first created. Now I hope it is clear why I have put the title of the following section in quotation marks.

3. The "Text"

John Cotton's defense of the inelegancy of the new version is often quoted, and I shall not break custom: "If therefore the verses are not always so smooth and elegant as some may desire or expect; let them consider that Gods Altar needs not our pollishings: Ex[odus] 20" (xx3verso). The very phrase is a vivid demonstration that elegance was at his command when he chose; if only the Founders had always written so well! It is a *defense*, however, not (as usually construed) a confession. Cotton Mather sounds the retreat in the *Magnalia Christi Americana* (1702), reporting that "afterwards, it was thought, that a little more of Art was to be employed" on the version, which Henry Dunster and Richard Lyon supplied.[39]

From such slight concessions descends our modern conviction that the first edition (perversely decreed the only legitimate representative of the "text") is the ultimate in bad poetry; its rugged printing and deficient aesthetics become proof of some primitive American strength, so that, as Winship remarks, it "looks the part that the fates assigned it to play."[40] (Nineteenth-century fates, perhaps.) "How Bad is the Bay Psalm Book?" asked Norman S. Grabo in 1961. "Pretty bad," he replied, adding feebly that so were all the other contemporary versions, some by distinguished poets.[41] In short, he declined to answer his own question.

Of one thing we may be sure: the Founders' tongues did not drop verse like manna; they revised and rethought their amazing English. This already appears from the first-edition errata. In Psalm 19, instead of "And from presumptuous-sins, let thou / kept back thy servant bee," we should read, "And from presumptuous-sins, kept back / O let thy servant bee." A few years ago, preparing an exhibition on the Mathers, I accidentally noticed a similar revision made by press correction. In Psalm 69, the Prince copy reads:

And let their eyes be darkened,
that they may never see:
their loynes also with trembleing
to shake continuallee.

The Harvard copy revises the last two lines of the quatrain:

with trembling also make their loynes
to shake continuallie.

Intrigued by this useless bit of knowledge, Michael Winship and I resolved to compare the four facsimiles, from Shurtleff in 1862 to the Evans microfiche. As expected, we found further variants.[42]

Because the translators' intentions have no place in our critical tradition, I suppose these variants have no literary significance. As the literary historian Sacvan Bercovich accurately but unkindly remarked when I showed him my proud discovery, "You can't tell which is worse." And Norman Grabo, in effect, agrees: Sir Philip Sidney's translation of the Twenty-Third Psalm might be printed as the Bay Psalm Book's, and no one would be the wiser, for they are both "pretty bad." The Bay Psalm Book is a "text" consisting of arbitrary, more or less black marks on more or less white paper that, in some real sense, we are forbidden to read.

For the historian of printing, however, the book remains a record of Stephen Day's labor and experience. The exaltation of Matthew Day over the head of his father has mysteriously improved our opinion of the Bay Psalm Book's composition. Isaiah Thomas, who ought to have known better, is frankly dismissive: "This specimen of Daye's printing does not exhibit the appearance of good workmanship."[43] Winship and Starkey, on the other hand, argue that the composition is actually quite good, certainly better than we would expect from an emotional locksmith who could not spell.[44] This locates the argument on a rhetorical level—what culture do the letters express? Whereas the only pertinent question is technological: what was Stephen doing in the metal?

Stephen's handling of running-titles is perhaps our most telling index of his lack of professional training. The division of a running-title into "The." on the verso and "Preface." on the recto is a good example, noted by Thomas. The alternation of the spelling "PSALME" in the recto running-titles, and "PSALM" in the versos, also struck him as "very singular."[45] Starkey explains it by supposing that the compositor used a single skeleton throughout,[46] but the conjecture is not convincing, and indeed Brian

McMullin informs me that the transfer of skeletons in seventeenth-century printing is the exception, not the rule. The peculiarity that Thomas noted lies in the compositor's mind, not in his hands. Stephen sees no real difference between text and running-titles: catchwords often catch with the running-titles, rather than with the caption-titles, when a psalm begins a new page; and indeed, a running-title may do double duty as a caption title (e.g., on A1v) (Figure 8).

The profligate use of roman capital P, S, A, L, and M ought to have created shortages, and in fact Stephen fairly often substitutes wrong-font italics for these letters in the text. Nevertheless, his supply of type ought to have met these demands: he had at least forty-nine capital roman L's, yet often resorted to italic when nearly half this supply of roman was still unused.[47] Perhaps he saw no difference, as his use of ligatured letters might suggest. He first discovered the "ssi" ligature toward the end of the book, as Nicolas Barker points out,[48] and he intermixed ligatured and unligatured settings of "ss" (Psalm 5), "si"(Psalm 60), and "sh" (Psalm 94). These lapses have gone unremarked, I suppose, because they have been tacitly attributed to shortages—and yet, to judge by the recurrence of a few identifiable pieces,[49] Stephen had enough type for eight quarto pages.

The evidence for casting off of copy is mixed, and here I am indebted to Mr. Paul R. Sternberg for correcting the errors of an earlier version of this paper. In prose, the material ran short at the end of the Preface, as we see from the exceptionally loose setting of **3 and **3V; the fact that Stephen might thus adjust both the inner and the outer formes shows that he set them *seriatim*, without casting off copy. In verse, however, the evidence favors casting off. In signature N, as Mr. Sternberg kindly pointed out to me in a letter, there is an extra line of text inserted in the direction line of N2, whereas N2V ends in a blank line; both errors might have been corrected by moving the extra line to its proper place on N2V, if composition had proceeded *seriatim*. This error, and the late insertion of six lines in the inner forme of signature P, may, of course, only reflect the fact that the outer formes were printed when the errors were discovered. But Mr. Sternberg also urges evidence from the pattern of reappearing sorts, which I hope he will publish in the near future.[50]

Certainly, lockup caused Stephen considerable problems. The ill-fitting initials, which are really meant to work with pica, and the frequent substitution of pica sorts, particularly in the numeration of the lines, resulted in an uneven block of type. The lines wave and buckle so alarmingly that the crossing of ascenders and descenders in a recent forgery of the *Freeman's Oath* was considered inconclusive proof of its modern manufacture. In Psalm 65, the

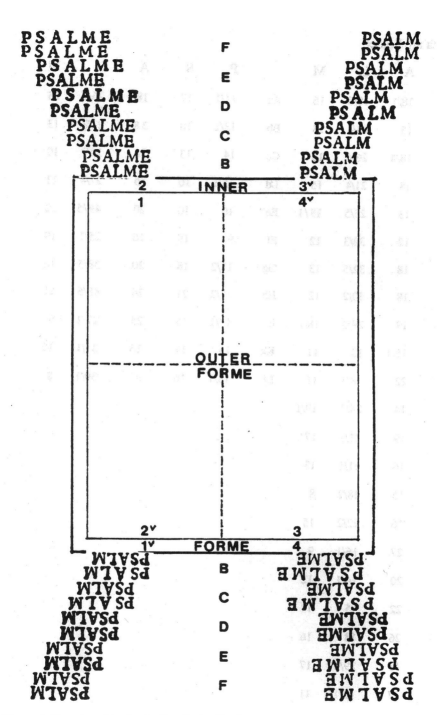

Figure 8. Running titles in the Bay Psalm Book.

whole column of type rose up beneath the initial. In the preface, Stephen follows his copy too literally, leaving references in the text that were surely meant to be placed in the margin. Marginal notes may have been more than he could manage.

To summarize, the evidence pretty consistently tells against Stephen's competence as a compositor and pressman, confirming Isaiah Thomas's verdict against that of Winship and Starkey. There is no need to make a mystery of the matter. Louis XVI, a man who was all thumbs, could manage a printing press, and so could Stephen Day, but they were rank amateurs.[51] If we assume that Stephen had ever observed the operation of a printer's shop before leaving England, perhaps while repairing the ironwork of a press, we can account for most of his modest achievement.

One of his blunders visibly affected the colony's plans for the press, I believe. In at least two of the surviving copies of the Bay Psalm Book, sheet D was turned the wrong way in reiteration. If the sample is representative of the copies printed, more than three hundred copies of the first edition were defective. In my edition of the Day-Green Accounts, I argue that these records of the Cambridge press begin at the expiration of Stephen Day's indenture, following which, they show, he printed thirty-three sheets of the Bay Psalm Book.[52] In short, his indenture expired just after he had completed signature D. The timing is probably coincidental, but one can imagine the thoughts that raced through the heads of President Dunster and the other Founders. A close analogy might be the sensations of a modern scholar when a computer program crashes, erasing hours of toil. Did the experience haunt them one year later, when they ordered nineteen copies of Nathaniel Ward's "Body of Liberties" to be copied out by hand? It was slow work, but it never risked such disasters.

We rather need to ask why Cambridge printing became so much more competent after 1643. By comparison with earlier productions, the 1647 *Theses*, the 1648 *Laws*, and the 1649 *Platform* are a pleasure to behold. This is not entirely the effect of the pretty new type with its abundance of swash capitals. It also appears in the heightened sense of form and hierarchy—the use of italic for the preface to the Cambridge *Platform*, for example; the nicely poised side-notes; the italicized quotations. Indeed, Stephen barely understood how to convey a new paragraph, apart from some verbal flag like "obj. 2," "Ans." or "Queston.," inconsistently capitalized and italicized. How did Matthew Day acquire this skill? Not, obviously, from his embittered father. Nor am I tempted by Winship's conjecture that an "experienced printer" accompanied the Glover party across the Atlantic, taught the Day children as they sailed, and then returned to England, his duty done.[53] A likelier source, as Starkey argues, is that shadowy master printer from Rhode Island, Gregory Dexter, who "about the year 1646 . . . was sent for to Boston, to set in order the printing office there," according to the Baptist historian Morgan Edwards.[54] Ezra Stiles confirms the account, adding that his services were particularly required for the almanac; I should say they were necessary altogether.

What conclusion may we draw, then, on this sesquicentenary of the Bay Psalm Book? To escape its nearly indestructible iconicity, I have conned its letters as certain metal sorts, not as an alphanumeric string. A simpler, more obvious metal form will perhaps make the implications of this "reading" clearer. The same trial that produced an account of the Reverend Jose Glover's printing shop also gave us a description of his silver. Both attest the quixotic errand in the wilderness of an accidental tourist who cannot be parted from the comforts of home. The silver particularly impressed the servants, including Stephen Day.

Let us compare the Bay Psalm Book to a piece from this collection, the great salt that his brother-in-law Richard Harris presented to Harvard in 1644.[55] The salt cellar is rich, chaste, and fashionable; the book is botched, antiquated, and shabby, despite its inordinate cost. Yet Glover's illusory expectations glitter in both objects, the silversmith's and the locksmith's. Had he lived to do the honors, what hall, what high table, what grand state occasion would Glover's salt have graced? We can only speculate, with a numbing sense of seventeenth-century Harvard's social and economic inadequacies. Like many Third World countries today, the Bay Colony imported a technology massively inappropriate to its economic infrastructure. Until John Eliot's mission to the Indians anchored it in social purpose later in the century, the printing press made about as much sense in New England as a DC-10 in Djibouti or Burkina Faso today. In Africa, such gadgets show the vision of figures known as the "Guide," the "Sage," the "Teacher," the "Chief of Chiefs," the "No.1 Peasant," and the "National Miracle."[56] In New England, we call them the "Founders."

Their name, of course, also has a typographical meaning, which is not inappropriate here. In the history of the first press, new fonts are associated with major changes in organization, production, and personnel. Large type did not betoken nearsightedness, age, and other disabilities in the seventeenth century; on the contrary, it bespoke social prestige and power. The gradually shrinking type traces with great precision the reality dawning in the collective mind of the colonists: England they could not afford to be, and there are things more needful than symbols. When the colonists demanded "a little more Art" for their psalm book in 1651, they were not rejecting the

literalism of the founders, as Cotton Mather believed. The revisions of the
second edition are quite consistent with the errata and press corrections of
the first. Its typography, however, was revolutionized. The Bay Colonists
learned the hard way that they needed the art of print, which is more than
a workman and an assemblage of press, type, paper, and words—in short,
the "print culture" beloved by their historians. God's Altar needs not their
pollishings, either.

Appendix 1. A Collation of the Bay Psalm Book Facsimiles

Sigla:

  1 (MB)   = *The Bay Psalm Book* (Chicago: University of Chicago Press, 1956)
  2 (MWA)   = Microfiche Evans 4, 1984
  3 (CSmH)   = *The Bay Psalm Book* (New York: Dodd, Mead, 1903)
  4 (RPJCB)   = *A Literal Reprint of the Bay Psalm Book* (New York: C.B. Richard-
                son, 1862)

Note: variants have not been verified against the originals.

Original Collation: (4to) *-***⁴, A-Ll⁴ (24-letter register, omitting J and U) = 148
leaves

Variant settings in the four facsimiles are noted as follows:
Forme *(o)
*3r:1 commaund-] 1,3,4; communicat- 2
   2 severall sorts] 1,3,4; special singing 2
   3 himselfe] 1,3,4; them the 2
Forme *(i)
*4r:5 cleare where] 2; cleared) there 1,3,4
   6 stoppeth mens] 2; stoppe all 1,3,4
Forme **(o)
**1r:5 i.] 2;it 1,3,4
Forme A(o)
Ps 4:5 Let . . . for sacrifices] 1,3; The . . . let sacrificed 2,4
Forme A(i)
Ps 6:6 goanes] 4; groanes 1,2,3
Forme B(i)
Ps 8:6 authoriy] 1,2,4; authority 3
Ps 10:18 ad] 2,4; adde 1,3
Forme E(o)
Ps 27:3 hosta] 2; hoasta 4; hoast 1,3
Forme G(i)
Ps 35:2 buchler] 1,2; buckler 3,4
Ps 35:5 Gcds] 2; Gods 1,3,4
Forme I(o)
Ps 40:8 beart] 2,4; heart 1,3
Forme K(o)

RT, K3r xl, xlv] 1,2; xlv 3,4
Forme Q(i)
Ps 69:23 Their loynes also with trembleing . . . continuallee] 1; with trembling also
make their loynes . . . continuallie 2,3,4
Ps 71:15 it] 1; forth 2,3,4
Forme W(o)
Ps 86:3 daily cry] 1; cry daily 2,3,4
Forme Ee(o)
Ps 119:25 cleav,s] 2; cleav's 1,3,4
Ff(o)
Ps 119:73,81 [Hebrew letters absent]] 3; [Hebrew letters present] 1,2,4

Appendix 2

Five right font/wrong font (roman/italic) sorts, distributed by signatures
     Note: roman character *maxima* are in boldface

	P	S	A	L	M
A	**17**	18	18/1	18/8	16
B	15/1	14	15	23/4	13
C	15	12	18/4	26/4	15
D	13	15	18	21/4	15
E	14	15	13	25/5	**19**/1
F	14	16	12	30/3	12
G	9	15	18	32/5	13
H	11	11	18	30/2	12
I	12	13	19	29/3	18/1
K	16	21	15/1	13	11
L	15	22	22	18/1	11
M	13	16	14	24/3	**19**/1
N	14	19	19	21/1	17
O	15	18	16	11/1	13
P	14/2	**25**	15	18/2	8
Q	14/1	12	16	22/2	15
R	12	22	27	16/1	9
S	13	18	20	14/1	12
T	12	19	22	15	11
V	15	16	26	18	16
W	15	21	13	29/2	17
X	10	18	17	19/1	11
Y	17/1	12	16	28/3	9
Z	17/1	14	19	29/3	11
Aa	11/1	17	18	26/2	15
Bb	13/1	10	**28**	21/3	13
Cc	14	13	21	14/1	10
Dd	15/1	10	15	27/4	11
Ee	16	10	20	**49**/5	12
Ff	9	19	16	25/1	19

Gg	17/2	18	20	38/5	16
Hh	17/2	21	24	48/5	11
Ii	12/1	15	25	27/2	9
Kk	15	11	16	31/1	12
Ll	13/1	16	9	30/1	8

Appendix 3. Recurrence of four identified pieces of type, by forme

		mI	dI	AI	ssI
A	(i)	Ps 7:4, 4	Ps 6:7, 1		
B	(i)	Ps 11:2,3	Ps 12:2, 1		
C	(i)	Ps 18:17, 1		Ps 18:19, 1	
D	(i)	Ps 22:6,1		Ps 19:13, 1	
E	(i)	Ps 25:19, 2	Ps 23:4, 3		
F	(i)	Ps 31:4,2	Ps 28(2):9, 4		
G	(i)		Ps 33:8, 3		
H	(i)		Ps 35:27,5		
	(o)	Ps 37:21,4			
I	(i)		Ps 39:6, 2		
	(o)	Ps 38:20,4		Ps 42:10, 1	
K	(i)	Ps 46:5, 1	Ps 44:3, 5		
L	(i)	Ps 49 (title)	Ps 50:14,1		
	(o)			Ps 50 (title)	
M	(i)	Ps 51:15, 1			Ps 51(2):13, 1
	(o)			Ps 51:10, 1	
N	(i)	Ps 56:4, 4	Ps 56:3,2		Ps 59:3, 2
	(o)			Ps 55:16, 1	
O	(i)	Ps 61:6, 2			
P	(i)	Ps 66:2, 2	Ps 68:17, 1		Ps 68:20, 4
Q	(i)		Ps 71:13, 1		
T	(i)		Ps 78:42, 1		
V	(i)		Ps 81:4, 3		
	(o)				Ps 82:1, 2
W	(i)	Ps 86:17, 4	Ps 85(2):4, 1		Ps 88:6, 2
X	(i)	Ps 89:50, 2			Ps 89:15, 1
Y	(o)		Ps 95:4, 1		
Z	(i)	Ps 96:11, 4			
	(o)				Ps 97:12, 3
Aa	(i)	Ps 103:18, 4			
	(o)				Ps 103:15, 1
Bb	(o)		Ps 105:25, 1		
Cc	(i)			Ps 107:39, 1	
	(o)		Ps 107:15,2		
Ff	(i)	Ps 119:69, 2			
Gg	(i)	Ps 119:175, 2			
Ii	(i)	Ps 138:7, 5			
Kk	(i)	Ps 142:7, 4			
**	(o)	**3r, 22			

Notes

1. See, e.g., Randall McLeod, "ALTVM SAPERE Parole d'homme et Verbe divin Les chronologies de la Bible hebraique in-quarto de Robert Estienne," in *La Bible imprimée dans l'Europe moderne*, ed. Bertram Schwarzbach (Paris: Bibliothèque Nationale de France, 1999), 83–141.

2. [I describe the collectors of Americana and the bibliographical consequences of their collecting in a chapter on learned culture in volume three of "A History of the Book in America" (forthcoming)].

3. Winship, *Cambridge Press*; Lawrence Granville Starkey, "A Descriptive and Analytical Bibliography of the Cambridge, Massachusetts Press from its Beginnings to the Publication of Eliot's 'Indian Bible' in 1663" (Ph.D. dissertation, University of Virginia, 1949); Zoltán Haraszti, *The Enigma of the Bay Psalm Book* (Chicago: University of Chicago Press, 1956). The only textual work since Haraszti are John H. Dorenkamp's two articles, "The Bay Psalm Book and the Ainsworth Psalter," *Early American Literature* 7 (1972): 3–16; and "The New England Puritans and the Name of God," *Procs. AAS* 80 (1970): 67–70. I am grateful to Professor Gwynne Evans for drawing my attention to them. In addition to the specific acknowledgements I make below, I am grateful to Jerry Anderson, Terry Belanger, Norman Fiering, Katharine Pantzer, Michael Winship, and John Lane for friendly assistance.

4. [Alternatively, Steven Day, the spelling Amory used in the original version of this essay but not consistently elsewhere.]

5. Gray Graffam, "A Discovery of Seventeenth-Century Printing Types in Harvard Yard," *HLB* 30 (1982): 229–31.

6. As Professor Terry Belanger of the University of Virginia [at the time of publication, Columbia University] pointed out to me (speaking from his own experience).

7. These are my twenty-line measurements; Starkey's differ slightly, but not significantly.

8. A professional printer has identified five different sizes of type on the title-page of the Bay Psalm Book alone; I can only make out three, however, and believe that he was misled by the italics, which are smaller on the body than the romans. Sidney A. Kimber, *Cambridge Press Title-Pages, 1640–1665* (Tacoma Park, Md.: Walter L. Kimber, 1954), 102.

9. Thomas, *Hist. Printing*, 43–44; Starkey, "Descriptive," xxiv–xxvii; Winship, *Cambridge Press*, 335. Jerome Anderson kindly drew my attention to a notice of Glover fundraising in England for Harvard College and a printing press, in May 1638: Kenneth W. Shipps, "The Puritan Emigration to New England: A New Source on Motivation," *NEHGR* 135 (1981): 95. Unfortunately, it adds little to our knowledge of Glover's motives.

10. W. Craig Ferguson, *Pica Roman Type in Elizabethan England* (Aldershot, Eng.: Scolar Press, 1989), 3–4; the j is also intrusive, possibly at an earlier stage of the font's history. Cf. R. B. McKerrow, "Some Notes on the Letters i, j, u and v in Sixteenth Century Printing," *The Library* 3rd ser. 1 (1910): 258–59, who dates the introduction of this "Ramist" letter in England to 1578; and Nina Catach, *L'orthographe française à l'époque de la Renaissance* (Genève: Droz, 1968), 128ff.

11. Mark H. Curtis, "William Jones: Puritan Printer and Propagandist," *The Library* 5th ser. 19 (1964): 38–66; I am indebted to Katherine Pantzer for additional information on both printers, information that figures in the revised STC. In particular, Jones did not die in 1626, as Curtis supposes, but in 1641.

12. No less an expert than Isaiah Thomas, indeed, described the type as "entirely new" (*Hist. Printing*, 54), but I am unable to account for his opinion. A number of pieces were certainly used and battered before the printing of the Bay Psalm Book began, including some hebrew *shins*. The italics are notably deficient in sorts, which the compositor made good from the romans, and there is a hebrew *ayin* that seems to have been whittled from wood. These are absolute deficiencies in the sense that the missing sorts are nowhere attested in the surviving products of the press.

13. President Chauncy to the Company, October 27, 1669, *Some Correspondence between the Governors and Treasurers of the New England Company in London and the Commissioners of the United Colonies in America . . . and Others between the Years 1657 and 1712* (London: E. Stock, 1897), 64. Compare the piddling order in 1710 for 30 lbs. of great premier roman and other type, to be used in a proposed edition of the Indian Bible: William Kellaway, *The New England Company, 1649–1776* (London: Longmans, 1961), 154.

14. Samuel Eliot Morison, *The Founding of Harvard College* (Cambridge, Mass.: Harvard University Press, 1935), 329.

15. For a scholarly edition of the documents, see *Pubs. CSM* 15 (Boston, 1925): 20–21, 174–75.

16. [George Brinley (1817–1875), a private collector of New England imprints.]

17. The exact figures are less important here than the order of magnitude: 480–500 (Starkey) or 500 almanacs a year (Winship) are unacceptable estimates. Starkey's discussion of the almanacs (pp. 56–57) is a useful corrective to Winship (p. 75), who argues that Day and Green estimated Dunster's profits from now lost documents; and his analysis of the evidence indeed suggests that the ratio of almanacs to *Theses/Quaestiones* was 3:1. Further it will not go, without some proof of the price at which the almanacs actually sold. Starkey assumes they sold for 1d each, the "normal price" of a single-sheet almanac in sixteenth-century England. Book almanacs sold for 2d, and this price rose to as much as 4d in the following century (Bernard Capp, *Astrology and the Popular Press: English Almanacs 1500–1800* [London: Faber and Faber, 1979], 41). At 2d, Starkey's algorithm works out to 240 almanacs a year, not 480, but this may be too low a price; my estimate of 180 almanacs a year would imply a price of about 3d. The algorithm operates on the cost of paper, however, and we have no evidence of the actual price at which colonial almanacs sold, much less of the press's margin of profit (if, indeed, the Founders ever thought in these terms). See the edition of the accounts, in my exhibition catalogue *First Impressions*.

18. Bailyn, *Merchants*, esp. 60ff.

19. David Grayson Allen, *In English Ways: The Movement of Societies and the Transferal of English Local Law and Custom to Massachusetts Bay in the Seventeenth Century* (Chapel Hill: University of North Carolina Press, 1981), 219–20.

20. Winship, *Cambridge Press*, 110.

21. In order to explain the Bay Psalm Book's extraordinary press run, Winship supposes that it also sold in England; Starkey, more sensibly, argues that the operators of the press did not expect to make a profit and left the distribution of their stock to time. Winship's conjecture encounters all sorts of difficulties: the Bay Psalm Book infringed the Stationers' Company's patent and was unlicensed to boot; the leaders of Massachusetts stoutly opposed the export of their manufactures, as Bailyn shows; the earliest evidence of any copy in England is the extracts from the

preface in Nathanael Homes's *Gospel Musick* (1644), who implies that he had only recently learned of it; and only one of the eleven surviving copies has an English provenance.

22. Littlefield, *Boston Printers*, I, 97–114; followed by Winship and Starkey, and by the American Antiquarian Society, *A Society's Chief Joys* (Worcester, Mass.: American Antiquarian Society, 1969), 18. There is much quibbling over the plain language of Stephen's claim. He was probably assisted by his three workmen and his son, but they worked under his direction and so far as we know (or can tell from their products) none of them had any special skill in printing. The conclusive fact for me is simply that the appearance of the press's products improved after 1643. In this context, the conjecture that Matthew actually ran the shop from the beginning raises more problems than it solves. Winship (p. 13) insists on the late testimony of Samuel Green, who described Matthew Day as "him that was brought over for [printing] by Mr Jose Glover"; this is directly contradicted by Stephen's indenture, however. Starkey (p. 6) rather dwells on Matthew's appearance in the imprint of the 1647 almanac, which is no evidence at all of his role in 1639.

23. Winship, *Cambridge Press*, 11; Thomas, *Hist. Printing*, 52.

24. *DAB*, entry under: Day, Stephen.

25. For the provenance of the eleven known copies, see Amory, *First Impressions*, arguing that the New York Public Library copy also comes from the Prince Collection.

26. Luther Farnham, *A Glance at Private Libraries* (Boston: Crocker and Brewster, 1855), 31.

27. Wilberforce Eames, *A List of Editions of the "Bay Psalm Book" or New England Version of the Psalms* (New York, 1885).

28. [The antiquarians' name for the English who settled on Cape Ann in the mid-1620s.]

29. [Henry Ainsworth, *The Book of Psalms, Englished* (Amsterdam, c. 1612); Ainsworth was among the radical Separatists who sought refuge in the Netherlands in the 1590s. In the 1540s Thomas Sternhold and John Hopkins prepared a translation that became widely used in the Church of England.]

30. For a discussion of regional differences, see "Psalmody in Coastal Massachusetts and in the Connecticut River Valley," in *The Bay and the River: 1600–1900*, ed. Peter Benes (Boston: Boston University, 1982), 117–31. This is not the issue, however: no one would ever call Isaac Watts's version the "River Psalm Book." Shurtleff's innuendo is political, not geographical.

31. Fairbanks and Trent, *New England Begins*, 2, no. 112.

32. Prince Collection, Boston Public Library, 21.15.

33. Starkey, "Descriptive" (p. 15), seems to believe that the translation was already projected in 1636.

34. Winship, *Cambridge Press*, 17, 24; 4 *Colls. MHS* 6 (1863): 99.

35. Graham Shaw, *Printing in Calcutta to 1800* (London: Bibliographical Society, 1981).

36. The list of "Miscellaneous Metrical Versions" in STC (2nd ed.) 2725f. is revealing. After 1603, several are published in Holland (STC 2731 (Dod), 2734.5 (Ainsworth), 2735 (Wither) and 2737 (Rous)); those that are published in England, with only one exception, are either patented (STC 2732, 2736–36a ("King James")) and

21724–25 (Sandys) or published "with permission of the Company of Stationers" (STC 2734). The one exception is Brathwaite's version (STC 3581). Failure to obtain a patent meant that the Stationers' Company simply appropriated the new version (see W. W. Greg, *Companion to Arber* [Oxford: Clarendon Press, 1967], 320–21). For Wither's earlier battle for his *Hymnes*, see now Norman E. Carlson, "Wither and the Stationers," *SB* 19 (1966): 210–15.

37. Wroth, *Col. Printer*, 2nd ed., rev. and enl. (Charlottesville: University Press of Virginia, 1964), 12–13.

38. David Cressy, *Coming Over: Migration and Communication Between England and New England in the Seventeenth Century* (Cambridge: Cambridge University Press, 1987), 44, 64.

39. Winship, *Cambridge Press*, 100; [the allusion is to the revised version of 1651].

40. Ibid., 30.

41. Norman S. Grabo, "How Bad Is the Bay Psalm Book?" *Papers of the Michigan Academy of Science, Arts and Letters* 46 (1961): 605–15.

42. See Appendix 1 for details. [Paul Sternberg has pointed out (in an email letter to me dated 5 January 2004) that the second variant is "an actual press variant," the first being an "editorial rewrite that occurred after the printing had been completed and thus was included in the errata." He adds that his own list of press variants "contains several that Amory does not have," noting that neither list "is based on complete collations of all known copies done from the originals" and that the only variant thus far discovered with any importance is the one concerning Psalm 69: 23.]

43. Thomas, *Hist. Printing*, 54.

44. Winship, *Cambridge Press*, 30ff; Starkey, "Descriptive," 17 (claiming that the defects have been "grievously overemphasized"). Some employees of the Société typographique de Neuchâtel were also subliterate: cf. Jacques Rychner, "Running a Printing House in Eighteenth-Century Switzerland," *The Library* 6th ser. 1 (1979): 15.

45. Thomas, *Hist. Printing*, 54.

46. Starkey, "Descriptive," 20–21; and for a sample of the variations in typesetting and type damage from one forme to another, see Appendix 2. I cannot rule out occasional transfers: the running title of I3r, "PSALME xl, xli," survived on K3r in an early state as "PSALME xl, xlv," and was corrected to "PSALME xlv" when Stephen noticed that there was only one psalm on the new page. This does not establish the transfer of an entire skeleton, however: Stephen simply reused part of what he saw as text.

47. See Appendix 2.

48. [Nicolas Barker], "A Scandal in America," *Book Collector* 37 (1988): 15. The first occurrence is on Cc2v.

49. See Appendix 3. I am much indebted to Paul R. Sternberg, who kindly sent me an account of fifteen identifiable pieces that extends and confirms these preliminary findings.

50. [Mr. Sternberg has not yet published his findings as this book was going to press.]

51. *L'Histoire de l'édition française*, ed. H.-J. Martin and Roger Chartier, 4 vols. (Paris: Promodis, 1982, 1984), 2: 125. My argument appeals to normal trade practice, and it is fair to note that Brian McMullin, viewing the slides that illustrated a version of this paper I delivered in Melbourne, felt that the typesetting was no worse than

that of many of Day's contemporaries. While deferring to McMullin's experience, I still find it hard to believe that a master printer would have taught Day to make such howlers, though he might have tolerated them.

52. Amory, *First Impressions*, 61–63. [The total number of sheets was 37, as James N. Green pointed out to me.]

53. Winship, *Cambridge Press*, 14.

54. Starkey, "Descriptive," 62ff.

55. Illustrated in Fairbanks and Trent, *New England Begins*, 3, no. 453.

56. David Lamb, *The Africans* (New York: Vintage Books, 1987), 47–48.

3. "A Bible and Other Books": Enumerating the Copies in Seventeenth-Century Essex County

"Ubiquitous in the personal libraries of New Englanders, yet rare in their institutional libraries, and entirely absent from our national retrospective bibliography before 1775, the Bible occupies a problematic position in the history of the American book." The ironies of this sentence (ironies, however, that ignore the publication of German-language Bibles in the colonies) resonate throughout the essay that follows. "A Bible and Other Books" transforms a well-practiced genre of scholarship, the description of books listed in probate inventories made after death.[1] Amory was the first to train a bibliographer's eye upon the entries that appear so commonly in these inventories, the maddeningly laconic "A bible and other books," and the first, therefore, to perceive that the inventories discriminate among three different formats of Bibles. Once he had worked out the differences, the data became the doorway to a discussion of the trade in imported Bibles and the solving of a bibliographical mystery (a false imprint). More remarkably, the data on formats enabled Amory to propose how the Bible was a social artifact as well as one deemed "religious." In doing so he moved beyond a blandly "religious" interpretation of New Englanders' reading and the religious/secular classification that others before him used in analyzing such inventories.[2]

Another kind of bibliographical information figures in the essay, Amory's awareness that some of the colonists owned "cheap, piratical editions" of the Bible printed in the Netherlands, many with supplements bound in with them, like the Book of Common Prayer. Moreover, in the absence of an effective book trade until almost the end of the century, the supply of Bibles was declining—indeed, declining sharply according to the Essex County inventories, for the "average number of Bibles per testator dropped by nearly fifty percent between 1650 and 1670 [and] the number of 'old Bibles' rose by a factor of four." "A Bible and Other Books" is thus a remarkable example of how bibliographical evidence opens out into a wider inquiry that transforms the very genre of which it is part. The appendices reproduce the information in the Essex county probate inventories but classified and arranged according to the analysis worked out in the body of the essay: differentiating formats of Bibles, English authors or publications from colonial authors, and arranging books into the categories of "divinity" and "other subjects."

SOURCE: *Order and Connexion: Studies in Bibliography and Book History*, ed. R. C. Alston (Cambridge, Mass.: D.S. Brewer, 1997), 17–37. Permission to republish has been granted by D.S. Brewer.

"It would be an interesting and by no means insuperable task for one of our industrious bibliographers," wrote Samuel Eliot Morison in 1936, "to make a catalogue of all the books that are known to have been in New England before 1700. My guess is that he would find about ten thousand separate titles, and that the number of copies of each work would range from several thousand of the Bible, and several hundred of the more popular works of puritan divinity, down to a single copy of the less common works."[3] The bibliographers whose work he so eagerly appropriated were a remarkable group, whose productions include Alfred C. Potter's reconstruction of John Harvard's library and Henry M. Dexter's account of Elder Brewster's; Worthington C. Ford's *Boston Book Market*; Arthur O. Norton's identification of books from the libraries of Harvard students; and Thomas Goddard Wright and Clifford K. Shipton's research in catalogues and probate inventories. [4] Morison extended their research from a variety of new sources to prove that seventeenth-century Harvard was a true university and not, as he put it, a divinity school, and that religion was not so overwhelmingly important in Puritan New England that it stifled an interest in science and literature. How many know, for example, that in 1707 Judge Samuel Sewall acquired a copy of Ben Jonson's works in Rhode Island; or that Charles Chauncy, president of the college at mid-century, owned a copy of Spenser? Morison is a mine of information of just this kind.

Morison's suggestion was never pursued, however; in part, perhaps, because he himself soon moved on to larger subjects than New England, but also in part because the interests of bibliographers were narrowing. Charles Evans, Wilberforce Eames, Douglas McMurtrie and the research he directed under the auspices of the Works Progress Administration in the 1930s, it seems, had refocused attention from the books that were actually in our early colonial libraries to those that were printed in the colonies. The study of such celebrated collections of books as the libraries of the Mathers or the Winthrops, the Prince Library (in which his "New England Library" formed only a small part), and Harvard College Library languished. Edwin Wolf's Lyell Lectures and Richard Beale Davis's *Intellectual Life in the Colonial South* were the first attempts in half a century to attack the problems,[5] and for New England, Morison's work has still not been superseded.

The immense value of Evans's work and its various descendants for bibliography is not in doubt, but their historical value is problematic. As G. Thomas Tanselle observes in his recent statistical analysis of Evans, the figures "do not necessarily tell one very much about what was being read in America or even what was available in bookshops," they "cannot be taken to represent the total number of items actually printed," and they "do not necessarily reflect the amount of printing performed."[6]

The historians of New England culture, too, seemed to have lost confidence in bibliography. In 1939, Perry Miller cited most of Morison's industrious bibliographers in his classic study *The New England Mind*,[7] but only, it would seem, to dismiss them: "Mere enumeration of volumes possessed by one or another seventeenth-century New Englander will not of itself declare what ideas were taken from them, still less how the appropriated material was worked into the Puritan metaphysic."[8] Not that their enumeration would have advanced Miller's argument much, for his "metaphysic" rested, for the most part, on an exceedingly elite and solidly connected group of six colonial authors: "in most instances," he noted, "it is a matter of complete indifference or chance that a quotation comes from Cotton instead of Hooker, from Winthrop instead of Willard; all [these] writers were in substantial agreement upon all the propositions which I am discussing in this book."[9] Those lonely copies of Spenser or Jonson, which Morison thought so promising for New England culture, have been thrust into outer darkness. Weaving Ramist technologia together with federal theology and Congregational church polity, Miller's synthesis left little room for Morison's anachronistic distinction between a university and a divinity school.

Today, in the burgeoning history of the book in England and America, Morison's suggestion takes on new importance, but it is no longer as easily answered as he imagined. Even an industrious bibliographer today would baulk at "browsing through six of our older libraries and pulling down likely volumes," as Morison described the research of his colleague Arthur O. Norton.[10] For one thing, quantities of older books, even at institutions as venerable as the Boston Athenaeum, the Essex Institute, or the American Antiquarian Society, have since been deaccessioned; for another, the exponential growth of libraries since 1936, the creation of satellite depositories, and the introduction of new classifications if, indeed, any classification is preserved at all, have rendered the shelves of our older libraries essentially unbrowsable.

Finally, however, the adequacy of any library for such research depends on its history and arrangement and the type of book we are looking for. Norton no doubt did a good bit of browsing, but he profited even more from the vast collection of textbooks then in the Essex Institute, and now divided between the Houghton Library and the Harvard School of Education. One's prospects for finding useful material would naturally be poorer if one were looking for Bibles. In 1723, Harvard held only five English Bibles, in a collection of some 3,500 volumes.[11] Congregational societies had no reason to collect Bibles, since their liturgy included neither epistles nor gospels. The premier American collections today, in the New York Public Library and the American Bible Society, and the not inconsiderable holdings of Harvard and the Congregational Library in Boston, were formed in the nineteenth and twentieth centuries, and include items of colonial ownership only by accident. With moderate industry, I have now located only thirty-two Bibles with some claim to a seventeenth-century colonial provenance.[12] Many more, I suspect, remain in the possession of historical societies, calendared as part of family archives, and inaccessible by title. Their systematic retrieval would be the work of a lifetime.

Morison's "guess" apparently rested on a rough analysis of the Middlesex and Essex County probate records made by Clifford K. Shipton, and on his own appraisal of the subjects represented in the Harvard College Library catalogue of 1723.[13] Since Harvard's holdings seem as unrepresentative of New England culture then as they are today, I shall confine myself here to the *Probate Records of Essex County, Massachusetts*, edited in three volumes by George F. Dow.[14] Seventeenth-century Essex was a small but relatively important part of the English colonies: in 1690, it had a larger European population than either Pennsylvania or New York, and outside Massachusetts, only Connecticut, Maryland, and Virginia outranked it.[15] As its name suggests, most of its settlers came from East Anglia, with contingents from Hampshire at Newbury and from Yorkshire at Rowley. Its wealth lay in farming, fishing, and shipping; its merchants traded salt cod, beef and pork, and barrel staves with Virginia, the Caribbean, and the Canaries, taking tobacco, sugar, molasses, and wine in return to Europe. After 1655, the Navigation Acts limited their trade in certain respects, but to judge by some of their creditors, the law was not always enforced.[16] English "returns" were overwhelmingly in various kinds of cloth and hardware, but might also include books, though I do not find any stocks in their inventories before 1681.[17]

Dow transcribed the records of 1044 Essex estates between 1635 and 1681, amounting to perhaps a quarter of the county's total mortality during this period.[18] I have selected 765 of these, for which either an inventory or an inventory and a will survive for descendants down to 1680.[19] About forty-eight percent of the estates in this sample had books, however vaguely described; this compares with the more urban Middlesex County, to the south, where, according to David D. Hall, sixty percent of the surviving inventories for roughly the same period mention at least one book, usually a Bible.[20] My sample contains mostly male testators and heads of families, the women being exclusively widows, and, of course, there are no children, and the average age of the testators is relatively high, compared with the population at large. This also means that they are comparatively wealthy, but their wealth ranges widely from a few pounds to over £8,000.[21] One testator had over £12 of books, in a total estate of only £27.[22] I am not sure at what age it was usual to own a book, but a Suffolk County testator left money to buy a Bible for each of his ten grandchildren when he or she reached twelve.[23] The enormous fertility of New Englanders, and the relatively high rate of infant mortality, suggest to me that my sample may well represent half of the potential book-owning population of Essex County, and that the main exclusions are probably women and servants, who would have had access to the books of the household. Interestingly, a number of the testators who owned books signed by a mark, so that they were unable to write, though, as Margaret Spufford observes, they may still have been able to read.[24]

The largest holdings of books are invariably described in a lump as a "library" or "study," worth from £30 to £100, which ministers like Nathaniel and Ezekiel Rogers, Edward Norris and William Worcester kept upstairs, out of sight. Here too there were Bibles, no doubt in Hebrew, Latin, and Greek as well as in English, but the inventories give few details because their significance is personal and professional, not social. Downstairs, in the "hall" or "parlour," beside the best bed, other testators held what are often called "a Bible and other books" worth a pound to a pound and a half. We learn no more of these collections unless he or she makes a specific bequest, or unless the same group of books is more specifically described in the inventory or will of the legatee; but we have learned enough. Heads of families were enjoined to read the Bible to their families by their ministers; by a note to Genesis 17:27 of the Geneva Bible; and by the statute of 34 & 35 Henry VIII c. 1; hence they display their one to five copies at the front of the house, with other tokens of social status.[25]

Intellectual historians like Morison and Miller are naturally impatient with a people who suppress their ownership of the works of Alstedius, Comenius, Zanchius, Pareus, Amesius, and other learned men, and parade their multiple copies of the Bible in obscure sizes and conditions, but their priorities are not those of seventeenth-century New England. The small size of these libraries, I think, gives added weight to the appraisers' and the testators' selections: titles seem to be specified quite at random, and they must represent between a quarter and a tenth of the collections from which they were taken. No one title, indeed, has much cultural importance, but their aggregate testimony must be reliable.

Thus no one doubts the importance of the Bible, for example, though if we took its measure from institutional libraries its numbers would be negligible. Without in any way deprecating federal theology, on the one hand, or Spenser and Jonson, on the other, we need not doubt that animal husbandry, herbs, and navigation were of consuming interest to some New England minds; and the inventories confirm it.

Down to 1680, these wills and inventories specifically describe 251 English

Bibles, one Latin Bible, seven New Testaments, and eighteen metrical psalms; at least twenty-nine European divines, represented in sixty-three books, and five colonial divines, in six; seven "sea books"; five "physic books," including the famous herbal of Rembert Dodoens; three books on animal husbandry by Markham, Mascall, and Blundeville, respectively; two on geography by Heylyn and Purchas; one history book, one political tract, one manuscript book of "mathematix," and one dictionary, probably English. The total ratio of 277 biblical books to sixty-nine from divinity and twenty-one from other subjects is over twice as strong in divinity and about seven times as strong in other subjects as Morison's "guess." At most twenty of these 367 books may have been printed in New England, if we generously suppose that all eighteen metrical psalms were colonial editions of the Bay Psalm Book.[26]

The preponderance of religion is striking, but the comparative paucity of secular books has no necessary connection with their value. Morison, as we have seen, assigned it a positive value, as does Gloria Main, who groups secular books together with items like wigs, tea-services, and clocks in an "index of amenity."[27] This makes sense for some secular books, I think, such as eighteenth-century novels, magazines, and Newtonian spin-offs, but not for the very utilitarian selection of the Essex inventories. The Puritans' leisure amusements more likely revolved about such speculative theologians as Aquinas, Thomas Brightman, and John Wing, for example. The tendency of historians to categorize books by subject should also be deprecated: compare the drastically limited subject categories of the appraisers, i.e., (A) the Bible; and (B) other books, being (1) good books; (2) sermon books; (3) physic books; (4) paper books; and (5) sea books. Indeed, the assignment of a topic is hopelessly subjective. We blandly call the Bible "religious," for example, without the slightest recognition of what religion—Jewish, Catholic, or Protestant—might be involved, or of the considerably different secular components these religions would assign to their reading of its contents. We might more usefully ask what a book is good for, where it resided, and how it was read.

Ubiquitous in the personal libraries of New Englanders, yet rare in their institutional libraries, and entirely absent from our national retrospective bibliography before 1775, the Bible occupies a problematic position in the history of the American book. Its uses were more than religious—necessarily so, as the bulk of the household's printed possessions.[28] It served as a primer, from which the mother taught her children to read, and as entertainment; Christian allegorizing could not abolish the literary value of Job, Jonah, Esther, or the Song of Songs, and, of course, Holy Writ did not include the Apocrypha, for Protestants. Little girls stitched the story of

Tobias in their samplers—which is not an inspired text, so that their samplers could not have aroused the Puritans' iconophobia.[29] Outside the household, the Bible's political and legal authority appears in John Cotton's proposed law code of Massachusetts Bay, "Moses His Judicialls." Well aware of the dangers of such a two-handed engine in an unlearned grip, the clergy incessantly, but not always successfully, tried to control its use through preaching. When we hear or read about Israel today, we are likely to think of the former British Mandate; Puritans thought rather of New England, and named their settlements Salem, Rehoboth, or Padanaram. This blurring of the boundary between the sacred and the profane is a typical consequence of the Reformation, of course, just as their separation, to which Morison and Main appeal, begins in the Enlightenment. "If God spare my life," William Tyndale told a bishop, "ere many years I will cause a boy that driveth the plough shall know more scripture than thou dost."[30]

The paradoxical authority of the Bible—alternately religious, yet secular; personal, yet political—and the impact of national publication on this authority may be illustrated by two frontispieces: one sacred, engraved by John Foster in about 1675, and one profane, by John Dunlop in 1792. These are personal statements, of course, but they may serve to illustrate two ways of looking at a single text and subject, as shaped by the Reformation and the Enlightenment. Indeed, they seem to portray two different objects. Dunlop's engraving appeared as a frontispiece to the first American edition of the Reverend John Brown's *Self-Interpreting Bible*, published in 1792 (Figure 9). Before a temple of Liberty, Peace, and Justice, sits America clutching a scroll labeled the Constitution, and leaning on a tablet inscribed with the name of Washington and other revolutionary heroes. Civil Liberty stands beside her, introducing Religious Liberty, on her knees, streaming light and presenting an open volume, with the improbable running title "Holy Bible." Or so I understand the allegory from the 1790 prospectus: Religious Liberty might equally well be Revelation, Truth, or Enlightenment, and the book might be anything, without its label. The original volume, measuring 42.5 × 25.5 × 9 cm., and weighing over seven kilos, is appreciably larger and evidently heavier than Religious Liberty's, but the authoritative folio format is what signifies. The allusion to the Bill of Rights is unmistakable: America's scroll, a format reserved for imperial charters in the colonies, whose local laws had invariably been recorded in manuscript or printed codices, proclaims the primacy of secular law over the revelation of the Bible, the independence of the new nation under God, and the derivative status of Religious Liberty, who is, after all, on her knees.

Brown's *Self-Interpreting Bible* was published by subscription, and boasts a list of some 1,400 names headed by George Washington; it is one of several such enterprises launched in 1790.[31] John Foster, however, was no entrepreneur, but a "meer mechanic," as Stephen Botein reminds us;[32] no doubt he sold Bibles, but he regarded preaching as a truer form of "publication." His engraving of Richard Mather was probably designed for insertion in a previously published edition of his *Life* (1670), by Increase Mather (Figure 5). In his left hand, the preacher holds a small-format book, probably duodecimo or less, open to show two columns to a page—the layout of small Bibles since the twelfth century, and by the seventeenth found in very few other titles. We can immediately infer from the history of its publication in the seventeenth century that his copy of the Bible does not include the Apocrypha, and that it is an Authorized Version, "appointed to be read in churches." So we are in church, or rather, meeting. In his right hand, Mather holds the spectacles that, at his advanced age, he needs to read the small type; he has just announced the text of his sermon, and removes them, in order to see his congregation, ranged before him according to their social status. Are they all there? Foster catches him looking. He did not really need the spectacles, of course, since he knows his text by heart; and the congregation mark the chapter and verse in their small Bibles, but not, or not yet, the sense. Foster depicts a text imbedded in the life of a particular church community, hierarchically doled out in small, incoherent, anxiously scrutinized portions. No light emanates from this black authority; the book is open, but, as if in a Bergman film, the words remain illegible, because the preacher has not yet begun to speak. We must distinguish, I think, the Bible as a continuous text or story, as it was read at home, from the Bible as chapter and verse, as it was read in meetings; even if the division of the verses into numbered paragraphs broke up the sense, as John Locke noted, family reading re-connected it.[33] Size or format is clearly a major index of this cultural difference: you cannot hold a fifteen-pound Bible between your thumb and forefinger, nor can a duodecimo or eighteenmo suitably represent the text for formal presentation; and it is not very useful to lump these objects together as "Bibles" or "religious books."

Indeed the Bible, uniquely among seventeenth-century texts, is fully provided for in a range of formats and prices, for a variety of purchasers and uses. The appraisers preserve these distinctions in the inventories, in order to justify their valuations. Theirs is the ultimate short-short-title catalogue, consisting of three titles: a "Bible"; a "Testament," or separate printing of the New Testament; and a "Psalm Book," or separately bound edition of the

Engrav'd for the American Edition   of Brown's Family Bible

FRONTISPIECE

Figure 9. Title page engraving by John Dunlop for first American edition of John Brown, *Self-Referencing Bible* (Philadelphia, 1792). Courtesy of the Houghton Library, Harvard University.

metrical psalms. It distinguishes three, and only three, "editions" of the Bible. A "great Bible" is in folio, worth, usually, over ten shillings; a "small Bible," in octavo or less, is rarely worth more than three shillings. Plain "Bibles," in between, are therefore quartos; if they are "old Bibles," however, they may be worth no more than the small formats. This tripartite scheme, of course, is also standard in the arrangement of most seventeenth and eighteenth-century book catalogues, and appears in the *Catalogus Librorum Bibliothecae Harvardianae* of 1723.

Unfortunately, the distribution of biblical formats in the inventories cannot be as precisely determined as one could wish because, as specific bequests show, the appraisers occasionally lumped one or more formats together in the plural "Bibles," or worse, "Bibles and other books." There are occasionally ambiguous descriptions, such as "a Bible and other small books," or a "woman's Bible." This last was probably in small format: one husband can refer to "my Smallest byble which was my wives," and one Bible I know of is a duodecimo bound in red morocco, gilt and clasped, which passed down through three generations of women all named Hannah,[34] part of their "Sunday go-to-meeting" dress, I suppose, and the expensive morocco binding and silver clasps would explain the exceptionally high valuation of five shillings.

The formats of the plural "Bibles" must be estimated by using the group's total valuation as a guide. This involves two somewhat doubtful assumptions: that the plural ordinarily specifies only two copies; and that the formats ordinarily have an intrinsic value; though, as we have seen, a splendidly bound and clasped small Bible might be worth as much as five shillings, and one folio, at least, was appraised at only 6 shillings. I suspect, too, that the appraisers specified "great Bibles" more readily than "small Bibles," so I have counted sixteen copies as "small" because of their low price, even though they are not specifically so described. Finally, a fair number of Bibles of indeterminable format must lurk under the blanket heading of "books," particularly in the larger collections, some fifty-one copies in all, if we assume that collections of "books" valued at over one pound ordinarily included at least one Bible; but I ignore these copies in my account. My final total of forty-six folios, 134 quartos, and seventy-one small formats, then, should be taken with several grains of salt—in particular, I suspect that I must have understated the number of small formats. Still, these figures are a considerable improvement over Morison's "guess," and represent the small private libraries of seventeenth-century New England more reliably than any figures we surmise from the copies that survive today. However inadequate a sample of the original stock, the thirty-two seventeenth-century

New England Bibles that I have located nevertheless provide an essential control for interpreting the inventories. Once more, the historically and culturally significant fact is not just a text, but a book or books: our historians, indeed, cite no more than three seventeenth-century New England Bibles, two of them of dubious provenance,[35] and they seem unaware of their actual contents. The text of the Bible, and the works that were normally bound with it, varied according to their bibliographical format, so that a "great Bible," a quarto "Bible," and a "small Bible" in the inventories not only have different texts and functions, but different textual supplements.

To begin with the text itself, the Geneva Bible was available only in quarto after 1611; the colonists favored the cheap, piratical editions printed by J. E. Stam in Amsterdam during the 1630s and 1640s, but falsely dated 1599.[36] Since the Synod of Dort had banned the Apocrypha in 1619, it is absent from these editions—another reason for their cheapness. The Apocrypha continued to be included in the larger-format English printings, but not in duodecimo or smaller, as already observed. As is well known, the Geneva Bible enjoyed a relatively full commentary, whereas the Authorized Version supplied only occasional variant readings, glosses, and textual parallels; in Stam's edition, it was also illustrated with woodcuts of Noah's Ark, Solomon's Temple, and other difficult objects. Such aids might help a busy parent or mistress explain a knotty passage to a child or servant, but the Dutch editions abounded in misprints even by the liberal standards of the age, and, of course, the Geneva Bible was less faithful to the originals. Just as today, one may hear a Revised Standard Version in church yet cling to one's old King James at home, so the Geneva Bible, however unauthoritative, was "familiar"—even Archbishop Laud quoted it. Conversely, the King James Version required the mediation of the preacher all the more urgently for its very authoritativeness, and this mediation in turn leveled the competition between the two versions, as Patrick Collinson has pointed out.[37]

Besides these textual differences, which can be roughly related to the books described in the inventories, the actual copies would have been bound up with various supplements: the Book of Common Prayer, John Speed's genealogical tables, Sternhold and Hopkins's metrical psalms, for the King James Bible, and Herrey's concordance, for the Geneva. As the surviving price lists show, these items were usually included in the price of binding, though the London customer might, perhaps, request the binder to omit them.[38] The colonial purchaser had no such option, unless he specially ordered his copy from England, for most books were imported bound.[39] Just as today a purchaser may take his automobile in the color the dealer has in stock, rather than order the color he prefers, or may pay extra for wire wheels he does not want in order to get immediate transportation, so the colonial customer's tastes in Bibles were shaped by his opportunities and the uniform practices of the trade. A stout, brass-bossed seventeenth-century Dutch folio edition in the library of the Massachusetts Historical Society, for example, is extra-illustrated with a suite of papistical prints by Claes Jansz Visscher, but I doubt that the purchaser was flirting with Rome. Format also determined what items might be bound together.

In a famous anecdote reported in his journal-history, Governor John Winthrop noted that mice had gnawed his Book of Common Prayer but left the Greek Testament and the metrical psalms with which it was bound miraculously intact.[40] This volume must have been in octavo, and it was almost certainly bound to Winthrop's special order, a circumstance that perhaps added piquancy to the divine rebuke. In the teeth of God and his congregations, however, the London trade continued to supply Bibles bound with Books of Common Prayer. Doubtless the Puritans had not just more Anglican prayer books than they could wish, but also more Authorized Versions, if Christopher Hill has accurately stated their preference for the Geneva Bible.[41] The Bay Psalm Book, too, the colonists' most celebrated effort to conform their service to God's Word, was available only in small formats, after the first edition; these would either have to be bound separately, or together with small format Bibles.

The Essex inventories, then, implicitly describe no more than eighty-nine Bay Psalm Books, as opposed to 180 metrical psalms in other versions, most of them Sternhold and Hopkins.[42] So the metropolitan book trade decreed. Swollen with supplements and the Apocrypha, the Authorized Version of the Bible became an almost cubical affair in quarto, whereas the Geneva Bibles are notably slender—almost half the thickness—in a lovely copy in filleted black sheep that belonged to Mariah Mather, and which has neither the Book of Common Prayer nor the metrical psalms. When a Suffolk County testator bequeaths his "thicke Bible," there can be little doubt of its text.[43] Folio Bibles are favored by ministers like John Norton, whose Cambridge folio, now in the Houghton Library, shows many minute annotations in his hand; small formats, I have argued, are usually personal copies, used as "proof" texts for sermons, but also by women and children, who may have no other book. The family format is in quarto, as many copies show that have a manuscript record of the family's births; deaths rarely figure, and christenings not at all. The earliest records are entered on the verso of the title page of the New Testament, and spread out from there, sometimes over several generations, but often enough for only one, in the Bibles I have seen. I wish I knew the origin of this custom, but it cannot be much earlier than Queen Elizabeth, since it presumes a wide lay ownership of Bibles. It contrasts with the Catholic practice of entering children under their saint's day in the Book of Hours.[44]

The symbolism is naively obvious: little Protestants are entered at the beginning of a *novus ordo saeculorum*, facing the genealogy of Jesus Christ in Matthew, and gathered together in a common place or visible church, in the Book of Life (cf. Rev. 13:8). Little Catholics, however, are individually arranged, in the order of an invisible army of saints, spread over the entire church year. Indian as well as European Bibles exhibit these annotations,[45] and I suppose the settlers brought the custom with them. Eventually, the printers made room for it in the Bible, as in the Family Bible printed by Mathew Carey in 1801. Strictly speaking, it departs from the New England Way, which required all members of a church to give a convincing account of their conversion to the congregation.[46] Yet here the parents humbly presume on the fact of their children's salvation—in Adam's fall, it seems, they sinned not at all. Not for the first time, one feels the distance between the New England mind and New England life.

Since Puritan Bibles were the product of London and Amsterdam, their numbers also tell us something about how they got to New England. The Stationers' Company, indeed, had never been known for its enterprise. Michael Sparke's *Scintilla* (1641) makes it quite clear how ineptly they managed the Bible trade. Because they had so successfully cornered production and sales in London, they neglected the provinces, from which most of the settlers came; one leading Stationer claimed in 1582 that he could supply all of England and Scotland with only eight to ten presses.[47] In the event, with many more presses, as Mary Pollard has shown,[48] they supplied them poorly, and the leading members of the Company never pioneered new modes of distribution.

Writing from the perspective of 1848, George Eliot takes it for granted that Captain Donnithorn of *Adam Bede* acquires his copy of Wordsworth and Coleridge's *Lyrical Ballads* from London, and not (as we might expect) from a bookstore in the county town, or even from the original publisher in Bristol. *Mutatis mutandis*, that was also how John Winthrop, Jr. and Increase Mather bought their books, using the Frankfurt *Messkataloge* and the *Term Catalogues* instead of the *Gentleman's Magazine* for information. Unlike their continental brethren, the great London booksellers never established factors for their wares in the larger provincial cities before the eighteenth century.

Books are extremely durable consumer goods, and I assume that any Bibles that arrived on our shores by 1640 would still have been around in 1680; but throughout this period, immigration to New England dropped, reaching a negative value by 1680,[49] so that this form of supply was failing. Thomas Shepard of Charlestown lamented, in an election sermon of 1672, "I wish this be not the condition of many Families, that either there is no Bible, or but a piece of the Bible, and that they can content themselves therewith";[50] in a better world, either the families would have been less contented, or Bibles would have been more plentiful, and I take it that the preacher was grieved for both. What is clear from the inventories is that if they had wished to better their condition, they had no real resource but the booktrade by 1680, and the booktrade was not supplying them. The average number of Bibles per testator dropped by nearly fifty percent between 1650 and 1670, the number of "old Bibles" rose by a factor of four, and Essex merchants before 1681 do not seem to have had any Bibles or indeed any books in stock. The only direct evidence I have discovered is a debt for one Bible, charged as £1 4 "beaver," an incredibly large sum, unless "beaver" was exchanged at a discount from sterling.[51] Even in Boston there were no booksellers before 1680, and the business of their two bookbinders was poor. Bernard Bailyn may have exaggerated the ascendancy of the New England merchants after the Restoration, but his hypothesis is vindicated, in a small way, by the development—or indeed the birth—of the New England booktrade.[52]

As a working model, then, I propose that down to 1680 few books were regularly imported, so that the colonial stock became "creolized"—that is to say, distributed fairly equally at all social levels. This part of the social pie was, for the moment, fixed, and the colonists shared it about. The selection of divinity specifically described in the inventories therefore affords no surprises. The only divines with more than two books are William Perkins, John Preston, and Richard Sibbes, more or less the selection of "federal theology" that Miller calls for, with Norton, Hooker, and Shepard supporting them; apart from Luther and Aquinas, there are no authors outside the Puritan fold. Having proved the obvious, however, let me complicate it a little: there is only one member of the Westminster Assembly—Anthony Burgess; no Samuel Rutherford, no Smectymnus;[53] only two books, by Richard Baxter and John Collinges, represent the Puritanism of the "Great Persecution" after the Restoration. This is a backward-looking selection, so we are looking at the books that the settlers brought with them, to which few have been added, and to an Elizabethan Puritanism that they anachronistically revered. These limitations of their inheritance were not without their consequences, even for the learned: would the New England mind have been quite so unanimous if New Englanders generally had had a wider, newer selection of books? The learned scarcely absorbed the literature of the "Great Persecution" before the eighteenth century, when figures like Benjamin Colman look back to Richard Baxter, Thomas Manton, and Edmund Calamy. The occasional copy of their works to be found in a minister's study stayed there, I suggest, because it was private, like the occasional copy of Spenser and Jonson.

It is therefore of considerable interest that around 1680 Hezekiah Usher imported some Bibles from Holland that appear to have been specifically printed for the New England market, though their bibliographical features have disguised the fact. The prevalence of European printing in colonial culture has inevitably meant that Evans is full of "ghosts" generated from advertisements and other unreliable sources. Far from exorcising Evans's haunted house, I would like to see it better inhabited. One such ghost, or rather *doppelganger*, a little duodecimo Bay Psalm Book printed for Hezekiah Usher in Boston, has received two entries in Evans: one copy with a correctly printed imprint is located in the American Antiquarian Society; the other, with imprint misprinted "Bostoo," is in the New York Public Library.[54] Both are bound with an eighteenmo Bible ostensibly printed in "Cambridge 1648," as is another copy formerly in the collection of Mr. Michael Zinman. Neither imprint is dated, but on the assumption that Hezekiah Usher, Sr., the publisher of the 1651 edition, also published this edition, the two copies have been variously dated between 1648 and 1669 and localized either in Massachusetts or England. In fact, both are printed from the same setting of type, with press-variant imprints, and duplicate settings of the final half-sheet; so they must be assigned the same date. As Brian McMullin has recently shown, moreover, the Bibles were probably printed in Amsterdam ca. 1680, and since Hezekiah Usher, Sr. had left business in 1669, the publisher must be the son, who appears in only one other imprint in Evans (1692).[55]

Why, one might ask, would a Bostonian go all the way to Amsterdam to reprint a text that had already appeared in at least three New England editions? The short answer, I believe, is that around 1680 there was a dearth of printers in Boston who could have handled formats as sophisticated as eighteens or even twelves. Richard Chiswell had recently reported to Hezekiah Usher's son John that "Bibles are very plenty and of divers sorts and very much cheaper than formerly of true English prints,"[56] and I suppose he placed the order with Amsterdam. The whole affair was defined by a market for the composite small Bible-cum-Bay Psalms, and is unintelligible when the components are considered separately. The 1670s and 1680s, I believe, were an important conjuncture for the history of the book in America: an affordable and plentiful supply of Bibles opened up at a time when ministers perceived a dearth, and when merchants like the Ushers were offered an opportunity. Here, at last, one might locate the beginning of something like an American market—the extension, no doubt, of London's and Amsterdam's, but defining their response by genuine demands, as it had never done before.

Appendix. Specific Books in Essex County Inventories and Wills, 1635–80

1a. Complete English Bible: Enumeration

	Fo.	Q.	Small
"Bible"[1]	24	86	26
"Old Bible(s)"[2]	(7)	(18)	
(2) "Bibles"[3]			
8–15s. = Q, S		8	8
£1 = F, Q	1	1	
(2) "Bibles" et al.[4]			
5–10s. = 2S			4
15s.—£1 = Q, S		4	4
£1 5s.—£1 10s. = F, S	6		6
£1 15s.—£2 = F, Q	4	4	
2 15s. = 2F	2		
"3 Bibles"			
8–10s. = 3S			6
12s. = Q, 2S		1	2
"3 Bibles" et al.			
£1–2 = Q, 2S		4	8
"4 Bibles"			
£1 = 2Q, 2S		2	2
"4 Bibles" et al.			
£1 13s. 4d. = 2Q, 2S		2	2
£2 = F, 2Q, S	1	2	1
"5 Bibles" et al.			
£2 = F, 2Q, 2S	1	2	2
TOTAL:	46	134	71

1 Includes 3 Bibles valued at over 10s., and 16 Bibles valued at 3s. or less, but not specifically distinguished as "Great" or "Small" Bibles.
2 Distributed into Folios and Quartos in proportion to the single Bibles.
3 Specified as "2 Bibles" in 6 of the 9 inventories; otherwise as Bibles.
4 Specified as "2 Bibles" in 13 of the 18 inventories; otherwise as Bibles.

1b. Complete English Bible: Distribution

	Fo.	Q.	Small	Old	Total Bibles	Estates	Bibles/ Estates
To 1640		1			1	1	1.00
To 1650	7	16	16		39	39	1.00
To 1660	3	22	17	4	46	66	0.70
To 1670	11	31	8	4	54	97	0.56
To 1680	18	46	30	17	111	164	0.68
Total:	39	116	71	25	251	367	0.68

2. Other Bibles and Psalms

Bible, Latin (Tremellius)
—, N.T. (Authorized)
—, N.T. (Geneva)
Metrical psalms

Testaments (7)
"Bible, with Beza's notes"
Psalm books (18)

3a. Divinity (European Authors)

Ainsworth, Henry, 1571–1623. *Annotations upon Moses & the Psalms*
Aquinas, St. Thomas, 1225–1274. *Summa theologica*, pt. 1 ("Aquinas his I am [i.e. primam] in folio")

Baxter, Richard, 1615–1691. *Call to the unconverted*
Bayly, Lewis, d. 1631. *Practice of piety*
Bolton, Robert, 1572–1631. works
Brightman, Thomas, 1562–1607. *Revelation of the Apocalyps*
Broughton, Hugh, 1549–1612. works
Burgess, Anthony, fl. 1652. *Spiritual refining* ("Concerning the tryalls of grace")
Burroughes, Jeremiah, 1599–1646. 2 books
— *Moses his choice*
Byfield, Nicholas, 1579–1622. works
Calvin, Jean, 1509–1564. *Institutions*
Collinges, John, 1623–1690. works
Dod, John,1549?-1645. works
— book
Downame, John, d. 1652. works
Dyke, Mr. works
Dyke, Daniel, d. 1614. *Deceitfulness of man's heart*
Gibbens, Nicholas, fl. 1600. *Questions & disputations concerning . . . Scripture*
Gouge, William, 1578–1653. book
Luther, Martin, 1483–1546. *Commentary upon . . . the Galatians*
Perkins, William, 1558–1602. *Works,* 3 v. (2, 1 impf.)
— books (2)
— *Exposition of the Creed*

Preston, John, 1587–1628.	works (3)
—	book (2)
—	*New Covenant* ("Of Gods alsufficiency")
Reyner, Edward, 1600–1668.	*Precepts for Christian practice* ("Of originall sinn")
Reynolds, Edward, 1599–1676.	*Meditations on the . . . Sacrament*
Rogers, Mr.	a book of his works
Rogers, Daniel, 1573–1652.	*Practical catechism* (author not named)
Rogers, Richard, 1550?–1618.	*Seven treatises* (2)
Sibbes, Richard, 1577–1635.	2 books
—	*Bowels opened* ("Upon the Cantickels")
—	*Bruised reed*
Smith, Samuel, 1584–1662?	*The Great Assize*
Symonds, Joseph ("Joshua")	books
Wing, John, minister at Flushing	*The Crown conjugal, or, The spouse royal*
Zanchi, Girolamo, 1516–1590.	"my three zauches . . . in old covers"; read "zanches."
Anon.	Concordance (perhaps Clement Cotton's?)
—	divinity books (2)
—	good books (4)
—	*A synascete* (MS) ("that old manuscript called a synassigh") sermon books [MS.?] (5)

3b. Divinity (Colonial Authors)

Cobbett, Thomas, 1608–1685.	book
Hooker, Thomas, 1586?–1647.	*Soul's preparation for Christ*
Norton, John, 1606–1663.	book
—	*Orthodox Evangelist*
Shepard, Thomas, 1604–1649.	*Theses Sabbaticae* ("Morality of the Sabbath")
Whiting, Samuel, 1597–1679.	Work

4. Other Subjects

Blundeville, Thomas, fl. 1561	book
Dodoens, Rembert, 1517–1585.	*Frumentorum . . .* [1566] ("Herball boke, Didimes moue mowtione")
Evans, Arise, b. 1607.	*Voice of the iron rod*
Heylyn, Peter, 1599–1662.	*Cosmography* ("Geogripha")
Markham, Gervase, 1586?–1637.	book
Mascall, Leonard, d. 1589.	*The government of cattle*
Purchas, Samuel, 1575?–1626.	*Purchas his Pilgrimage*
Anon.	Book of mathematics (MS)
—	Dictionary
—	history book
—	"paper books" (3) (i.e. blank books)
—	physic books (4)
—	sea books (7+)

Notes

1. A useful bibliography of such studies appears in Perry Miller and Thomas H. Johnson, *The Puritans* (New York: American Book Company, 1938), 829–31. Some of the uses to which such studies can be put are indicated in Norman Fiering, *Moral Philosophy at Seventeenth-Century Harvard* (Chapel Hill: University of North Carolina Press, 1981).

2. Amory may not have known that his restlessness with such categories was shared by other historians of the book, notably Robert Darnton. See "Reading, Writing, and Publishing in Eighteenth-Century France: A Case Study in the Sociology of Literature," in *Historical Studies Today*, ed. Felix Gilbert (New York: W.W. Norton, 1972).

3. Morison, *Intellectual Life*, 149.

4. Alfred C. Potter, "Catalogue of John Harvard's Library," *Pubs. CSM* 21 (1920): 190–230; Henry Martyn Dexter, "Elder Brewster's Library," *Procs. MHS* 2nd ser. 5 (1889): 37–85; Arthur O. Norton, "Harvard Textbooks and Reference Books of the Seventeenth Century," *Pubs. CSM* 28 (1935): 361–438; For Wright see below, note 11; Shipton's calculations are included in Morison, *Intellectual Life*, 142.

5. Edwin Wolf II, *The Book Culture of a Colonial City: Philadelphia Books, Bookmen, and Booksellers* (Oxford: Clarendon Press, 1988); Richard Beale Davis, *Intellectual Life in the Colonial South, 1585–1763*, 3 vols. (Knoxville: University of Tennessee Press, 1978).

6. "Some Statistics on American Printing, 1764–1783," in *The Press & the American Revolution*, ed. Bernard Bailyn and John B. Hench (Worcester, Mass.: American Antiquarian Society, 1980), 319–20.

7. Perry Miller, *The New England Mind: The Seventeenth Century* (1939; Cambridge, Mass.: Harvard University Press, 1954), 510, n. 12.

8. Ibid., 92.

9. Ibid., ix; and see George Selement, "Perry Miller: A Note on His Sources in *The New England Mind: The Seventeenth Century*," *WMQ* 3rd ser. 31 (1974): 453–64; and cf. James Hoopes's comments in his edition of the notes, *Sources for The New England Mind: The Seventeenth Century* (Williamsburg, Va.: Institute of Early American History and Culture, 1981). I do not find Hoopes's objections to Selement's analysis very convincing.

10. Morison, *Intellectual Life*, 149.

11. These were: two folio Authorized Versions, one printed in Oxford, 1680, and one with the Geneva notes (Amsterdam, 1642 or 1643); a "Matthew" Bible (London, 1541), imperfect; Samuel Clarke's annotated folio (London, 1690); and a quarto Geneva Bible, with the Book of Common Prayer (London, 1610). The Geneva Bible was bought after 1700: cf. Thomas Goddard Wright, *Literary Culture in Early New England, 1620–1730* (New Haven, Conn.: Yale University Press, 1920), 118.

12. [A list that, alas, is not recoverable].

13. Morison, *Intellectual Life*, 142, 147.

14. Salem: Essex Institute, 1916–20; hereafter cited as *PREC*. Harriet S. Tapley, *Salem Imprints, 1768–1825* (Salem, Mass.: Essex Institute, 1927), publishes a useful selection (275–90).

15. William A. Davisson, "Essex County Wealth Trends," *Essex Institute Historical Collections* 102 (1967): 291–342, at 292.

16. James Browne (1676), *PREC*, 3, 63: "Due from Abra. Kick in holland . . . 880 Guilders"; see also Ford, *Boston Book Market*, 8, n. 2, for an order from Holland. Governor John Winthrop, Jr. acquired part of Dr. Dee's library in Hamburg, but it was lost at sea. Julian Roberts and Andrew G. Watson, *John Dee's Library Catalogue* (London: Bibliographical Society, 1990), 66.

17. William Bowditch (1681), in *Records and Files of the Quarterly Courts of Essex County, Massachusetts*, 9 vols. (Salem, Mass.: Essex Institute, 1912–1975), 8: 221. Tapley, *Salem Imprints*, mistakes this collection for a private library ("the largest collection of books in Salem in the seventeenth century," 268), because she misunderstands its use of "books" to mean "titles." But "Eleven books called Rutherfords Letters" means eleven copies of his *Joshua redivivus* (3rd ed., 1675). For the usage (not recorded in the OED), see R. W. Chapman, ed., *The Letters of Samuel Johnson*, 3 vols. (Oxford: Clarendon Press, 1952), 3, 471; and the "study" of Ezekiel Rogers, worth £100, must have had many more books than Bowditch's collection.

18. Gloria L. Main, "Probate Records as a Source for Early American History," *WMQ* 3rd ser. 32 (1975): 87–99, at 97–98; Davisson, "Essex County Wealth Trends," 294.

19. The following holdings are counted as a single estate, because of bequests: *PREC*, 1, 152 (William Averill, 1653) = 201 (Abigail Averill, 1655); 154 (William Stevens, 1653) = 3, 19 (Samuel Stevens, 1675); 162 (William Bacon, 1653) = 230 (Rebecca Bacon, 1655); 185 (William Auger, 1654) = 2, 250 (Benjamin Auger, 1671); 189 (William Fiske, 1654) = 2, 371 (Phineas Fiske, 1673); 211 (Robert Moulton, 1655) = 2, 27 (Abigail Moulton, 1666); 218 (Humphrey Bradstreet, 1655) = 2, 31 (Bridget Bradstreet, 1666); 288 (William Jeggles, 1659) = 2, 94 (Elizabeth Jeggles, 1667); 335 (Ezekiel Rogers, 1661) = 3, 289 (Mary Rogers, 1678); 356 (Hugh Burt, 1661) = 2, 361 (Ann Burt, 1673); 419 (Thomas Sallows, 1663) = 445 (Grace Sallows, 1664); 433 (Robert Rogers, 1664) = 3, 155 (Susannah Rogers, 1677); *PREC* 2, 75 (Samuel Sharp, 1664) = 95 (Alice Sharp, 1667); 126 (Richard North, 1668) = 223 (Ursula North, 1671); 159 (James Axey, 1669) = 209 (Frances Axey, 1670). The holdings in the following estates may overlap substantially, but it is difficult to say how, and they have been separately counted: *PREC*, 1, 169 (Thomas Scott, 1654) = 258 (Thomas Scott, 1657); 85 (George Abbott, 1647) = 301 (Thomas Abbott, 1659); 97 (John Balch, 1648) = 264 (Agnes Balch, 1657); 123 (Hugh Burt, Jr., 1650) = 356 (Hugh Burt, 1661).

20. David D. Hall, "A Note on Book Ownership in Seventeenth-Century New England," in *Worlds*, 248. Shipton counted bookholdings by estates (whether or not an inventory survived), and his figures are not strictly comparable.

21. Unlike England, where probate was limited to estates worth £5 or more, the colony required probate only where the testator held land, and colonial land was widely distributed and cheap. William Blackstone, *Commentaries*, 2, 487–88, 509.

22. Robert Johnson (1649), PREC, 1, 117.

23. *Suffolk County Wills*, ed. William B. Trask et al. (Baltimore: Genealogical Publishing Company, 1984), 294.

24. Margaret Spufford, *Small Books and Pleasant Histories* (London: Methuen, 1981), 27ff.

25. I follow the analysis of social space by Robert Blair St. George, "'Set Thine House in Order': The Domestication of the Yeomanry in Seventeenth-Century New England," in Fairbanks and Trent, *New England Begins*, 2: 159–86.

26. For details, see appendix. Samuel Whiting's "work" (*PREC*, 2, 245) must have been printed in Cambridge, Mass.; John Norton's "Bock" (*PREC*, 2, 31) may have been.

27. Gloria L. Main, "The Distribution of Consumer Goods in Colonial New England: A Subregional Approach," *Proceedings of the Dublin Seminar for New England Folklife* 12 (Boston: Boston University, 1989), 165.

28. Christopher Hill, *The English Bible and the Seventeenth-Century Revolution* (London: Allen Lane, 1993), 7ff.

29. Fairbanks and Trent, *New England Begins*, 2, no. 319b; the catalogue notes that the preliminary drawing may have been done in England. See also Tessa Watt, *Cheap Print and Popular Piety, 1550–1640* (Cambridge: Cambridge University Press, 1991), chap. 4, for the persistence of the older ideology in print.

30. *The Acts and Monuments of John Foxe*, ed. Stephen Reed Cattley, 8 vols. (London, 1837–41), 5, 117. [As found in Foxe, the statement is indirect dialogue and Tyndale is speaking to "a certain divine."]

31. I am most grateful to James N. Green for allowing me to read his unpublished paper on this subject.

32. Stephen Botein, " 'Meer mechanics' and an Open Press: The Business and Political Strategies of Colonial American Printers," *Perspectives in American History* 9 (1975): 130–211.

33. D. F. McKenzie, *Bibliography and the Sociology of Texts* (London: British Library, 1986), 46ff.

34. *PREC* 1, 120. "Hannah's" Bible is in the Andover Theological Seminary, Newton, Mass.

35. John Alden, "The Bible as Printed Word," in Ernest S. Frerichs, ed., *The Bible and Bibles in America* (Atlanta: Scholars Press, 1988), 9–28; Harry S. Stout, "Word and Order in Colonial New England," in *The Bible in America*, ed. Nathan O. Hatch and Mark A. Noll (New York: Oxford University Press, 1982), 19–38; David Cressy, "Books as Totems in Seventeenth-Century England and New England," *Journal of Library History* 21 (1986): 92–106.

36. A. F. Johnson, "J. F. Starn, Amsterdam, and English Bibles," *The Library* 5th ser. 9 (1954): 185–93; P. G. Hoftijzer, *Engeise boekverkoepers bij de beurs* (Amsterdam: APA-Holland University Press, 1987).

37. Patrick Collinson, "The Sense of Sacred Writ," *Times Literary Supplement*, April 9, 1993, p. 3.

38. Mirjam Foot, in *De Libris Compactis Miscellanea* (Aubel and Brussels: Bibliotheca Wittockiana, 1984). For earlier "reformed" texts bound with the Geneva Bible, see Patrick Collinson, *The Elizabethan Puritan Movement* (London: Cape, 1967), 165, 365.

39. Hugh Amory, "Under the Exchange: The Unprofitable Business of Michael Perry, a Seventeenth-Century Bookseller," *Procs. AAS* 103 (1993): 31–60, reprinted in this volume. Jeremy Condy may have been the first Boston bookseller to purchase his stock in sheets. Cf. Elizabeth C. Reilly, "The Wages of Piety," in *Printing and Society in Early America*, ed. William L. Joyce et al. (Worcester, Mass.: American Antiquarian Society, 1983), 88.

40. John Winthrop, *The History of New England from 1630 to 1649*, ed. James Savage, 2 vols. (Boston: Phelps and Farnham, 1825), 2, 24.

41. Hill, *The English Bible*; Stout, "Word and Order," 20, n. 4, claims that it is "well known" that the Bay Colony clergy cited the Authorized Version, giving some specific examples. One would like fuller and more detailed evidence for the generality of the practice.

42. Hall (*Worlds*, 249) notes that "psalm books do get cited" in the Middlesex inventories, "though not as frequently as the supply would indicate they should be." By the "supply," he alludes to the 1700 copies of the 1640 Bay Psalm Book, which, if evenly distributed, would have blanketed every house in New England. One should also take into account the supply that came ready bound with the Bible, however, which in any case provided the music for both versions.

43. *Suffolk County Wills*, 131; Mariah Mather's Bible is in the Massachusetts Historical Society.

44. Christopher De Hamel, *A History of Illuminated Manuscripts* (Boston: Godine, 1986), 164.

45. An Eliot Indian Bible (1663) at the University of Virginia has family records on the verso of the N.T. title-page; I have not seen this copy, and do not know whether the records are European or Indian.

46. [Describing the personal quest for grace (not, strictly speaking, a conversion) was a condition in most churches of becoming a "full" church member, and therefore being eligible to participate in the Lord's Supper, but a much larger share of the population, indeed in most towns the majority of people, became church members via infant baptism. Amory was far from alone in overlooking this distinction.]

47. Sheila Lambert, "The Printer and the Government, 1604–1640," in *Aspects of Printing from* 1600, ed. Robin Myers and Michael Harris (Oxford: Oxford Polytechnic Press, 1987), 3.

48. Mary Pollard, *Dublin's Trade in Books,* 1550–1800 (Oxford: Clarendon Press, 1989).

49. David Cressy, *Coming Over: Migration and Communication Between England and New England in the Seventeenth Century* (Cambridge: Cambridge University Press, 1987), 69.

50. Thomas Shepard, *Eye-salve, or, a Watch-word From Our Lord Jesus Christ Unto His Churches* (Cambridge, Mass., 1673), 42.

51. *PREC*, I, 119.

52. Bailyn, *Merchants*; and see Stephen Foster, *Their Solitary Way: The Puritan Social Ethic in the First Century of Settlement in New England* (New Haven, Conn.: Yale University Press, 1971).

53. [Acronym made up of the initials of the names of the five authors, the first being Stephen Marshall, of *An Answer to a book entitled An humble remonstrance* (London, 1641)].

54. Evans 49 and 96; Thomas. J. Holmes, *The Minor Mathers: A List of Their Works* (Cambridge, Mass.: Harvard University Press, 1940), entries 53cc–53dd.

55. B. J. McMullin, "Format and localization: the eighteenmo in the seventeenth century," *Bibliographical Society of Australia and New Zealand Bulletin* 9 (1985): 139.

56. Ford, *Boston Book Market*, 85; Ford's transcriptions are not reliable, and need to be corrected by Roger Thompson's addenda, *Procs. MHS* 86 (1974): 67–78.

4. Under the Exchange:
The Unprofitable Business of Michael Perry,
a Seventeenth-Century Boston Bookseller

The inventory of Michael Perry's bookstore that was taken after Perry's death in Boston in 1700 has been widely cited by historians. But until Amory studied it closely, no one had fully understood what this text tells us about trade practices at the end of the seventeenth century. Perry's shop included books in which his own imprint appears, but as Amory demonstrates, some of these are examples of shared printing or of an exchange of sheets. The broader story that emerges from this close study of imprints is that the slow rate of sales, the limited scope of the market, and the virtual impossibility of exchanging books (or sheets) with the English trade made local printers and booksellers loath to risk too much on any single item. This, then, is an example of bibliographical analysis turning into economic history. It is also an example of bibliographical analysis helping to resolve a difference of interpretation, the Botein-Foster debate, as Amory frames it: did the colonists rely on locally printed books or on imports, and what was the impact on the local reading public of the English "congers" that controlled the rights to certain titles or kinds of books? The essay concludes with appendices in which Amory re-edited the inventory in order to classify the books according to the categories of analysis indicated in the essay. That is, he was hoping to demonstrate the nature of Perry's business as printer and bookseller and to clarify which editions were printed locally and which were imported. Anyone using these appendices should pay close attention to the "note" that precedes them in which Amory defined the meaning of "edition" and "issue."

SOURCE: *Proceedings of the American Antiquarian Society* 103 (1993): 31–60. Reprinted with the permission of the American Antiquarian Society.

At the end of the seventeenth century, Boston booksellers clustered around the Town House, where the Old State House now stands. Here, at street level, was the merchants' exchange; above them stood not only the courts, but also the armory and the public library; below them lay a once-new, pre-literate world. In this symbolic situation, American goods, arriving from Roxbury Neck along Cornhill Street, met European credit, ascending along King Street from the harbor. The centrality of the Town House was not just geographical and commercial, however, but social and even intellectual. At either end of town lay traditionally rival areas, whose younger male inhabitants bonded in a ritual brawl once a year on Guy Fawkes Day.[1] In the North End, at Second Church, twinkled the liberal wit of the Mathers; in the South End, at Third Church, glared the systematic learning of Samuel Willard. Boston's printers worked in those intellectual extremes, but the booksellers occupied the center, near First Church, the pulpit of the moderate Benjamin

Wadsworth. Their imprints located them "under the Exchange" or "near the Old Meeting House," on either side of Cornhill Street. Here, the Artillery Company and the governor, council, and House of Representatives assembled for annual election sermons; here, since 1679, the Boston ministry by turns had delivered lectures every market day (Thursday). These discourses provided regular jobs for the booksellers in the vicinity.

Michael Perry was baptized in First Church on February 15, 1666, but never became a member.[2] Following an apprenticeship to the prominent merchant and bookseller John Usher,[3] he set up business under the stairs at the west end of the Exchange in 1694. On July 12, he had married the widow of the wealthy Robert Breck, Joanna, whom John Dunton, the eccentric English bookseller who visited Boston in 1686, called "the Flower of Boston." She brought Perry not just beauty, but the wealth he needed to set up shop; and she carried on as a bookseller in her own right after his death. The premises had just been vacated by the bookseller Samuel Phillips, who moved into a large brick shop across the way, measuring twenty feet by twelve. In 1699, Perry entered into partnerships with Nicholas Buttolph and with his cousin Benjamin Eliot, who continued in business at the same premises until 1703, when he moved into "greatly enlarged accommodations" measuring nine feet eight inches by four feet one and one-half inches.[4] Perry's first apprentice was Judge Samuel Sewall's son Sam, who contracted chilblains in the tiny shop and had to quit.[5] Unfortunately, Perry enjoyed only a brief career, and his sole importance for book history came at the end of it: he died intestate and insolvent in 1700, aged thirty-four; and therefore the Suffolk County Probate Court, at the request of his widow, ordered a detailed inventory of his estate.

The inventory has been printed three times to date, with varying degrees of accuracy, most usefully by Worthington C. Ford, who identifies many of the entries and supplements their information with transcripts of letters and invoices of books sent from London in 1674–85 to Perry's former master, John Usher.[6] These documents are our only direct evidence for the operation of colonial American bookselling in the seventeenth century, apart from scattered advertisements. Ford used them mostly to illustrate the variety and intellectual interest of the books available to seventeenth-century Bostonians, without much considering the commercial forces that produced them and brought them over. Stephen Botein and Stephen Foster have cited Ford's data to explore the place of the English book in American culture, but they reach surprisingly different conclusions.

Botein, in common with most American historians, assumes that the majority of the books in America were English-printed, and that American printing is thus a supplement to make up for temporary shortages, or to furnish texts of local interest such as the colonial laws.[7] In this model, the colonial press is equated in principle with the British provincial press and operates within the parameters set by the socalled "topping booksellers" of London through the sharebook system, familiar from the work of Cyprian Blagden, Graham Pollard, and Terry Belanger.[8] Share books were copyrights, typically of steady sellers, held by a more or less numerous group of partners who bought and sold their shares at trade auctions. By this arrangement, they monopolized the supply of the most valuable properties, spread the capital needed to keep them in print, and maintained prices. The system canonized the stock available for resale to American booksellers, Botein argues, while denying them the discounts that would have allowed their market to expand and thrive. In time, other arrangements, notably the dumping of remainders on the American market, ensured a cheaper supply of books and maintained the "anglicization" of colonial culture down to 1776 and for some time beyond.

Stephen Foster objects that our earliest documents, including Perry's inventory, contradict Botein's initial assumption.[9] The Usher invoices show that English books arrived in "dribbles and drabbles" of from twenty to fifty copies at a time. The English wholesalers who appear in the Usher invoices, Robert Boulter and Richard Chiswell, held their properties in partnerships known as "congers," which absorbed most of their own production, leaving only small and insignificant numbers available for export. And the American trade responded by printing new titles or reprinting the London properties most in demand. Perry's stock, unlike that of an English provincial bookseller, contains quantities of locally printed items, which outnumber imports by ten to one.[10] In seventeenth-century New England, Foster concludes, the general reading public perforce read colonial authors and colonial editions, so that English books and English ideas never threatened "the unity of the Puritan enterprise."

Thus, for Botein, the London monopoly operated to depress trade by keeping prices high, whereas for Foster, it worked to restrict production and distribution, in either case with radically different cultural consequences. Botein's thesis is general, but focused on the eighteenth century; Foster's thesis is apparently limited to the seventeenth century, but he never explains when or why London books eventually became more common. In my opinion, congers and share books kept standard properties in print, making wholesaling and a backlist possible. That such monopolies restricted trade seems clear, yet Botein and Foster exaggerate their impact. The failure of the colonies to communicate their needs and the endemic difficulties of credit must have been as important as the inelasticity of London supply.[11] Neither scholar considers the older, even more tightly controlled London monopolies, such as the Queen's/King's printer's patent in Bibles, service books, and proclamations or the exclusive property of the Stationers' Company in almanacs, law books, schoolbooks, and psalms, known as the English stock, monopolies that, far from constricting, provided staples of the American trade, and on which American printing only exceptionally (if invariably, in psalms and almanacs) infringed. New books, moreover, were not monopolized either by the sharebook system or by congers: their sheets might be freely exchanged for those of other booksellers, or distributed by trade subscription before publication. Hence the colonial bookseller's stock fell into various categories, subject to different conditions of production and distribution, and these must be considered separately, not in a lump.[12]

Foster's argument, however, raises some vital questions. He must be right that colonial-printed copies regularly outnumbered imports in colonial stocks; Elizabeth Carroll Reilly has found confirming evidence as late as 1770 in the papers of the Boston bookseller Henry Knox.[13] And colonial imprints unquestionably were cheaper. But must we conclude, with Foster, that the colonial press was meeting a need that the London trade was unable to satisfy, or that English books were consumed by a small elite, whereas the productions of Willard and the Mathers reached out to the broad masses? And can Botein's estimate of the power and prestige of English printing still be sustained, in view of its numerical unimportance? These are the issues I will explore in the context of Perry's inventory and its associated documents, particularly some unpublished records of his debtors and creditors.[14]

Perry was one of the smaller Boston booksellers, even though he published editions of the Bay Psalm Book and the Massachusetts laws. The strongest indication of this, apart from the mere size of his shop, is his investment in bookbinding, for binders were usually the poorest members of the trade. The inventory lists turkey leather, calf, sheep, both plain and red, and forel, or unsplit sheepskin, for covers of various strength and luxury; pasteboard and "scale" or scabord, a kind of oak veneer used for stiffening covers; vermilion and sap green for sprinkling edges; leaf brass for gilding; painted paper (also used for wallpaper) for wrappers; packthread; and 261 pairs of clasps for Bibles. These articles, together with Perry's bookbinding tools (worth fifteen shillings), are valued at nearly twenty pounds, though his entire stock of American printing was only worth about sixty-five pounds. British printing and even British blank books, we may note from the Usher invoices, arrived in the colonies bound, so that Perry's investment only gave a return on American sheets.[15] These were not limited to the sheets that Perry himself printed, for he might bind the productions of other book-sellers, taking their sheets in payment. Reilly provides later parallels from Jeremy Condy's accounts.[16] Twenty pounds was thus Perry's working capital, considered merely from the bookselling side of his business.

It is also observable, though no one so far has observed it, that Perry could never have carried on a bindery in his tiny, damp shop below the stairs of the Exchange. He also leased a house nearby in Pond Ward, south of Summer Street.[17] The inventory assigns no value to either of these premises, because he leased them; and it does not distinguish the books in the bindery from those in the shop. Thus the bindery is virtually invisible and only emerges when we consider that the shop could not have had the "Garretts," chamber, and kitchen mentioned in the inventory. Hence we may picture Perry's simple home: the bindery itself; a bedroom, which poor Mrs. Perry shared with quantities of hornbooks, ink powder, spectacles, and parchment; an attic stuffed with unbound sheets and assorted stationery; and a kitchen, which also contained a bed for an apprentice or servant. Perry's circum-stances were too modest for a slave or a horse, the usual indexes of prosperity.

The insolvency proceedings dragged on for five years or more.[18] The record of the court's final distribution is now lost, but the estate could hardly have paid out more than fifteen shillings in the pound. At least half of the thirty customers who owed Perry money at his death (Appendix 2) were from Boston and vicinity. They included merchants, a magistrate, farmers, a brewer, three women, and seven members of the Ancient and Honorable Artillery Company, but no ministers and no Harvard graduates.[19] Ten other customers lived at some distance from Boston, in an area of 135 miles from north to south, and over 100 miles westward: Francis Pope of Newport, Rhode Island, George Vaughan of Portsmouth, New Hampshire, and Eben-ezer Gilbert of Hartford, Connecticut, among them. Altogether they owed Perry nearly £100; his assets were worth only £334, about a third of it in books.

His largest creditors were all Boston merchants: John Usher, Capt. Ben-jamin Gillam, Nicholas Roberts and Co., and Joseph Coysgarne (see Appendix 2);[20] and they in turn shipped fish, meat, and pipe staves to London, Lisbon, or the Caribbean, taking sugar, wine, and, of course, books in return.[21] Perry's business was too small to generate a return in goods, credit, or cur-rency that would have been acceptable in London, so that he had to rely on such general merchants for his stock. Nor could he furnish the assortment of learned, recent publications that a minister would require. Ministers like John Wise, in Chebacco (now Essex), Increase Mather, in Boston, Thomas Shepard, in Charlestown, and John Allin, in Woodbridge, New Jersey, imported their books by special order directly through Usher.[22] This basic division of the colonial trade into general merchants and bookseller-stationers continued well into the eighteenth century. Daniel Henchman, characterized by Isaiah Thomas as "the most eminent and enterprising bookseller that appeared in Boston, or, indeed, in all British America before the year 1775," did not deal directly with London until 1724.[23] Not until the late 1730s was the transition of his business to general merchandising fully achieved by his son-in-law Thomas Hancock.

Perry's holdings of English books are thus not representative of the dealings of a merchant at Usher's level; and Usher, in turn, would have few or no American imprints, which were worthless for exchange in London. Usher indeed sent 190 copies of the 1672 edition of the Massachusetts *Laws* to Richard Chiswell of London in 1674, for "nouelties," as he put it; but Chiswell did not ask for them, and probably Usher had found them unsaleable even in Massachusetts, where his seven-year copyright was running out.[24] There are three other Boston booksellers at Perry's level—that is, they often share imprints, and they are occasionally mentioned as bookbinders: Nicholas Boone, and Perry's partners, Benjamin Eliot and Nicholas Buttolph. When two of them club together to publish a title, such as Samuel Willard's *Man of War* (1699), we may infer that they split the edition between them. This practice, and the occasional sale of American sheets in London, might somewhat moderate the disproportion of American to English copies in the overall stock of such books in Boston. And booksellers like Elkanah Pembroke or James Gray, who appear in only a single imprint or none at all, might have stocked far fewer American books than Perry.

All the titles with three or more copies in Perry's inventory are described in Appendix 1, which should account for the books that he either printed himself or acquired in multiple imported copies. I omit the ninety-nine other titles of which Perry had a copy or two, which tend to be older publications assessed much below their original price; I suppose they represent remainders that the London trade dumped on the colonial market, or perhaps secondhand colonial copies. Their inclusion would swell the count of London editions, particularly in the miscellaneous category I call "other books." Indeed, there are only two American-printed books among them, a Connecticut election sermon worth tuppence, and Samuel Lee's *Joy of Faith* (1687), which was also issued in London.

The identification of English and American editions is generally straightforward, though the inventory does not, of course, supply imprints. When there is a choice, I assign any titles in quires or sheets to Boston presses, for London books came bound or at least stitched; and I assume that a title worth a shilling or more is probably of London printing. Since Boston printing greatly outnumbers London printing, we may suppose that the very numerous schoolbooks used for instruction in English were printed in Boston, though sometimes no record of their editions survives outside of Perry's inventory. In a few cases, Perry might have acquired his copies from Amsterdam, Dublin, or Edinburgh, but direct access to these markets was forbidden by the Navigation Act of 1663. Usher imported his Amsterdam-printed English Bibles through Chiswell in London;[25] and the export of Scottish books to the colonies only dates from the 1740s.[26]

Foster assumes, logically enough, that the larger the number of copies in Perry's stock, the better he expected the title to sell; but actually matters were more complicated. The numbers of steady sellers like the Bible or schoolbooks are purely accidental, being determined by the state of the stock at Perry's death. My editing of the inventory may have eliminated a popular title that was temporarily in short supply, and the exceptionally high numbers of *Shorter Catechisms* may merely mean that Perry had recently replenished his stock. As for unique editions, the numbers and state of Perry's stock often suggest slow sales: it is not altogether good that Perry still had eighty-nine copies of Cotton Mather's *Early Religion Urged* (1694) after six years; and the majority of Perry's American books were in sheets or quires, unbound—the raw material for his bindery, perhaps, but as yet unsuited for sale in his shop.

An annual supply of twenty to fifty English books, moreover, compares rather better with an American edition than Foster would indicate. The edition, after all, needed time to sell, and the older titles in Perry's stock go back from three to six years. In a four-year period, something like 80–200 English copies would arrive and sell out, or their importation would not have continued. John Usher was not the only Boston merchant who imported books, moreover: Perry ran up as large or larger accounts with three other Boston merchants. Between them, they could easily have supplied 320–800 copies of a popular title in the time it took a single Boston edition to exhaust itself. Foster's estimate of 1,000 copies per edition may be accepted, though Perry's editions, to judge by his stock, were often no larger than 500.[27] To take Willard's *Man of War* once more as an example, it looks as though Eliot and Perry each took 250 copies, about 100 of which Perry had sold by his death. The point, however, is that even an edition of 500 copies was an ample supply for a city of some 1,300 families and 7,000 souls.

Such numbers can only indicate possibilities, of course, since the documentation is so fragmentary and accidental. They need to be assessed against the larger picture of colonial culture. Students of the book trade in colonial

Philadelphia or Williamsburg or Charleston should find few surprises in Perry's inventory. The late Edwin Wolf spoke truly in his Lyell lectures when he claimed that the books of colonial Philadelphia were typical of other colonial cities as well.[28] The alterity of New England has always fascinated and disturbed historians, but in future it may well be that we will labor to explain why, for all the cultural differences that separated their owners, colonial libraries were so unexpectedly uniform. The explanation that leaps to hand is that the London trade was in fact very little concerned to cater to colonial tastes.

Perry's stock does not entirely conform to Wolf's proposed norms, of course. There are no almanacs, for Perry died in July, when his supply must have been exhausted. His divinity is decidedly sectarian: no Quaker titles; for Catholics, only one copy of the *Imitatio Christi*; for Anglicans, six copies of the Book of Common Prayer, and one of Jeremy Taylor's *Contemplations of the State of Man*, which was ever popular with the Puritans as well. English law books are practically absent: no Dalton's *Country Justice*, Care's *English Liberties*, Coke on Littleton; no blank forms, except for ninety-six quires of bills of lading. Indeed, apart from the Massachusetts *Acts and Laws*, Perry's only legal title was a copy of Charles Molloy's *De Jure Maritimo et Navali*, a great favorite in the colonies. Three hundred of Perry's 304 copies of the Massachusetts *Acts and Laws* were in quires; it must have sold very slowly, as indeed, Usher's edition did. Merchants like John Usher or Samuel Sewall had a wider variety of legal titles, but retailers like Perry could not afford them. Magistrates as well as ministers, I suppose, supplied their needs by special order, as John Adams did fifty years later.

When London and Boston competed, they battled over staple fare, signaled by asterisks and daggers in Appendix 1. Here, indeed, Boston printing is generally a supplement, furnishing the peculiar primers, psalters, psalm books, and laws that New England culture required; but they were occasionally reprinted in England, Scotland, or later, New York and Philadelphia, when the New England presses failed. Perry's stock of English-printed popular literature—two chapbooks, and some small-format Bibles—is strikingly limited; merchants like Usher probably distributed a broader assortment of these perennials to town and country stores, and peddlers like James Gray hawked them around the countryside.

As for the "other books," as I call them, both London and Boston imprints appear in unique editions, or single years only, and are heard of no more. Such constantly changing novelties are, of course, important in their own right: they may have brought customers in to browse who then departed, as usual, with a *New England Psalter* or a Bay Psalm Book. But their market was brief and limited. London printings of "other" books, I suppose, were purchased by the tradesmen, merchants, and sea captains who wished to be au courant with British culture. An unknown author, possibly Samuel Sewall, addressed this audience in his *Epitomy of English Orthography*, a very elementary treatise of which Perry had 100 copies. Sewall wrote, as he tells us in the preface, "for the Benefit of my Countrymen who retain a Smattering of the Latine and Greek Tongues," but who have been "dismissed from School, some to Clerkship, others to Merchandize or Trade." He believed there were many such: their numbers roughly corresponded to the 250 weekly copies of a colonial newspaper, of which they and the colony's ministers and magistrates were the first readers.

Despite their cheapness, the market for "other" Boston imprints was primarily urban. The tradesmen, sea captains, and merchants who owed Perry money are only the upper stratum of his custom, distributed over an anomalously wide area; we learn nothing from the insolvency proceedings of the many more numerous and less wealthy customers who paid cash, and who therefore surely resided in Boston. The sale of colonial imprints (apart from almanacs) was thus more intensely civic and localized than the sale of English books. We naturally assume that their cheapness recommended them to humbler purses, but it is only an assumption. Popular literature, like oral literature, is relentlessly conservative, and small libraries (including parish libraries) inclined to a few costly but socially venerated titles—the Bible, of course, a commentary on the Bible, or Foxe's *Book of Martyrs* are what we should expect, not an assortment of recent publications, however cheap.

Lastly, there are the schoolbooks, where London and Boston divide the market. Most of Perry's Bibles probably were destined for grammar schools in duodecimo, and in 24mo for dame schools. He had none of the quarto Bibles that served for family reading, and only a single folio Bible, suitable for serious Congregationalist study and annotation or perhaps an Anglican lectern. His English-printed schoolbooks were for grammar schools, and for boys.[29] In 1700, there were only fifteen grammar schools in New England, six of them in the Boston area.[30] This represents a cohort of perhaps forty or fifty Boston boys a year, so that the "dribbles and drabbles" of such books imported annually from London were doubtless adequate. Perry had twenty or thirty times as many schoolbooks for the children who attended "dame" or "petty" schools, and these were all printed in America. In this rather special case, Foster's thesis makes sense, and indeed suggests certain reservations about the prevalence of a classical education in the colonies.[31]

Foster, however, expressly excludes schoolbooks, Bibles, psalm books, and almanacs from his analysis, which is limited to books "with something resembling a mental content," or that presented "an imaginative rendering of doctrine."[32] He observes that American presses invariably reprinted the most frequently imported titles of this description, and argues that London was therefore unable to meet colonial demand. The same phenomenon, of course, is also observable in Scotch and Irish "piracies," yet in all these cases, the demand for titles that were reprinted originates in London, not in Boston, Edinburgh, or Dublin. Products of intellectual distinction certainly originated from the colonial press, but they were rarely reprinted in England and they almost never became steady sellers, even in the colonies. The typical long-term productions of the colonial press were serials: newspapers, almanacs, sessions acts; the Boston trade had no proper backlist before the *Boston Catalogue* of 1804.[33] Down to this period, colonial printers were unable to wrest a niche for their "piracies" from the London trade; as in Edinburgh and Dublin, "piracies" remained sporadic, brief intrusions in the steady current of London production. Of the devotional works in Perry's stock, on which Foster places such emphasis, only John Flavel's *Token for Mourners* reached more than two colonial editions.

Congers and sharebooks, I suspect, were most effective in controlling the exchange of sheets, the usual method of "publication" in seventeenth- and eighteenth-century England, but these limitations could hardly have affected Boston booksellers, whose sheets had little market value in London except as "nouelties." Indeed, none of the titles in Perry's stock, or for that matter in Usher's, belonged to Richard Chiswell's conger, as Foster's thesis demands.[34] The schoolbooks, psalm books, and Bibles that formed the staple of Perry's business were vested in the English stock of the Stationers' Company and the Bible patentees. These monopolies indeed made them costly.[35] An American-printed reader like the *Shorter Catechism* cost only a third as much as one printed in London, and this sufficiently accounts for its preponderance at the dame-school level. At a more advanced level, however, in grammar schools, the market was much more restricted: here the long purse of the London trade took its toll. Boston might pass off 500 copies of Cotton Mather's latest sermon, but the trade was not prepared to wait ten years to sell a comparable number of copies of Ovid's *Metamorphoses*.

Even on the imperfect evidence of Perry's inventory, then, Botein and Foster's models both require adjustment. The stream of English steady sellers must, in time, have overwhelmed the occasional, feverish colonial "piracies," as David D. Hall argues, supporting Botein.[36] Foster's model better explains the sale of schoolbooks, where London and the colonies divided the market, but Foster's explanation is mistaken, and meant in any case for very different properties. Britain retained control of Bibles, of technical literature like law books or navigation books, and of chapbooks right down to the Revolution. British imports thus constituted the most widely owned titles, and the ones that, by any reckoning, contributed most to colonial knowledge and imagination.

The numbers of colonial editions in Perry's stock begin to be meaningful when they are restored to their contexts of production, distribution, and, above all, bankruptcy, which all of the commentators on the inventory ignore. Perry is named in twenty-two imprints, but in five of these merely as a distributor ("sold by M. Perry"). Here, even if he had Nicholas Buttolph's sheets in his attic, they would not appear in his inventory, because they were not Perry's property. He and his partners supplied the paper for the seventeen other items, which were therefore said to be "printed for" them. Of the titles that he probably undertook on his own account or in partnership, five have no imprint, have lost their title pages, or have perished utterly.[37] Five of the twenty-two titles in which he invested do not appear in the inventory: two election sermons, Cotton Mather's *Johannes in Eremo* (1695), and Samuel Willard's *Law Established by the Gospel* (1694) and his *Truly Blessed Man* (1700).[38] Even when an edition was "printed for" him, however, Perry did not necessarily assume the entire risk. Thus the Province took 200 copies of the Massachusetts *Laws* (1699, 1700) and all of Samuel Torrey's and Samuel Willard's election sermons of 1694 and 1695. Cotton Mather's friends financed *Johannes in Eremo* and, seemingly, his *Good Man Making a Good End* (1698) as well. Since the appraisers of Perry's estate did not consider a single copy of Willard's *Truly Blessed Man* to be Perry's property, its sponsors must have taken the entire impression of this recent title, a substantial (653 pages) series of sermons on Psalm 32.

The printed sheets themselves, as we have seen, might be exchanged for services or for the properties of other booksellers. Perry had only twenty copies of John Williams's *Warnings to the Unclean* (1699), but it is scarcely credible that he had nearly sold out an impression of 500–1,000 copies in a single year. Either the author and his friends had absorbed a good part of the edition, or Perry had exchanged quantities of its sheets for other properties, like Nicholas Buttolph's 450 copies in sheets of Stubbs on conscience. If an edition appeared at Perry's expense, he would customarily allow the author fifty free copies for the manuscript; other parts of the edition went to pay for the binder's or the printer's services.[39] It is surprising that Bartholomew Green and John Allen, who did all of Perry's printing after 1694, do not appear among his creditors. In a currency-poor economy, such an instant and complete balancing of accounts could only have been effected in sheets. The real size of a colonial edition is distorted by a kind of value-added tax, which does not apply to English imprints.

When we set aside the government printing and the editions printed for the author or his friends, the remainder of Perry's production is mostly topical or practical: Judge Sewall on spelling for tradesmen; Increase Mather's two execution sermons on the scandalously impenitent Sarah Threadneedle; the adventures of Élie Neau among the papists; the curious bereavement of Mary Hooper; funeral sermons on John Bailey; the fearful, fresh, yet hopeful judgments of God on New Englanders and their offspring, retailed by Cotton Mather. Doctrinal or devotional offerings like Samuel Willard's *Spiritual Desertions* (1699) are unusual.

Perry certainly published some of these titles at his own expense: he and Eliot "entreated" Cotton Mather for the manuscript of *The Family Well-Ordered*, for example, a Thursday lecture. Other arrangements divided the risk of publication. The Artillery Company perhaps took what they wanted of Willard's *Man of War* from Eliot, and Perry overprinted an issue of his own, paying for the paper but getting the print for nothing. In a market crammed with vanity publications, such ventures tempted fate. Perry's death and insolvency froze his assets for five years, and in the meantime, his partners' shares sold off, new editions of his steadier sellers, like Stubbs, might be published, and the topical became ever staler. The Boston fire of 1711 devoured what was left. No wonder, then, that many of his more marketable titles are of absolute rarity today.

Not that the market in general controlled their production and reception. Oral publication sufficed for the vast majority of colonial sermons, especially the congregations' regular Sunday fare; parents had carefully examined these portions of doctrine with their families, and they rarely appeared in print. Bostonians overwhelmingly preferred to print discourses that were external to the ordinary business of their churches, delivered to uncovenanted audiences or on historic occasions: meetings, lectures, executions, elections, funerals, and weddings. The audiences, families, friends of the preacher, or the preacher himself, often encouraged their publication with subventions.[40] That—and not extensive popular demand—is why Willard and the Mathers accounted for such a high proportion of colonial editions. Their sponsors bought into the editions and distributed copies gratis.[41]

Sermons are usually undedicated and few of them, to judge from surviving copies, were formally presented to distinguished public figures or the author's peers, "well bound" in calf or turkey, or "very neatly" in kid.[42] Like nineteenth-century religious tracts (a few would be reprinted in the nine-teenth century for this purpose), most, one imagines, were stitched or in painted paper wrappers. They rarely survive in this condition today, how-ever, because they were rebound in tract volumes or used for waste paper after reading (like magazines). A few copies survive in their original sheep over scabord, and these, I think, may well have been purchased, but they are hardly common. Clifford K. Shipton rightly celebrates Judge Sewall's "inex-haustible pocketful of printed sermons which [he] spread broadcast over the colony,"[43] yet even he met his match in Cotton Mather, who shamelessly enlisted the help of the entire Provincial legislature in the good work. Their resources were incomparably larger than a colonial bookseller's; indeed, sponsors seem to have regarded bookselling as a desperate last resort. In 1704, we find Sewall dispensing a remainder of five dozen copies of Willard's *Fear of an Oath* (1701) among the Boston booksellers, including a dozen copies to Nicholas Boone, for whom they were ostensibly printed.[44]

Depending on the distance between donor and recipient, such gifts might carry various messages of respect, affection, condescension, or re-proach. One would give much to know what passed through the mind of Joseph Sewall's sweetheart when the Judge gave her Cotton Mather's *Adver-sus Libertinos* (1713), for example.[45] Others, like the unregenerate sailors on whom Cotton Mather lavished his good advice, were fiercely resentful.[46] Evi-dence of actual purchase is hard to come by, but to judge by bindings, the boughten copies usually went to children. In suspiciously fine original sheep—an inexpensive and rather fragile binding—they are often adorned with childish inscriptions, such as "Benjamin French his Book god give him grace."[47] The hand is Benjamin's, but he speaks in anxious and elderly accents. English books may have had a relatively restricted circulation, but at least their numbers responded to a genuine, unmediated need and interest.

The colonial production of print, in short, was initiated by the magis-trates, the church, private groups, authors, and occasionally by the book-sellers. The closest English analogy to Puritan publishing is probably the program of the Quakers, who, however, centralized the supply of their pub-lications, instead of printing them locally. Pennsylvania, of course, was a proprietary colony, but there seems no reason why the New England Com-pany could not have provided a similar program of publications—the Eliot tracts and the Andros tracts, indeed, are close parallels. Foster draws a pathetic picture of print-starved, working-class Puritans, driven by the ideol-ogy of the Reformation to develop something to read that their society was unable to supply except by local imprints. The hunger for reading was easily satisfied by rereading the same book, however, and the socially sanctioned object for this purpose was the Bible, not the productions of Willard and the Mathers. Their sermons circulated to record religious or social obligations—like Gideon Bibles in motels, or twenty-liter drums of kerosene among the Melanesians—not to convey knowledge or to stir imagination.[48] The monotonous generality of Perry's stock, and the mediocrity of his custom, should reassure us that his inventory adequately represents this culture, and its dependence on the English trade.

Note to the appendices that follow: The original entry in the inventory is quoted in a note, if the title is difficult to recognize from this description. When the number of copies is bracketed, it represents a total of two or more entries in the inventory; I have added the date of editions, if the evidence permits the date to be so limited, and supply the unit price in parentheses at the end of the entry. "Edition" is here used as a technical term, meaning a unique setting of type, whatever the bookseller may claim on his title page; "issue" is a part of such an edition, with variant date or publisher. This definition is not used in Wing, so that the separate issues of L'Estrange's *History of the Plot* (1679) in 1679, 1680, and 1689 are all described as "editions." In a sense used here, frequent *editions* imply large markets and readership; multiple *issues* imply inadequate capitalization and slow sales.

Appendix 1

London Imprints

Prices in sterling

* = also reprinted in colonial America

SCHOOLBOOKS

[14]   *Æsop's fables* (English and Latin) / ed. C. Hoole (2s.)

19   *Institutio Graecæ grammatices* / William Camden (18d.)

Cf. Pauline Holmes, *A Tercentenary History of the Boston Public Latin School, 1635–1935* (Cambridge, Mass.: Harvard University Press, 1935), 340. This is the most widely used Greek grammar; Richard Busby's is also possible, though Mather Byles's copy, cited by Ms. Holmes, seems to be an 18th-century abridgment.

[18]   *Catonis Disticha* / ed. C. Hoole (10d.)

Includes the *Dicta septem sapientium* / Seven Sages and the *Sententiæ* (English and Latin) of Publilius Syrus.

7   *De officiis* / Marcus Tullius Cicero (16d.)

8   *Epistolæ* (Selections) / Marcus Tullius Cicero; ed. J. Sturm (6d.)

6   *Orationes* (Selections) / Marcus Tullius Cicero (18d.)

A Harvard copy of the 1700 ed. has the signature of Samuel Plaisted (*A.B.* 1715) dated 1710/11.

5   *Janua linguarum* / Johann Amos Comenius (6d.)

    5 *Janua trilinguis* / Johann Amos Comenius (3s.)
 [14] *School colloquies* / Maturin Cordier; ed. C. Hoole (2s.)
   43 **Sententiae pueriles* / Leonhard Culmann; ed. C. Hoole (8d.)
   11 *Ονομαστιχον βραχυ = *Nomenclatura brevis* / Francis Gregory (1s.)
   14 *Lillies rules construed* / William Hayne
         2 Wing L2268, etc.; bound with William Lily's *Short introduction of gram-mar* (16d.)
 [74] *The common accidence examined and explained* / Charles Hoole (8d.)
         "Accidence": Hoole's (2 Wing H2674, etc.) seems the likeliest text. A Harvard copy of the 1657 edition of Hoole belonged to Elisha and Middlecott Cooke, both of whom attended Boston Latin; it is bound with Hoole's *Terminationes et exempla declinationum & conjugationum,* and a separate edition of his translation of Lily's *Propria quæ maribus,* in contemporary sheep, as issued. The quarto accidences imported by Usher in 1685 (Ford, *Boston Book Market,* 149) must be John Brinsley's (2Wing B4699–4703), though the last quarto ed. was in 1669. Brinsley went out of print with a 15th ed. in 1687, and Usher's valuation is less than half Perry's.
 [74] *Terminationes et exempla declinationum & conjugationum* / Charles Hoole
         Bound with his *Common accidence examined,* as issued (8d.); post-Restoration editions include his translation of Lily's *Propria quae maribus.*
 [43] *Brevissima institutio grammatices* / William Lily
         Bound, as issued, with his *Short introduction of grammar* (1s.-16d.)
 [43] *Short introduction of grammar* / William Lily (ls.-16d.)
         Bound, as issued, with Lily's *Brevissima institutio grammatices*; includes 14 copies @ 16d. "with construing books," i.e., *Lilies rules construed,* by William Hayne (a Clark Library copy dated 1678 and a Harvard copy dated 1685–87 are so bound).
    4 *Metamorphoses* / Ovid (2s.)
         Harvard has a copy of the 1684 ed., with the signature of Joshua Moody (A.B. 1707)
    5 *Tristia* / Ovid; ed. Jan Minell (8d.)
         Harvard has a copy of the 1697 ed., with the signature of John Tufts (A.B. 1708) dated 1702.
   12 * *England's perfect schoolmaster* / Nathaniel Strong (1s.)
    7 Virgil / variorum (1s.)
   20 *Complete English scholar* / Edward Young, schoolmaster (10d.)
BIBLES, PSALTERS, ETC.
 [18] Bible (12mo);with the Bay Psalm Book (3–4s., in various bindings).
         With "N:E:Psalms," presumably in a European ed., since Bibles were ordered and delivered bound.
   11 Bible (24mo) (4s.)
    4 Bible (Latin) (6s.)
    3 New Testament (16d.)
    8 New Testament (Latin) (18d.)
    5 * Metrical Psalms / Tate and Brady (1s.)

[6]   * Book of Common Prayer (not separately priced; in various bindings)

GOOD BOOKS

16   *Call to the unconverted / Richard Baxter (10d.)
        Reprinted in Boston, 1717, 1731.

4   *Navigation spiritualized / John Flavel (18d.)
        Reprinted in Boston, 1726.

23   *Saint indeed / John Flavel (10d.)
        Reprinted in Boston, 1726; also reprinted in Scotland before 1701.

12   *Token for mourners / John Flavel (10d.)
        Reprinted in Boston, 1707, 1725, 1729 and 1730.

[17]   *Great concern / Edward Pearse (1s.)
        "Pearce on death": reprinted in Boston, 1705, 1711; also reprinted in Ire-
        land before 1701. One other (secondhand?) copy (not counted here) is
        appraised at 3d.

[13]   *Great assize / Samuel Smith (1s.)
        Reprinted in Boston, 1727; also reprinted in Scotland before 1701.

11   *Christ's certain and sudden appearance to Judgment / Thomas Vincent (15d.)
        Reprinted in Boston, 1718; Philadelphia, 1740; not reprinted in London
        after 1695.

STEADY SELLERS

3   *Pilgrim's progress / John Bunyan (1s.)
        Also printed in Boston, 1681; the relatively high price and low quantity,
        however, suggest a London ed.

[26]   Mariner's new calendar / Nathaniel Colson (18d.-2s.)
        Includes 8 copies @ 2s. "with practice," i.e., Richard Norwood's Sea-
        man's practice; a NYPL copy is so bound, and four editions were so
        issued in 1710-13. See Thomas R. Adams, Non-cartographical Maritime
        Works Published by Mount and Page (London: Bibliographical Society,
        1985), no. 72.

5   Fortunatus (8d.)
        Chapbook.

13   Epitome of navigation / Henry Gellibrand (18d.)

4   Geodæsia / John Love. 1688 (8d.)
        Reprinted in 8 London editions, 1715–71.

8   Seaman's practice / Richard Norwood.
        Bound with Nathaniel Colson's Mariner's new calendar (2s.).

13   Sea charts (3s.)
        Probably John Seller's or John Thornton's.

3   Seven wise masters of Rome / Seven Sages (English) (8d.)
        Chapbook. Cf. also Catonis Disticha, under SCHOOLBOOKS above.

8   Compleat compting-house / John Vernon (15d.)

8   Mariner's compass rectified / Andrew Wakely (2s.)

3   Whole duty of a woman (2s.)
        Compiled in part from The ladies calling, by Richard Allestree; an 8th
        London edition appeared in 1735.

3   Systema agriculturæ / John Worlidge (3s.)

OTHER BOOKS

18   *Sermon preach'd before the . . . House of Commons . . . 16 Apr. 1696 /*
     Samuel Barton. 1696 (1d.)
     Not in the *Term Catalogues*; hence selected by a London wholesaler.

[35] *Helps for faith and patience /* James Burdwood. 1693 (1s.)

[5] *Last legacy /* Henry Care. 1688 (3d.)
     Only one copy survives (Bodleian).

7   *Looking-glass for persecutors /* Samuel Clarke [1599–1683] (3d.)
     2 eds., 1674 and 1675 (1s.)

30   *Collection of papers relating to the present juncture of affairs.* 1688 (1d.)
     Pt. 1 of 12 pts.; printed in 3 eds., 1688; collected and reissued in 1689.

3   *God the guide of youth /* Timothy Cruso. 1695 (3s.)

3   Πλανηλογια = *Succinct . . . discourse of . . . mental errors /* John Flavel. 1691
     (2s.)

17   *Life in God's favour /* Oliver Heywood. 1679 (3d.)

5   *History of the life, bloody reign, and death of Queen Mary.* 1682 (3d.)
     3 eds., 1682; no doubt an episode of anti-Catholic hysteria.

11   *History of the Plot /* Sir Roger L'Estrange. 1679 (3s.)
     Reissued with cancel t.p.'s in 1680 and 1689.

7   *Immoderate mourning /* John Owen, chaplain. 1680 (3d.)
     Not in the *Term Catalogues*.

4   *Meditations on the fall and rising of St. Peter /* Edward Reynolds.
     1677 (6d.)
     "Fall and riseing of St: Peter."

3   *Of the day of grace /* John Shower. 1694 (6d.)
     Two issues, with variant imprints: London; and Worcester.

5   *Thanksgiving sermon . . . April 16, 1696 /* William Stephens. 1696 (1d.)

18] Ποιμνη φυλακιον = *Pastor's charge /* Samuel Stodden. 1694 (8d)
     Not in the *Term Catalogues*.

8   *God, a Christian's choice /* Samuel Winney. 1675 (2d.)

5   *Apology for Congregational divines /* [Samuel Young]. 1698 (3d.)

Boston Imprints

Except as noted, printed by B. Green and J. Allen for M. Perry
† = also printed or reprinted in England

SCHOOLBOOKS

[690] †Hornbooks: 222 gilt (1d.) and 468 plain (1/2d.)
       No colonial editions are otherwise documented. Samuel Sewall
       imported 12 doz. from London in 1700 (*Letterbook, Colls. MHS* 6th ser. 1
       (1886), 248). Unless that was an exceptionally small order, the numbers
       in Perry's stock seem too large for London printing.

[856] †*New England primer* (2d.)
       The earliest surviving edition, enlarged with the Westminster Assembly's
       Shorter catechism, is dated 1727; in this form it was already being adver-
       tised in 1691. Includes 300 copies in quires (1d.)

[124]   *New England psalter* (9d.)
> "Psalters with Proverbs," "Psalters": the Psalms and Proverbs, in the Authorized Version; printed as a reader for children. First printed in Boston, 1682 (Evans 311 [advt.] = 2 Wing B2551A [a ghost]); the earliest surviving edition is dated 1730. Includes 25 copies in quires (5d.)

[1428]   †*Shorter catechism* / Westminster Assembly (1643–1652) (1d.)
> Presumably the 1699 ed., of which only one imperfect copy survives (AAS); f. S. Phillips.

31   † *Shorter catechism, with Scripture proofs* / Westminster Assembly (1643–1652) (2d.)
> Eds. appeared in 1693 (sb. B. Harris) and 1698 (adespoton)

PSALTERS

[304]   †*Bay Psalm Book.* 1698 (18d.-2/6, in various bindings)
> "Psalm books": includes 225 copies in quires (10d.). There was also an ed. f. S. Phillips, 1695.

LAW BOOKS

[304]   †*Acts and laws; with the Charter of* 1692 / Massachusetts (Colony). 1699[–1700](1s.)
> "Law books": 4 copies stitched; the rest in quires. Two items, continuously paged: Evans 867/8 (f. M. Perry and B. Eliot) and Evans 917 (adespoton). Perry and Eliot submitted their bill of £20 on Jan. 24, 1699/1700 for the first item, delivering 200 bound copies—fifty free, and 150 at cost; and Joanna Perry as executrix and Eliot submitted a bill of £6 3s. for the second item on Nov. 18, 1700, of which the Province allowed £6. Massachusetts State Archives, Executive Council Series 3 (1698–1703): 90, 168; the Province still owed Perry's estate £1 5s. 8d. at his death (below, Appendix 2).

GOOD BOOKS

[373]   †*Call to delaying sinners* / Thomas Doolittle. 1700 (6d.)
> Includes 200 copies in quires (3d.); f. B. Eliot. Only one imperfect copy survives (AAS). Reprinted Boston, 1726; 14th ed., London, 1750.

[486]   †*Conscience the best friend upon earth* / Henry Stubbs [1606?-78](4d.)
> 2 eds., dated 1699 and 1700, both printed by B. Green and J. Allen for Nicholas Buttolph; only one copy of the 1699 ed. survives (JCB). Includes 450 copies in sheets (1d.). Reprinted Boston, 1714; not reprinted in London after 1702.

OTHER BOOKS

32   *Thirty important cases* / Cambridge Association of ministers. 1699 (1d.)
> sb. the booksellers.

100   [*Epitome of English orthography.* 1697] (1d.)
> The only surviving copy (AAS) has no t.p.; the mutilated signature at the end of the pref. may be read: [S.S]ewa[ll].

6   †*Sion in distress* / Benjamin Keach. 1683 (3d.)
> The price suggests this Boston ed., of which there are two issues, f. S. Phillips, or f. T. Baker; not reprinted in London after 1692.

  9   [*Lamentation of Mary Hooper.* ca. 1694?] (1d.)
        For Mary H., see O. E. Monnette, *First Settlers of ye plantations of Piscat-
        away . . .* (Los Angeles: Leroy Carman Press, 1930), Pt. 5: 829; her two
        sons died of mushroom poisoning in Aug. 1693. No copy survives, so it
        is impossible to say whether this is by Mary H. (as Shipton and Mooney
        suppose) or about her; and given the presence of the title in Perry's
        stock, Shipton and Mooney's New York imprint is implausible.
 36   *Christian thank-offering* / Cotton Mather. 1696 (1d.)
        Only one copy survives (JCB).
[89] *Early religion urged* / Cotton Mather. 1694 (2d.)
[223] *Family well-ordered* / Cotton Mather. 1699 (5d.)
        Includes: 23 copies listed as "Duty of Parents and Children" (a para-
        phrase of the running-titles), and 150 copies in quires (1d.); f. M. Perry
        and B. Eliot.
[51] *Good man making a good end* / Cotton Mather. 1698 (4d.)
        "Mr. Bailys life": includes 17 copies bound with "old Mr. Mathers ser-
        mon," i.e. *David serving his generation* (6d.)
152   [*Remarkable judgments of God* / Cotton Mather. 1697] (1d.)
        Reprinted in the *Magnalia Christi Americana* (1702) under title *Terribilia
        Dei,* but the only surviving copy (Harvard) has no t.p.
[59] *Warning to the flocks* / [Cotton Mather]. 1700 (1/2d.)
        f. the booksellers.
 17   *David serving his generation* / Increase Mather. 1698
        Bound with Cotton Mather's *Good man making a good end* (6d.);
        adespoton.
[61] *Folly of sinning* / Increase Mather. 1699 (5d.)
        f. M. Perry and N. Buttolph.
[34] †*Order of the Gospel* / Increase Mather. 1700 (6d.)
        Includes 9 copies listed under the running-title as "Order of churches,"
        and 25 copies in quires (3d.); two issues, f. Nicholas Buttolph, or f. B.
        Eliot.
[268] [*Presen*]*t from a farr countrey [to the] people of New England* / Élie Neau. 1698
        (1d.)
        "French Lettr.": the words "French Letter" are prominent on the t.p.
        Neau was a New York Huguenot who had been captured in the
        Caribbean and imprisoned for recusancy by French authorities; Cotton
        Mather prints his account with a translation and comment. 2 copies sur-
        vive (AAS, JCB), one wanting the t.p. and much else.
[147] *Man of war* / Samuel Willard. 1699 (2d.)
        2 issues, f. B. Eliot, or f. M. Perry.
[140] *Morality not to be relied on for life* / Samuel Willard. 1700 (2d.)
        f. B. Eliot.
[30] *Peril of the times displayed* / Samuel Willard. 1700 (6d.)
        sb. B. Eliot.
[224] *Spiritual desertions discovered and remedied* / Samuel Willard. 1699 (6d.)
        Includes 125 copies in quires (3d.); f. M. Perry and B. Eliot.
 20   *Warnings to the unclean* / John Williams. 1699 (2d.)

Appendix 2

ACCOUNT OF PERRY'S CREDITORS, MAR. 18, 1701

	£	s.	d.
Capt. Gilbert Bant	8	5	0
Capt. Benjamin Gillam	65	4	10
Gabriel Bernon	3	18	0
Andrew Faneuil	3	10	9
Samuel Keeling & Co.	36	19	1½
John Borland	6	8	9
Samuel Baker	13	10	0
Peter Barbour		15	8
Nicholas Roberts & Co.	78	13	0
Joseph Coysgarne	102	0	11½
David Jeffries	5	10	8
Benjamin Eliot	21	3	9
Stephen Minot	38	12	8¾
William Vaughan, Esq.	19	14	7
John Usher, Esq.	61	0	3
John Nelson	20	0	0
Francis Foxcroft	29	12	0
Duncan Campbell	3	18	7
Total:	518	18	7[¾]

ACCOUNT OF DEBTS RECEIVED, APRIL 1702

	£	s.	d.
John Cutler	2	4	10
Samuel Sheppard	16	16	6
The Province, by Capt. Southack	1	5	8
Ebenezer Gilburt	3	0	0
Benjamin Davis		13	6
Richard Gerrish	4	15	0
Jose Appleton	2	6	1
Thomas Holland	1	2	0
Samuel Prince	1	9	10
Seth Pope	2	12	4
Simeon Stoddard	6	0	0
Waterhouse Fernly	1	18	0
Francis Pope		4	0
Mr. Whetcombe		2	6
Captain Belcher	2	0	0
Total:	46	10	3

ACCOUNTS RECEIVABLE ("MANY OF WHICH DEBTS BEING DOUBTFUL")

	£	s.	d.
Elizabeth Gidding	2	3	3
Charles Storey	3	14	8

James Meinzeis	6	10	10
John Noble	1	7	4
Elizabeth Redford	3	0	0
James Cornish	3	4	3
Ebenezer Gilburt	2	1	6
Samuel Shrimpton	1	7	7
John Haskett	4	13	0
Sampson Sheafe	2	18	4
John Houlden	2	15	6
Tamazin Harris	3	0	0
Robert Eliot	10	1	9
Francis Pope		4	0
John Pratt		9	0
Samuel Lockwood		12	0
Benjamin Pemberton	3	1	1
George Vaughan		14	4
Total:	51	18	5

The author is most grateful for comment and criticism by David D. Hall, for the privilege of reading the typescript of James N. Green's Rosenbach lectures, which has greatly influenced his treatment of publication, and to John Bidwell, who supplied particulars of Clark Library copies and proposed the identification of Hoole's *Accidence*.

Notes

1. Walter Muir Whitehill, *Boston: A Topographical History* (Cambridge, Mass.: Belknap Press, 1959), 29.

2. *Records of the First Church of Boston, 1630–1868*, ed. R. D. Pierce, *Pubs. CSM* 39 (1961): 344. [More correctly, Perry never became a "full" church member, though remaining in membership thanks to his baptismal covenant.]

3. Cf. a deposition by Michael Perry stating that he was living with Usher in 1690, Massachusetts State Archives, Mass. Archives Series, 8: 87; Littlefield, *Boston Booksellers*, supposes (p. 72) that Perry was apprenticed to Samuel Phillips, his predecessor in his shop.

4. Littlefield, *Boston Booksellers*, 188–89.

5. Sewall, *Diary*, 1: 321, 327.

6. Ford, *Boston Book Market*, 163–82. First printed in *John Dunton's Letters from New England*, ed. W. T. Whitmore (Boston: Prince Society, 1867), 314–19, and again in Littlefield, *Boston Booksellers*.

7. Stephen Botein, "The Anglo-American Book Trade Before 1776," in *Printing and Society in Early America*, ed. William L. Joyce et al. (Worcester, Mass.: American Antiquarian Society, 1983), 48–82.

8. Cyprian Blagden, "Booksellers' Trade Sales, 1718–1768," *The Library* 5th ser. 5 (1951): 243–57; Terry Belanger, "Booksellers' Trade Sales, 1718–1768," *The Library* 5th ser. 30 (1975): 281–302; Graham Pollard, "The English Market for Printed Books," *Publishing History* 4 (1978): 7–48.

9. Stephen Foster, "The Godly in Transit," in *Seventeenth-Century New England*, ed. David D. Hall and David Grayson Allen, *Pubs. CSM* 63 (Boston, 1984), 185–238, esp. 219–31.

10. For some other English provincial stocks, see also John Feather, *The Provincial Book Trade in Eighteenth-Century England* (Cambridge: Cambridge University Press, 1985), 75–80 and 125–29. Unfortunately, none of these booksellers lived in a town such as Norwich or Exeter, whose commerce and population were comparable to Boston's.

11. Cf. Ian K. Steele, *The English Atlantic, 1675–1740* (New York: Oxford University Press, 1986), chap. 2.

12. Cyprian Blagden, *The Stationers' Company: A History, 1403–1959* (Cambridge, Mass.: Harvard University Press, 1960), 63, 92–94; for lists of items that were in the English stock in 1692 and 1695, see John Johnson and Strickland Gibson, *Print and Privilege at Oxford to the Year 1700* (Oxford: Oxford Bibliographical Society, 1946), 75–77, and the Stationers' Company, *Transcript of the Registers . . . from 1640–1708*, 3 vols. (London, 1913–14), 3, 457–61, and cf. a broadside price list of ca. 1695, reproduced in Blagden, "Booksellers' Trade Sales," 187.

13. I refer to a draft of a chapter on Knox in her Ph.D. thesis, in progress, which she generously allowed me to read. [Elizabeth C. Reilly, "Common and Learned Readers: Shared and Separate Spheres in Mid-Eighteenth-Century New England" (Ph.D., dissertation, Boston University, 1994), chap. 3.]

14. I have used the microfilm of the Suffolk County Probate Register, 14: 287 (Boston Public Library, call. no. *F72.S9. M43), checked against the original documents in the Massachusetts Judicial Archives, Suffolk Co. Probate Records Series, Docket 2600.

15. Cf. Ford, *Boston Book Market*, 108–51, where most of the titles are annotated "Ca[lf]," or "sh[eep]," or "b[oun]d," and only occasionally "st[itched]."

16. Elizabeth Carroll Reilly, "The Wages of Piety: The Boston Book Trade of Jeremy Condy," in *Printing and Society in Early America*, ed. Joyce et al., 83–131. [Amory usually preferred Jeremiah to Jeremy as the spelling of Condy's first name, but I have regularized the usage in this essay and elsewhere to Jeremy.]

17. Thwing Index (Massachusetts Historical Society).

18. Cf. a writ attaching the goods of William Haskell of Middleboro, dated January 1, 1704/5; Massachusetts Historical Society, Miscellaneous Bound Papers.

19. The only possible minister or Harvard graduate is Samuel Shepard, minister of Woodbridge, N.J. (A.B. 1685); but I suppose that Perry's customer was Samuel Shepard of Haverhill, Mass. (d. 1707), a blacksmith. The sole Boston magistrate was Simeon Stoddard, a member of the Provincial Council.

20. Report of the commissioners for insolvency, Docket 2600 (above, n. 14). For John Usher, see Littlefield, *Early Boston Booksellers*; Capt. Benjamin Davis (d. 1704) was a founder of the Brattle Street Church and a member (1673) of the Ancient and Honorable Artillery Company of Boston. Nicholas Roberts (d. 1710) was a Boston merchant; Joseph Coysgarne (occasionally spelled Coysgaine or Coysgame), a Huguenot merchant, operated briefly in Boston in partnership with Peter Signac, ca. 1699–1703. Cf. Charles W. Baird, *History of the Huguenot Emigration to America*, 2 vols. (1885, repr., Baltimore: Regional Publishing Co., 1966), 2: 214 and the Thwing Index.

21. William T. Baxter, *The House of Hancock* (Cambridge, Mass.: Harvard University Press, 1945); William T. Baxter, "Daniel Henchman, a Colonial Bookseller," *Essex Institute Historical Collections* 70 (1934): 1–30.

22. Ford, *Boston Book Market*, 81, 108–20, for these accounts. Ford (p. 24) wrongly identifies the bookseller as John Allen, who did not come over from England until 1686, though the account (p. 81) is dated 1679.

23. Account of Thomas Cox, in Henchman ledger I (1712–ca. 1735), fol. 234. The original ledgers are now in the New England Historic Genealogical Society and the Boston Public Library; the author has used the microfilm at the American Antiquarian Society.

24. Ford, *Boston Book Market*, 13.

25. Chiswell notes that these Bibles were "very much cheaper than . . . the true English prints." Ibid., 85.

26. William McDougall, "Scottish Books for America in the Mid-18th Century," in *Spreading the Word: The Distribution Networks of Print*, ed. Robin Myers and Michael Harris (Winchester, UK.: St. Paul's Bibliographies, 1990), 21–46.

27. Press runs tend to be quantified in multiples of a ream of paper (500 sheets). I would put less weight than Foster on the 1,700 copies printed of the Bay Psalm Book (1640), a vanity publication, or the 1,800 ballad versions reportedly printed and sold in a year of Wigglesworth's *Day of Doom*, a white whale. What Cotton Mather might consider a reasonable edition size, when he and his friends paid for it, would also differ from the sober calculations of a bookseller who did not have money to burn.

28. Edwin Wolf II, *The Book Culture of a Colonial American City: Philadelphia Books, Bookmen, and Booksellers* (Oxford: Clarendon Press, 1988); and see Richard Beale Davis, *A Colonial Southern Bookshelf* (Athens: University of Georgia Press, 1979).

29. Thus, the inventory lists blank copybooks as a matter of course "for boys," and the title of Culnann's *Sententiae pueriles* implies the same limitation.

30. Robert Middlekauff, *Ancients and Axioms: Secondary Education in Revolutionary New England* (New Haven, Conn.: Yale University Press, 1963), esp. 8 n.: Boston, Cambridge, Roxbury, Watertown, Charlestown, Dorchester, Salem, Ipswich, Hadley, Bristol (now in Rhode Island), and Plymouth, in Massachusetts; New Haven, Hartford, Fairfield, and New London, in Connecticut. Ten other Massachusetts towns had schools but "failed to supply grammar masters for varying periods . . . between 1700 and 1720" (p. 34 n.).

31. "Anyone who went to school (and . . . most did) began the learning process through Latin authors, unless he was an apprentice or a black." Davis, *Colonial Southern Bookshelf*, 100, cited approvingly by Wolf, *Book Culture*, 47. For assumptions about the numbers attending grammar school, see contra, Margaret Spufford, *Small Books and Pleasant Histories* (London: Methuen, 1981), 19–37.

32. Foster, "Godly in Transit," 221, 228.

33. [Edward Cotton], *A Catalogue of All the Books Printed in the United States* (Boston, 1804).

34. These are listed in "A Catalogue of Mr. Richard Royston's Copies," appended to the 1703 ed. of William Cave's *Antiquitaties Christianae*; see further *The Notebook of*

Thomas Bennet and Henry Clements, ed. Norma Hodgson and Cyprian Blagden (Oxford: Oxford Bibliographical Society, 1953), 76–100; and cf. their list of conger copies entered in the *Stationers' Register, 1688–1707* (pp. 203–8), none of which appear in Perry's or Usher's lists either.

35. Ford, *Boston Book Market,* 48, argues for their cheapness, but does not substantiate his opinion.

36. Hall, *Worlds,* 47–49.

37. These are the Session laws for March 1699 (Evans 917) and Increase Mather's *Good Man Making a Good End,* both adespota; Samuel [or more likely, Stephen] Sewall's *Epitome* and Cotton Mather's *Remarkable Judgments,* which have lost their title pages; and the *Lamentation of Mary Hooper.* I have not counted the American schoolbooks, which are more or less incomparable, and which are likely to have been published "by the booksellers," as they were in England.

38. These are Evans 711–12, 724 (which includes 725 and 727), 739, and 965. Evans 724 has the ambiguous imprint "for and sold by M. Perry," but in fact appeared by subvention.

39. Rollo G. Silver, "Publishing in Boston, 1726–1757," *Procs. AAS* 66 (1956): 17–50, at 19, 28. The author's "payment" was generous, since an English publisher would surely have given nothing.

40. Holmes, *Cotton Mather,* suggests how widespread the private publication of Mather's works was: the author himself paid for nos. 34, 47, 50, 67, 71, 78, 127, 132, 134, 144–45, 149, 227, 235, 240, 269, 320, 322, 375, 396, 405, 411, 447, 455; Edward Bromfield for nos. 8, 111, 136, 229; Sir Henry Ashurst for no. 88; Eliakim Hutchinson for no. 18; Samuel Mather for no. 408; Samuel Penhallow for no. 273; Thomas Prince for no. 435; Madam Saltonstall for no. 31; Samuel Sewall for nos. 334 and 389; John Winthrop for nos. 14 and 53; relatives of the deceased for nos. 13, 29, 113, 166, 222, 420, 448; and various pious private groups, including one headed by Obadiah Gill (a shipwright and minor bookseller, for obvious reasons), for nos. 9, 28, 48, 55, 68, 80, 138, 156, 159, 169, 188, 202, 218, 221–22, 243, 248, 281–82, 311, 317, 322, 330, 337, 381, 385, 406, 410, 446, 456–57, 462; and these are just the instances for which we have documentation. I ignore publications financed by the church and state, and various subscriptions, all unsuccessful.

41. Hall, *Worlds,* 45–46.

42. Sewall, *Diary,* 1: 390, 2: 687, 767.

43. Shipton and Sibley, *Biographical Sketches* 4 (1933): 249.

44. Sewall, *Diary,* 1: 495. In 1713–17, Henchman credited Joanna Perry for some copies of Willard's *Truly Blessed Man,* printed for her husband in 1700 (Henchman ledger I, fols. 17, 90). These must represent a similar kickback, since no copies of this work appeared in her husband's inventory. Note, too, that Willard was still "in print" after seventeen years.

45. Sewall, *Diary,* 2: 709.

46. Holmes, *Cotton Mather,* no. 340.

47. This example is taken from Houghton Library *AC6.M4208.703d; the formula is common. Other Houghton copies with childish signatures are *AC6.W6618.700f; *AC6.W6618.699s; *AC6.W6395.670meb; and *AC6.Sh472S.1692.

48. Nicholas Thomas, *Entangled Objects: Exchange, Material Culture, and Colonialism*

in the Pacific (Cambridge, Mass.: Harvard University Press, 1991). In Thomas's analysis, a presentation copy is a totally different object from one acquired by purchase, since they come "entangled" with different social contexts. A Melanesian object may become entangled in a European museum, and a European object (like drums of kerosene) in Melanesian society. A book historian must constantly undo and reknit the severed ends of objects entangled in imprint programs, American Studies, and Rare Book Rooms.

5. Printing and Bookselling in New England, 1638–1713

"Printing and Bookselling in New England, 1638–1713" draws on the three essays that precede it in this collection, incorporating their arguments and discoveries into a narrative that fits within the organization of *The Colonial Book in the Atlantic World*, where it was originally printed, somewhat abridged, as chapter three.

Revisiting the history of the first English-language press in North America, Amory trained his iconoclastic eye on every aspect of a story that had been told by Isaiah Thomas in *A History of Printing in America* (1810) and, with more precision though not in every respect accurately, by George Parker Winship, Lawrence Starkey, and William Kellaway, among others. One task was accomplished with ease, demonstrating the relative insignificance of the Cambridge printers compared with the output of the printers who set up shop in Boston after 1675. A second was to clarify the sequence of printers and the presses on which they worked, a modestly triumphal piece of analysis. A third was to specify the relationship between church and commonwealth, on the one hand, and printers and booksellers on the other. Here, influenced by Sheila Lambert and Michael Treadwell's rethinking of "freedom of the press" in seventeenth-century England,[1] he noted a circumstance that is too readily overlooked, that printers and booksellers in the seventeenth century relied on state regulation to curtail competition within the trade. The sections dealing with censorship or state control are also marked by Amory's uneasiness with orthodox Puritanism. As in the essay on "A Bible and Other Books," he did not want to pursue Samuel Eliot Morison's suggestion that the colonists created a healthy secular (or humanist) culture, but he was also well aware (as that other essay demonstrates, citing Bibles that included the Book of Common Prayer) of the contradictions that emerged from any close study of the book trade. A few of his asides about Puritan culture are out of step with current scholarship, as I have indicated in two notes of my own. Nor do the details of his narrative sustain the assertion, for which there is warrant in some of the scholarly literature, that a pious, well-regulated press gave way to more "secular" forms of enterprise: the close connections between Increase and, especially, Cotton Mather and the leading printer in early eighteenth-century Boston belie such an argument.

Where the voice in this essay becomes more distinctively his own is in Amory's analysis of two famous imprints, the Bay Psalm Book and the minister-poet Michael Wigglesworth's *Day of Doom* (1662).[2] The challenge in both instances was the same, to make sense of the quantities of copies printed and sold, quantities that, on the face of it, made little sense in the context of the near-inactivity of the Cambridge printers, the almost equally "unadventurous" Boston trade, and the very limited scope of the market. Extending a calculation begun in the essay on Michael Perry's inventory, Amory figured out the rate of sales of local imprints as compared with the rate of sales of books imported from overseas. These efforts, which included assembling a box of books matching in weight the English customs figures in order to estimate the scale of importations, led to a contrarian conclusion, that local books were "in print" for a long time, in part because they sold much more slowly than imported items. A telling example was the broadside edition of the Massachusetts capital laws issued in 1642 and, according to Amory, still in print in the mid-1670s when the selectmen of Watertown distributed copies of the broadside to each household. The production and distribution of law books, from the "Body of Liberties" of 1641 (produced in nineteen scribal copies, one for each town) to the 1648 *Laws and Liberties* and its sequels in Massachusetts, Connecticut, and Rhode Island, served as perhaps the clearest evidence of the utilitarian constraints on the book trade. Other feats of analysis arose out of Amory's description of bookselling. The presence of certain names in imprints ("printed for" x or y) was, he argued, evidence of private patronage, not of bookselling as a commercial activity.

SOURCE: Chapter 3 of *The Colonial Book in the Atlantic World* (2000), reprinted with the permission of Cambridge University Press (New York), and including material eliminated from that version (ms., American Antiquarian Society).

1. Freedoms and Licenses

The colonizing of New England happened in a rush. The "separatist" Pilgrims found a haven at New Plymouth in 1620. The Massachusetts Bay Company, a joint-stock venture chartered in 1629, initiated the "Great Migration" of 1630, founding Boston and several neighboring towns in that year. As more people arrived during the 1630s, they dispersed up and down the coast and as far inland as the settlements that became Hartford, Windsor, and Springfield along the Connecticut River. In 1640, when the first book was printed in British North America, New England contained five separate jurisdictions: New Plymouth; Massachusetts Bay, which claimed the future territories of Maine, New Hampshire, and Vermont (the last also claimed by New York); Connecticut; New Haven; and an aggregation of towns and land-grants that were later incorporated under a royal charter as Rhode Island and Providence Plantations. In 1662 Connecticut merged with New Haven, and in 1679 New Hampshire split off from Massachusetts as an independent royal colony. Together with New York, which England had annexed from the Dutch, the resulting five New England colonies were jointly administered as the Dominion of New England under Sir Edmund Andros, from 1686 to 1689. Thereafter, they were rearranged into four, a royal charter having incorporated Massachusetts Bay and New Plymouth as the Province of Massachusetts in 1692. The islands off the southern coast of Massachusetts formed a fiefdom of the Mayhew family, administered at first by New York, and later by Massachusetts, but in a sense an extension of the anarchic townships of Rhode Island.

Despite this chaotic scatter of jurisdictions, from which yet others later split off, the localized origins of the Great Migration in East Anglia, Hampshire, and Dorset, the motives that impelled emigration, together with the covenanted character of New England churches, enforced a highly homogeneous culture, at least outside of the Quaker and Baptist settlements of Rhode Island; in the United Colonies of Massachusetts, Connecticut, and New Plymouth, communication (and indeed communion) was essentially equivalent to agreement. In his influential study, *The New England Mind: The Seventeenth Century* (1939), Perry Miller observed that "it is a matter of complete indifference or chance that a quotation comes from Cotton instead of Hooker, from Winthrop instead of Willard; all writers were in substantial agreement upon all the propositions which I am discussing in this book."[3] Few historians today would agree that anything like this unanimity prevailed in reality: we are dealing with folk who openly preferred hypocrisy to sincere dissent, yet who failed to admit a substantial fraction of the population to their platforms, compacts, and covenants. Unanimity, in short, was largely maintained on paper, and the access of dissent to print was precarious. From the arrival of a press in December 1638 down to 1689, the Massachusetts General Court and later, the governor and council of the Dominion of New England not only limited the number of presses and confined them to either Cambridge or Boston, but also directly controlled their management. Dissident opinion had no alternative but to go overseas: John Eliot might exhibit his views by writing to England, but Thomas Lechford, Roger Williams, and other critics had to remove themselves and their opinions bodily from New England in order to break into print.

In these respects, New England's censorship differed little from Old England's, though it was more visible, more effective, and culturally more accepted. Some marginal titles, moreover, were imported that would not have been licensed for printing: the Book of Common Prayer, for example, was regularly bound up with the Authorized Version of the Bible, which New Englanders owned at least as frequently as the Geneva Version.[4] The Bay Colony suppressed a Cambridge edition of the *Imitatio Christi* in 1669, though a 1658 Leiden edition would find its way into Harvard College Library by 1723. The merchant John Usher imported a salacious novel, *The London Jilt*, a pornographic classic, *Venus in the Cloister*, and the Earl of Rochester's libertine *Poems*.[5] Massachusetts and Connecticut ports were officially closed to Catholic, Quaker, and Baptist books, but Benjamin Lynde, a future Massachusetts Chief Justice, had acquired copies of Dryden's agnostic poem, *Religio Laici* (1682) and his allegorical apology for Catholicism, *The Hind and the Panther* (1687) shortly after their publication.[6] Such importations imply that the ultimate constraint on the books that the colonists read was rather the Licensing Act of 1662, in force to 1679, when it lapsed for six years, and again from 1685 to 1695, when it lapsed altogether.[7]

The Licensing Act certainly complicated existence for English Catholics and Nonconformists, but it also enforced trade privileges that went back to the beginnings of the Stationers' Company; the only new element was the enactment of these privileges by Parliament, instead of by royal decree. In the colonies, too, the licenser's propriety and the printer's property went hand in hand; if anything, the licensed printer preferred more, not less, prior restraint on his trade. Sergeant Samuel Green in Cambridge treated his license to print English as a privilege from which the printer of Indian, Marmaduke Johnson, should rightly have been excluded. Timothy Green would not settle for a mere monopoly over Connecticut printing; he demanded and got a contract guaranteeing him £50 a year—more than the salary of the deputy governor—and a free supply of paper. The Boston merchant John Usher secured a seven-year privilege on his edition of the 1672 Massachusetts *Laws*, apparently to protect it from overprinting by Samuel Green, the colony printer.[8]

The colonial press, especially in Cambridge, thus took on some of the features of a mint, setting an official seal of authenticity on a text. The market for books was a separate matter, of secondary concern to the authorities, and managed by merchants and booksellers. New England's characteristic separation of printing from bookselling owed something to its institution of censorship, which divided the world of the covenanted from the world of the commercial, "a plantation of religion," as John Higginson insisted in his election sermon of 1663, from "a plantation of trade." The colonies' abandonment of this ideal, pilloried as a shameful "declension" in many an election sermon, is a tale of two cities, a gradual triumph of Boston merchants, royal governors, and the English Board of Trade over the Cambridge press, the General Court, and the "New England Way" of its Congregational churches.[9]

Technologically, Boston and Cambridge were roughly on a par: from 1639 to 1692, there were one or two presses operating in Cambridge; from 1675 to 1713, one to three presses in Boston; and in New England as a whole down to 1713, there were usually two, and occasionally three or four presses. During this period, Boston presses printed eighty-one percent of the New England editions still surviving, and in only half the time it took Cambridge to print nearly all the rest: with 361 editions in Cambridge, of which 116 are now lost, we may compare forty-eight editions in New London, of which twenty-three no longer survive, and some 1,239 editions (including separate issues of the *Boston News-Letter*) in Boston, of which ninety-six have perished.[10]

Despite uncertainties in the assignment of lost editions, the measure of Boston's commercial importance seems assured.

Intellectually, no Boston imprints have the stature of the Bay Psalm Book (1640), the *Platform of Church Discipline* (1649), or the Eliot Indian Bible (1661–63), all of them first printed in Cambridge, and yet these early monuments were oddly specialized.[11] The Cambridge press contributed nothing to medicine, science, or technology, and little to belles lettres, politics, or news; its production centered on ecclesiastical and municipal laws, Indian texts, and practical divinity. It printed no schoolbooks but catechisms, and most of its poems were funeral elegies that the mourners cast in the grave; even regular sequences of blank forms, the ubiquitous staple of later printers, date only from the 1680s. The exceptions that are sometimes urged are unconvincing: is *Gods Terrible Voice in the City of London* (1667)—an account of the Great Fire and plague of 1665 by the London minister Thomas Vincent—really "the first American medical work?" Is the Earl of Winchilsea's *True and Exact Relation of the Late Prodigious Earthquake & Eruption of Mount Aetna* (1669) the "prototype" of "Eye Witness news?"[12] The eye that witnessed and the voice that spoke in these events was divine. In their accounts of New England culture, Thomas Goddard Wright and Samuel Eliot Morison have tried to lighten the grim Cambridge statistics by balancing them against English printing and book exports, but it will not work. Of a total of 157 Evans entries down to 1670, Wright acknowledges, only four were secular poems and eight were works of "History, Biography, etc." where "etc." must do duty for news-sheets on the London plague, Mount Etna, and other signs of God's displeasure.[13] Nevertheless, he continues, works by New Englanders or about New England were printed in London or circulated in manuscript in America—and in any case, there were, undeniably, imports. Boston imports.

Boston's strength was in history and biography, and in its sheer uncovenanted diversity: Thomas Thacher's *Brief Rule* for dealing with "the small pocks or measels" (1678); Benjamin Harris's almanacs, his *Public Occurrences* (1690), and *Protestant Tutor Enlarged* (1685); *The New-England Primer Enlarged* (1691) and *The New England Psalter* (1682), long-time staples of the trade; to say nothing of *Pilgrim's Progress* (1681). How did Bostonians ever live without *The Names of the Streets . . . within the Town of Boston* (1708)? How did they wage war—and they fought continually—without *An Abridgment of the English Military Discipline* (1690)? A number of these titles, including the *Abridgment*, were reprints of London properties, but the colonial editions were often "enlarged," or, in the case of the *Abridgment*, improved for the colonial market. The editor (Benjamin Harris?), who engagingly ascribed it to that Protestant martyr the Duke of Monmouth, decorated the title page with a cut of the royal arms and the pious motto, "God Save KING William & QVEEN Mary"; the recency of their ascent to the throne had caught the printer short, but he made do with the (barely recognizable) arms of Charles I.[14] These Boston imprints are, quite simply, the first of any practical importance for the lives of "the Common People of New England" to whom Thacher addressed his broadsheet.

The ascendancy of the Green family provides a technological link between the two cities. This "dynasty of printers," as it is often called, has been celebrated in family genealogies that omit any non-printing progeny, and even in a supposed "descent" of their presses, but they owe their genes to a government monopoly. Sergeant Samuel, the founder of the family fortunes, had five sons, three of whom had no innate inclination for printing: Joseph became a tailor, Jonas a mariner, and Samuel Jr. carried on "a convenient way of trading" and cattle ranching in Hartford and later, New London, Connecticut, for about six years before his father forced him to return to Boston to take over its printing in 1681.[15] The Greens eventually secured the contracts for Massachusetts, Connecticut, New Plymouth, and New Hampshire, and they gratefully internalized the values of these masters. Bartholomew, the most productive and least prolific of his clan, operated from 1685 to 1732, ever loyal to this past. He "always spoke of the wonderful spirit of piety that prevailed in the land of his youth with a singular pleasure," his obituarist reported, and was "cautious of publishing anything offensive, light or hurtful" even after the licensing regime had loosened. A certain lack of enterprise accompanied these beliefs, which Isaiah Thomas, that Revolutionary patriot and empire-builder, found puzzling: "He [Bartholomew] was the most distinguished printer of that period in this country, and did more business than any other of the profession; *yet he worked chiefly for the booksellers* [emphasis added]."[16] That was no way to get ahead in 1776, but Bartholomew appears as the printer of some 1,073 entries in NAIP, about a quarter of all the titles printed in the continental United States down to his death in 1732, nearly all of them printed for the colonial government, booksellers, or private customers. His brother Samuel Jr. was just as unadventurous. The only books in his estate were ten dozen psalters (£4 10s.), forty-six and one third dozen "larger catechisms" (£16 19s.), six dozen "smaller catechisms" (9s.), and fourteen "Bookes and wast paper" (10s. 9d.)—the last item possibly forming his personal library. Here is a concrete explanation of the Greens' "singular pleasure" in the "wonderful spirit of piety" of early New England.

2. Cambridge and Boston Presses

Our records are exceptionally complete for the Cambridge press because it was a tool of government and of John Eliot's mission to the Indians, on which the authorities reported progress to the sponsoring English agency, the New England Company. The first press and £60 worth of paper belonging to it were also the subject of a lawsuit by the rightful owners in 1654 against Henry Dunster, president of Harvard College, who managed it for the authorities.[17] This documentation, and the majesty of its product for the early church and state, have naturally won the Cambridge press the affection of later bibliographers, despite the much more varied and commercially valuable production of Boston.

Jose Glover, a wealthy Surrey clergyman, brought over the first press and £60 worth of paper, and secured the services of Stephen and Matthew Day, a locksmith and his son from Cambridge, England, possibly to operate it. Our earliest notice of the arrival of the press is a letter dated Dec. 10, 1638 from the Harvard overseer and clergyman Hugh Peter, to a correspondent in Bermuda: "Wee have a printery here, and thinke to goe to worke with some speciall things, and if you have any thing, you may send it safely by these." Peter sounds a little at a loss what to do with it, for Glover had died on the passage over, and his plans died with him. His property passed to his wife, who married the new president of Harvard College, Henry Dunster, in 1641 and died two years afterwards, leaving him five little Glovers. According to tradition, the press was set up in the president's house in 1639, where Dunster managed it as his property, receiving money for its product and leasing it on the decease of Matthew Day in 1649 to the College Steward Samuel Green for ten shillings a sheet; the college later claimed that the press and "all its impressions" since its arrival were Harvard property.[18] Nevertheless, Glover's heirs sued Dunster in 1654 for an accounting of the profits and recovered £20 for the press and £30 worth of paper, amounting to 120 reams. This seems to be a judgment that Dunster had managed the press as their stepfather and guardian during their minority, and not as president of Harvard, an office in any case he had resigned in 1654.[19]

This record, unfortunately, leaves many questions unanswered. If the college owned "all the impressions," for example, why would Green have paid Harvard 10s. a sheet for printing them? Or was the fee limited to the printing he undertook on the side—the almanacs, commencement exercises, and ex-libris that, in later years, at least, the students paid for? And when the government or Hezekiah Usher supplied the paper for a supplement to the laws or a new edition of the Bay Psalm Book, surely they, and not Harvard College, owned those "impressions"? Or did the 1654 decision somehow effect a transfer of the press and its remaining product to the college? At the statutory rate of 8s. per 100 copies of a sheet, Green—or in at least one recorded instance, Henry Dunster—would have received 48s. a sheet on a run of 600 copies; if Green's ten shillings were a kickback, did it operate regardless of the size of the edition? All that seems clear is that the college, Green, and the colony were entangled in a common public enterprise, though Green moonlighted from time to time, just as employees today abuse the office xerox and the company letterhead. Well into the eighteenth century, the college printer will not be held to his bargains, if they pinch him, and the government was surprisingly lenient on violations of the law by the printer of the New England Company if he promised to reform.[20] Government, college, and Indian printing were never carried on at arm's length, but collusively. Downy private enterprise only just peeps forth from beneath these sheltering wings.

Glover's plans for his two indentured servants are not recorded. Stephen had only contracted to serve for two years, and immediately afterwards left to explore for black lead in the valley of the Blackstone River. He strongly resented his time as prototypographer of British North America, and demanded and got extra compensation for it from the colony. The literature of emigration, moreover, might lead us to believe that the colony wanted locksmiths far more urgently than printers; perhaps Jose Glover planned to operate the press himself. A late tradition reports that the Days were "assisted" by Gregory Dexter, a London printer who had moved to Rhode Island in 1643.[21] This transient initiation may have sufficed to teach them the "mystery" of printing, but the authorities made little demand on their time, and all the early printers combined more important occupations with occasional stints at the press. The elder Green, indeed, was generally known as "Sergeant Green" from his joy in the maneuvers of the Ancient and Honorable Artillery Company, a Boston militia; Samuel Jr., his better-equipped Bostonian son, was "Printer Green."

The peculiar type, faulty spelling, and frequent misprints of the Bay Psalm Book (1640) prompted its historian George Parker Winship to joke that it "looks the part that the fates assigned it to play"; yet the type was English, "a very good letter," in Isaiah Thomas's opinion, and the composition was not much worse than London's rather low standard.[22] One might rather urge a certain amateurishness in the signatures, which follow an English register of twenty-four letters, including W, whereas London books followed a Latin alphabet of twenty-three (I/J and U/V were represented by a single letter in both languages down to 1640). The Days also treated the running-heads idiosyncratically, setting them afresh for every sheet as though they were the first words on the page, and occasionally making the catch-words "catch" with the headlines, whereas a London printer would have reused the same setting of the headlines, treating them as a "skeleton" of the page and not as part of the text. These are not grave faults, but we may fairly ascribe them to the Days' innocence of their craft.

A press was symbolic of larger, more plaintive needs, one suspects, than the need for printing. The image of New England that enticed the settlers over changed from a welcoming paradise to a "howling wilderness" as the reality struck home;[23] the press was a visible sign that they had never left—perhaps even a promise of return. In 1669, when a Royal Commission was challenging the validity of the Bay Colony charter, President Charles Chauncy anxiously addressed the New England Company, begging them to transfer the Indian press and its types to the college. He wrote in Latin, to make sure they saw the point: "we fear (alas!) that if the printing press fall to wreck, or in any wise fail us, and the Characters be taken from us, not only, to begin with, will America be without printers, & the Academy with its Scholars suffer damage in the progress of its Studies, & our very meetings with opportunity for taking Degrees be hindered, but also the Common weal & the Civil laws passed for the general good will, to the unspeakable, almost irreparable, loss of the Christian Religion and the Churches of the whole Community of New England, utterly perish & come to destruction."[24] His concern for the commonweal was genuine enough, at a time when England had unleashed the Clarendon Code against his co-religionists and dispatched a commission to review the charter and administration of Massachusetts. The presidential rhetoric, however, surely exaggerated the needs of Harvard College, which had subsisted on a meager annual diet of two broadside *Theses* and *Quaestiones* and a sixteen-page almanac since 1639—a total of from two to two and a half printed sheets a year. All the printed texts assigned to the students were imported from Europe; others they copied out. They commonplaced their reading, and they wrote out the college laws in manuscript, multiple copies of which still survive.[25]

Besides these anxieties, justified or unjustified, the proliferation of printers in the aftermath of the Indian Bible would have worried the president. The project grew out of John Eliot's mission to the Massachusett Indians. In 1659 the New England Company had unleashed a second press and Marmaduke Johnson, a competent printer, on a colony long accustomed to the unskillful and subservient Samuel Green. Eliot carried out the translation with the assistance of two converts, Job Nesutan and John Sassamon, and printed it with the help of a third, James Wowaus, known as James Printer. 1,500 copies of the New Testament were printed in 1661, of which 200 were provisionally bound up in limp vellum; and 1,000 copies of the Old Testament in 1663, of which forty copies were sent in sheets to England for presentation to the officers of the Company, and other dignitaries, bound in full morocco, or to be lodged with learned institutions. As of August 1664, only forty-two complete Bibles had been bound in America, and the binder was complaining that he could not afford to bind any more.

The size and speed of the project were unprecedented: the first edition alone (including the metrical psalms) required 353 reams, more paper than the entire output of the press down to 1660, and it was completed in only three years. Its effect on its intended audience is not much contested: Samuel Eliot Morison called it "the most notable—and least useful—production of the press at this period"; other historians have often seen it as an instrument of domination over an ambivalent and demoralized group of Indians— James Printer later joined King Philip, the leader of a native insurrection in 1675.[26] The binding of 200 New Testaments suggests that Eliot had converted no more than 200 families by 1661, and few of the surviving Bibles have an Indian provenance. It seems that production was calculated to ensure an ample future supply after Johnson had returned to England, and certainly the only occasion for a second edition was the wanton destruction of most of the first edition in King Philip's War.

Johnson declined to return to England, however, and launched into initiatives of his own. The first trained printer in the colonies, he had been apprenticed to the printer John Field of Cambridge, England, in 1645 and freed in 1652. The next printers of such competence were John Allen in 1686 (who was never apprenticed as a stationer, but had worked for George Larkin, a London printer) and Thomas Fleet in 1713. Johnson was a constant thorn in the side of the commissioners who supervised the progress of the Bible: he sought "to draw away the affections" of Green's daughter, though he had a wife still living in England, and he "absented himselfe" from the press;[27] when he returned to England in 1664 with instructions to buy a new supply of type for the "improvement" of the Indian press, he bought more type and a third press on his own account, which remained idle and unlicensed long after its arrival. There was simply not enough work for two printers without the Bible, and both Johnson and Green, for sheer want of copy, began to reprint London pamphlets, completing some fourteen exceptionally vendible titles in 1667–68 before the magistrates investigated. The magistrates may have objected to the use of the college and Indian presses for private profit; they may have felt that colonial reprints were a kind of piracy; or they may simply have rejected commerce as such; no official order suppressing this promising line of new titles is recorded, but it ended abruptly in 1668, and surviving copies are suspiciously rare.

Green and Johnson were thus cast onto other shifts, one to earn and the other to protect his living. Their first instinct was to lighten the competition: Johnson petitioned the General Court for permission to operate his own press in Boston, and Green counter-petitioned to suppress his rival's operations in Cambridge. Despite the perfect symmetry of their requests, neither obtained his wish. For a while John Eliot, who felt an uneasy responsibility for Johnson's predicament as the Indian printer who had no Indian to print, tried to supply or translate enough for his support. Eventually, Johnson gave up the unequal effort and entered into partnership with Green in late 1668. In 1671, the partnership broke up, and Johnson began to work for Edmund Ranger, Joseph Farnum, or John Usher, and Green for John Tappan, John Ratcliffe, or William Avery, all of them in Boston.

"In 1672," says Winship, summarizing this development, "all at once, smaller shops specializing in books and stationery hung out their signs."[28] It is a pretty thought, but based solely on the deceptive evidence of imprints. Ratcliffe had been working as a binder since 1662, and as we shall see, neither Avery, Tappan, nor Farnum specialized in books and stationery, though they commissioned books. Hezekiah Usher was a merchant who had occasionally paid for both colonial and London printing since 1647. His son John took over the business in 1663.[29] When the English bookseller John Dunton visited Boston in 1686, John was his main competitor.

The printers, however, had broken out of the cage where the magistrates had confined their craft. In 1673, Harvard leased the Indian press for 30s. a year to Johnson (a bitter blow to Green); and in 1674, the magistrates finally accepted the fait accompli and permitted Johnson to set up a press in Boston. His triumph was brief: he died a few months later, and his latest imprint was still dated from Cambridge, but there was no turning back. Despite a final petition by Samuel Green to lock up printing again in Cambridge, the magistrates allowed John Foster, a Harvard graduate, to purchase and operate Johnson's press. In Green's opinion he was "a young man, that had no skill of printing but what he had taken notice by the by," but it was skill enough for him as it had been for Green, and before his untimely death in 1681 he had produced the first printed portrait, of Richard Mather, and the first printed map of New England.

His widow sold the press and its equipment to Samuel Sewall, then at the beginning of his career as merchant; the General Court granted him the "management" of the press and prohibited others from setting up a second press without their permission. Though Sewall actually printed a catechism and a sermon on his own—and proudly dispatched some hundreds of copies of the catechism to his native town of Bishop's Stoke in England—he ordinarily "assigned" the operation of the press to others: John Ratcliffe, James Glen, Samuel Green, Jr., and Richard Pierce. Green moved to Boston from New London in 1681 and took over the government printing from his father, who had previously shared it with Foster.[30]

In 1684, when Sewall became a magistrate of the General Court, the Court released him from the "management" of the press, which he sold to Green. Benjamin Harris later described it as "the best furnished PRINTING PRESS, of those few we know of in America," and its fonts included the Greek, pointed Hebrew, and black letter that Johnson had cadged from his employers.[31] Green petitioned the General Court for permission to succeed Sewall as "manager" in 1685,[32] but its decision is not recorded and the evidence of imprints is confused. In 1685, Green printed the New Plymouth *Laws* and began an abortive edition of the Massachusetts *Laws*, but Pierce printed William Adams's election sermon. The revocation of the colony charter and the advent of the Dominion of New England threw the colony into turmoil, and when the air cleared in 1686, Pierce was appointed the government printer for the Dominion of New England.[33]

Little is known about Pierce beyond his bare name in imprints, which begin in 1684, when he was presumably working under Sewall's "assignment," though the imprints do not say so. In his history of early Massachusetts printing, George E. Littlefield supposed, logically enough, that Pierce got the government press along with the government contract, but if so, he certainly did not acquire Johnson's types and ornaments.[34] Unlike the younger Green, Pierce used romanized Greek and Hebrew, and his only black letter was a handsome great primer, which makes a brief appearance in Michael Wigglesworth's *Meat out of the Eater* (1689), whereas Green had smaller, pica "blacks" as early as 1686. The astrological characters Pierce used in Tulley's *Almanac* for 1691 are entirely different from those that Green used in the *Boston Ephemeris* for 1685. His long primer is a little smaller (20 ll. = 60 mm.) than Green's (62 mm.), as we can see in Cotton Mather's *Wonderful Works of God Commemorated* (1690), in which Pierce printed "The Way to Prosperity" (2A–C8) and Green printed the initial "Thanksgiving Sermon" and "Appendix" (A4 B–E8 2D4). An entrenched bibliographical dogma holds that presses may be distinguished by their stocks of type and ornaments; by this criterion, we may assume that the Dominion allowed Pierce to set up a press of his own in 1685, an assumption that, as we shall see, helps explain the continuity of printing in 1690, when Johnson's press was destroyed.

In 1686 Pierce cut a seal for the Dominion, and in 1688, a rather crude Royal Arms, for use at the head of proclamations—a public identification with Governor Edmund Andros's regime that would soon cost him his contract.[35] The printing of the Massachusetts *Laws* was suspended while the General Court haggled over the drafting of an article on "Courts," and collapsed with the arrival of Andros, who preferred to engross them on parchment; in the end the colonists (who had no intention of obeying them) cunningly complained that they did not know what the law was.[36] The Dominion fell in 1689, and a provisional Council of Safety took up the reins of government, leaving the future of the colony hanging before order was finally reimposed by the new charter in 1692. In the interim, the Council of Safety restored the government printing to Samuel Green, Jr. and then transferred it to Benjamin Harris and John Allen, after Green's death in July 1690. Pierce continued printing down to 1691, when he either left Boston or died; he may have worked as a journeyman for Harris and Allen, as he had previously done for Sewall.

At the Cambridge press, Sergeant Green had apprenticed his younger son Bartholomew in the early 1680s, when he needed help with a large (2,000 copies) edition of the Indian Bible; Bartholomew appears as a partner with his father in Cambridge imprints from 1691, about the time when his indentures should have expired. He seems to have split his time between his father's office in Cambridge and his brother Sam's in Boston, where he completed some government orders in August 1690, after his brother's death. The business of the Cambridge press shrank to printing commencement exercises, an annual almanac, and an occasional Indian title, and Sergeant Green finally closed it down in 1692. Cambridge had never been able to support two printers for long; Marmaduke Johnson complained that he was unable to use more than the "one third part of his time" after he had completed the Bible.[37]

Samuel Green, Jr.'s press was destroyed by fire in September 1690 and, though Bartholomew saved some of the type, Harris and Allen remained in possession of the only remaining press in Boston. Bartholomew Green did not finally receive permission to settle in Boston until June 6, 1693,[38] and he presumably used their press in 1692 to print Samuel Lee's *Great Day of Judgement* and, with Allen, Cotton Mather's *Blessed Unions*. The latter imprint foreshadows Harris's return to England in 1694, when Green and Allen took over the press and the government contract. Green himself had only one press, as appears from the inventory of his estate (1733), where it was valued at £15; and Allen had no other press before 1707, when he set up printing on his own. Harvard's two presses remained idle after 1692, the "Indian College" that housed them was torn down in 1698, and printing would not be permanently re-established in Cambridge for over a century. Harvard later acquired fresh fonts of Hebrew and Greek, which it provided for the printing of Judah Monis's *Dickdook Leshon Gnebreet* (1735), Stephen Sewall's *Hebrew Grammar* (1763), and the Harvard *Pietas et Gratulatio* (1762), but not until 1913 did the university acquire a "learned press" of its own.

Despite the plethora of printers in imprints, then, Isaiah Thomas is probably correct to say "there had never been more than two printing houses open at the same time in Boston" before 1700.[39] Green and Allen protected their monopoly by voluntarily declining to print any "Books of Controversy" without the approval of the Lieutenant Governor or their "particular Friends and Imployers," Increase and Cotton Mather. This became clear from a public scuffle over the printing of a reply to the Mathers. The casus belli was a "Manifesto" (1699) by the newly founded Fourth (Brattle St.) Church, a liberal congregation that admitted members without a public relation of their conversion, a deviance from "the New England Way" that Increase Mather attacked in *The Order of the Gospel* (1700). When Green refused to print the church's anonymous riposte, its principals resorted to the press of William Bradford in New York, adding some venomous remarks on the Mathers' control of the press in a preface.[40]

Prior restraint of free speech had certainly loosened, since critics of the New England Way no longer had to emigrate in order to put their attacks in print, but the colony had always followed a more liberal standard for imports than for native printing. Solomon Stoddard's *Doctrine of Instituted Churches* (1700), defending the indiscriminate admission of parishioners to holy communion, and Robert Calef's *More Wonders of the Invisible World* (1700), attacking the Mathers' hushed handling of the Salem witchcraft trials, were printed in London. William Bradford, in New York, printed George Keith's Anglican responses to the venerable Samuel Willard (1702) and Increase Mather (1703). All of these pieces circulated in Boston, prompting Increase Mather to lament that the glory of New England had departed, but the pattern of foreign attack and native reply was at least as old as John Norton's *Heart of N-England Rent* (1659).

Legally, the control of the press had been transferred from the General Court to the governor, which at least ensured that New England did not observe a peculiar standard of public decorum: the *Boston News-Letter* (1704–75) and almanacs were "Published by Authority," and Samuel Shute affixed his imprimatur to books as late as 1719 during his unhappy tenure as governor. The importation of controversial literature was one thing, however, and the admission of a hostile press into the colony was another. A "wicked company of *Manifesto*-men," Cotton Mather learned in 1703, "a year or two ago, procured a Press and Letters, to be sent for, unto London," but the governor apparently denied permission to operate it and they were obliged to sell the plant to Bartholomew Green and John Allen.[41] There was no officially appointed "manager" of the Boston press after 1692, but with the help of Green and Allen, the Mathers held all the cards; from 1695 down to 1713, the only printers in all of New England were the Greens or their associates.

Timothy Green, the youngest and laziest of Sergeant Samuel's sons, began to print books in 1700 and sold them at a shop in Middle (now Hanover) Street in the North End, near Second Church, where the Mathers presided. Perhaps at first he used Green and Allen's office, where he was certainly at work in 1700; but later he may have taken over the "Manifesto-men's" press. He continued printing, specializing in the Mathers' writings, down to 1707, when Allen, who had disappeared from Boston imprints for three years, opened a third office in Pudding Lane near the State House. This competition from their former associate seems to have disconcerted the Greens. Bartholomew proposed to assign the Connecticut government printing to Timothy, if he would move to New London, but Timothy declined, declaring that he did not wish to exchange "a certainty for an uncertainty," and Bartholomew was obliged to equip the colony with his brother-in-law, Thomas Short.[42]

To judge by his imprints, Timothy avoided competition with Allen by concentrating on bookselling after 1708, a year in which he printed only one piece, Cotton Mather's *Winthropi Justa*. "It has been said of him," Thomas remarked, "that whenever he heard a sermon which he highly approved, he would solicit a copy from the author, and print it for his own sales"—adding, severely, that he thus ended up with bushels of unsaleable sermons.[43] Timothy's record of printing in Boston can make this gossip more precise: of eighty-two editions that he printed between 1700 and 1714, sixty-three (seventy-six percent) were written by the Mathers, and almost all of these were heavily subvened by Cotton and his friends.[44] Timothy printed nine of the eleven pieces that Cotton published in 1704, when he ran what was virtually an in-house press for Second Church. The Great Fire of 1711 destroyed Allen's shop, Short died in 1712, Timothy moved to New London two years later, and the Mathers switched their custom to Thomas Fleet. The destruction of the stock of most Boston booksellers in the Great Fire must have been some comfort to Bartholomew, but two new printers sprang up in Allen's place.

3. Boston Booksellers

The Greens and the Mathers are good examples of what the historian Edmund S. Morgan called Puritan "tribalism," associations that fitted smoothly into their intellectual and contractual commitments; they may even have been related by marriage, since Cotton's sister Mariah was married to Capt. Bartholomew Green of Charlestown.[45] The younger Greens' businesses were infinitely more diverse than that of their father, whose "spirit of piety" they looked back to. Like his father, Bartholomew was set in motion by his customers' interests and ambitions, but the number and interests of these customers had proliferated, and his "spirit of piety" was sometimes at odds with theirs. Just as New England town meetings, unable to reach total agreement on the location of a meeting-house, divided into different towns and separate meeting-houses, so printers, if they were unable to work under a single roof, set up shop as distant as practicable from one another:[46] in Cambridge and Boston (1675–91); in the north, south, and middle of Boston (1700–13); in Massachusetts and Connecticut (1708–14). The printers form a striking contrast with the booksellers, a group of much more varied religious and social beliefs, who clustered together, companionably, beneath the Boston Exchange.

The Exchange was a wooden structure in the marketplace, also known as the "Town House," erected under a bequest of the merchant Robert Keayne in 1657. On the ground floor, where most of the booksellers had their tiny stalls, was an open concourse where the merchants gathered to exchange news and transact business. Above it were rooms for the legislature and the town library. The route connecting Boston to the country led into the square by Cornhill (now Washington) Street, where it met King (now State) Street, ascending from the harbor and the merchants' warehouses. The booksellers' imprints refer to the London Coffee House, the Blue Anchor Inn, and the "Old Meeting House" (First Church), ranged about the outside of the square. Every Thursday, a market day, the preachers of Boston and the adjacent communities preached a lecture in rotation at First Church, providing a prime source of texts for the booksellers. The justices met in quarter sessions in the "Court Room" of the Blue Anchor Inn, and merchants exchanged news and read the latest gazettes at the London Coffee House.

These addresses advertise the booksellers' valuable association with the center of church, state, and commerce, but there were a few outliers. Duncan Campbell, down at Dock Square at the northern end of Cornhill, was the postmaster, but his son John, the publisher of the *Boston News-Letter*, moved closer. Nicholas Buttolph set up shop a little farther out on Marlborough

Street (another section of Washington Street) next to his brother-in-law Robert Gutteridge's coffeehouse. There, at the corner of School Street, the pupils of the famous Boston schoolmaster Ezekiel Cheever, merchants interested in foreign news,and the congregation of Third Church came together.

These booksellers were not, of course, the only persons or agencies that distributed books. Since Isaiah Thomas, booksellers have usually been defined as the persons in imprints "for whom" the books were printed, and most of them certainly are to be discovered in this fashion. Nevertheless there were also persons who paid for printing who were not booksellers, though they do appear in imprints, and persons who distributed books who do not appear in imprints, both booksellers in the usual sense and private customers.

The books that were printed in Cambridge and Boston were distributed over a wide area, from New Hampshire to the Barbados, privately, officially, and commercially. Increase Mather's *Essay for the Recording of Illustrious Providences* (1684) and his *Two Plain and Practical Discourses* (1699) were simultaneously issued in Boston and London. The largest editions of books distributed outside their place of production were the early laws and election sermons of Connecticut, New Plymouth, and New Hampshire, all of them printed in Boston or Cambridge for official distribution in these jurisdictions. John Eliot's *Communion of Churches* (1665) was "not published, only committed privately to some godly and able hands to be viewed, corrected, amended, rejected, as it shall be found to hold weight in the sanctuary balance, or not," according to his preface; his collection of *The Dying Speeches of Several Indians* [ca. 1683–85?] was "printed, not so much for publishment, as to save charge of writing out of copyes for those that did desire them." The imprint of neither piece announced that it was to be had in Roxbury. None of Cotton Mather's sermons acknowledged (as they might have, in England) that they were "printed for the author"; many of them were, however, as some naughty people pointed out, to his irritation.[47]

When such private interests find their way into imprints, they show that Boston printers served divers other communities. The imprint of the church covenant of the First Church in Salem stated that it was printed "for themselves and their children" in 1680. Nathaniel Porter of Windsor, Connecticut, sponsored a sermon of his pastor's in 1707; and "Capt. Benjamin Marston, Merchant in Salem," commissioned an almanac for the latitude of the Barbados in 1712. *A Thankfull Remembrance of Gods Mercy . . . at Quabaug or Brookfield* (1676) was "published by Capt. Thomas Wheeler" of that town, a little west of Worcester. Nehemiah Walter, a Roxbury minister, delivered a sermon on *Unfruitful Hearers Detected*, "published by some of the hearers"

under that title in 1696. Clearly these are cases of private printing; even if
Capt. Marston hoped to get something for his almanacs, he was obviously
not in a regular way of bookselling.

The largest genre of such sponsored texts was the catechism, printed
both in New and Old England. The earliest such New England printing was
Edward Norris's, "published for the use of the Church of Christ at Salem" in
1649. James Fitch's *First Pinciples [sic] of the Doctrine of Christ* (1679) was
"published at the desire and for the use of the Church of Christ at Norwich"
in Connecticut; James Noyes, "late teacher of the Church of Christ at Newbury," prepared his popular catechism "for the use of the children there," and
another catechism "for the children of Bermuda" (1699) was written by
Sampson Bond, "late minister of that island." Other New England editions
were for John Fiske of Chelmsford, Massachusetts (1657), Seaborn Cotton of
Hampton, New Hampshire (1663), and the catechism of Samuel Stone of
Hartford, printed "for John Wadsworth in Farminton," Connecticut (1684).
Before the Boston press allowed an alternative venue to Cambridge in 1675,
New England ministers also resorted to London, where the catechisms of
Ezekiel Rogers of Rowley, John Norton of Ipswich, Thomas Shepard of
Cambridge, Richard Mather of Dorchester, and John Davenport of New
Haven were printed.[48]

When the person who sponsored the book did not identify his occupation, he may easily be mistaken for a bookseller, though in fact this might
not have been his chief calling. John Tappin (or Tappan), a feltmaker, died
worth £5,000, of which only £16 were in "Bibles and other books" (possibly a private library); he had married Mary, widow of William Avery, and
William, Mary, and John each appear in one or two imprints (1672, 1679, and
1682). William was a physician who set up the first apothecary's shop in
Boston. William Gibbons, who reprinted Samuel Stone's catechism in 1699,
was a Boston feltmaker. Obadiah Gill was a shipwright who, according
to Cotton Mather, clubbed together with other godly persons to sponsor
worthy books, including, of course, Cotton's;[49] he appears in two imprints.
Elkanah Pembroke, by profession a weaver but repeatedly described as a
"shopkeeper" in his numerous lawsuits, also appears in two imprints (1699,
1712), the second printed by William Bradford in New York, when Pembroke
had moved to Newport, Rhode Island. Joseph Farnum (otherwise Farnham), a shopkeeper, and Thomas Baker, otherwise unknown, "printed" only
one title apiece; another shopkeeper or stationer, Joseph Wheeler, is master
of only two imprints, one no longer extant.[50]

Private persons, like Gill and his associates, not only "printed" (i.e.
sponsored) books but also distributed them. In 1704, Sewall, after three

years of steady benefaction, dispensed a remainder of five dozen copies of Samuel Willard's *Fear of an Oath* (1701), one dozen of them to Nicholas Boone, "for whom" they were originally printed, and yet Sewall appears in only one imprint after 1684.[51] Cotton Mather saw print as a means of preaching to a wider audience than Second Church, though this "audience" did not always find the message congenial. "I will now have my Agents in several parts of the Countrey, to lodge the Book where it is intended," Mather wrote in 1711. His agents ranged from good Mr. Penhallow in Portsmouth down to Connecticut, and by 1706 they were distributing some fifty dozen sermons a year.[52] Such pious work was not necessarily limited to distributing New England editions. The best customers for Dunton's imports in 1686 were ministers, and John Usher imported London books for the Reverends Thomas Shepard, Jr. in Charlestown, and John Wise in Chebacco (Essex) in quantities that suggest that they were also acting as distributors, and possibly trading for profit. Governor Thomas Prence of New Plymouth left a parcel of a hundred psalm books and fifty "smale paper bookes" (exercise books), to be bound and distributed to the four Old Colony schools that he had recently established.[53]

The wealth of the trade varied enormously, from Hezekiah Usher's estate of £15,538 down to Michael Perry, who died some hundreds of pounds worse than nothing. In a Boston tax-list of 1687, we find six booksellers assessed from 1s. 10d. (Samuel Phillips) to 3s. (Benjamin Harris and Joseph Brunning); Samuel Sewall, a merchant and magistrate, paid 14s. 10d. or roughly five times as much. John Usher, merchant, treasurer of the Dominion of New England, and later lieutenant governor of New Hampshire, was even wealthier, though he too kept his shop under the Exchange. Books may have formed a relatively small part of Usher's or Sewall's business, which stretched across the Atlantic to London, the Azores, and down to the Caribbean. Because they had credit in London, however, they could provide English books to the humbler members of the trade. Other Boston booksellers who appear in only one or two imprints may well have been persons who dealt principally in English books: James Cowse, a stationer, or Job How, who came over with Dunton, perhaps qualify here. Samuel Sewall, Jr. was certainly apprenticed to a bookseller, though he appears in only two imprints; Richard Wilkins, a major customer of Dunton's, appears in only four, and Hezekiah Henchman (d. 1692), father of the leading printer and bookseller of the next generation, in none. John Hayward, a scrivener whom Sewall reproved for wearing a wig, seems to have dealt in schoolbooks in a small way, to judge from his account with Usher, but he appears in no imprint.[54]

If we define a bookseller as someone who traded sheets with other booksellers, the core of the trade was small: their stock may be represented by the inventory of Michael Perry's estate, in 1700, containing a wide selection of both English and American imprints. Ignoring single titles in the inventory, some of which may form Perry's personal library, his stock may be divided into schoolbooks; Bibles, psalters, and New Testaments; local law books; practical divinity; and miscellaneous titles. The schoolbooks for instruction in English, including catechisms, were all American reprints of English properties; those for grammar schools were imported from London. There were no English law books, which were little cited in colonial courts before the Dominion of New England, though in 1689 Perry had supplied some to John Usher and the Dominion. Anything resembling English literature—*Pilgrim's Progress*, chapbook histories like *Fortunatus* and the *Seven Champions of Christendom*—was all printed in England, though *Pilgrim's Progress* had already received an American edition in 1681. Otherwise literature is represented only by Latin school texts of Ovid, Virgil, or Cicero. There is an interesting group of practical handbooks on navigation, accounting, and husbandry. Newsbooks (in which remarkable providences, books of wonders, and execution sermons may be included) divided fairly equally between London and Boston printing. Perry had a stock well worth browsing, even in a shop of less than thirty-six square feet.[55]

On Perry's level, as of 1695 we might include Duncan Campbell, Nicholas Buttolph, and Perry's cousin Benjamin Eliot. Somewhat earlier, there were Joseph Brunning or Browning, Benjamin Harris, Samuel Phillips, and John Griffin; and somewhat later, Nicholas Boone, who eventually also undertook printing, Eleazar Phillips, and Timothy Green. Samuel Phillips, who had advertised a very similar stock to Perry's at the end of Solomon Stoddard's *Safety of Appearing at the Day of Judgment* (1687), moved into a much larger "Brick Shop" (240 square feet) next to the Meeting House in 1694; probably he was switching his business to imports, which required more space to display. Brunning was the son of Mercy Brunning, an English refugee bookseller in Amsterdam, Harris was a Baptist, Campbell was from Scotland, John Griffin was the third person to be buried by the Book of Common Prayer in Boston, and Dunton himself was Presbyterian. This is a remarkably "mixed" group of people for seventeenth-century New England, a settlement of tribalist landsmen who found even French Huguenots a little strange; but the trade pitched its tents on the wide-open Atlantic, where King Street led down to the harbor and out to the great world.

Benjamin Harris may be singled out from his fellows as a bookseller who was also an author and publicist. A London bookseller and radical

Protestant with a hatred of the Catholics, especially James, Duke of York, he had already been in trouble with the English authorities during the Popish Plot and Exclusion crisis for printing the *Protestant Intelligence* (1679–81) and Henry Care's *English Liberties* (1682). After James succeeded to the throne in 1685, Harris prudently moved to Boston, opening a bookstore and the London Coffee House near the Exchange. Coffeehouses had been one of the main venues for political discussion and the distribution of unlicensed news. His *Publick Occurrences* (1690) may or may not be the first Boston newspaper (only a single number issued before it was suppressed by the Boston authorities); his *Protestant Tutor* (two editions, 1682; reprinted in Boston, 1689), a violently anti-Catholic tract for children, is supposed to be one of the ancestors of the *New England Primer*; and he was the publisher of some overtly political pieces (then a new genre, in Boston) attacking the Andros regime and praising the Prince of Orange. He launched a series of Boston almanacs by John Tulley of Saybrook, Connecticut, in 1687, which shocked and entertained Bostonians by prognostications of the imminent death of Louis XIV, instead of the sophomoric verse and disquisitions on comets that filled their Cambridge counterparts. It would be nearly thirty years before another printer, James Franklin, ventured into public political controversy.[56]

Richard Wilkins, too, is less typical of the Boston trade. He came over from Limerick with his son-in-law John Bailey, a Nonconformist who had been ejected from his ministry there, and settled in Boston around 1683. It seems unlikely that Wilkins was ever actually a bookseller in Limerick, as Thomas supposed, since John Bailey stated that new books were unobtainable there. Dunton, with whom he had been in correspondence, does not describe him as a bookseller, and his business, which he carried on until his death in 1704, may have been fairly indiscriminate, in cloth, haberdashery, books, and other dry goods.[57] Only four Boston imprints bear his name: his son-in-law's farewell sermon to the congregation in Limerick (1689), with a preface by Increase Mather; two pieces by Increase Mather (1693, 1696); and Samuel Sewall's *Phænomena Quædam Apocalyptica* (1697). The intensely focused authorship of these pieces indicates that Wilkins published them more out of conviction than for commercial profit, and their dates cover only a small part of his bookselling career.

A little eighth-sheet broadside "Advertisement" mounted at the back of a Harvard copy of Cotton Mather's *The Triumphs of the Reformed Religion in America. The Life of . . . John Eliot* (1691), printed for Joseph Brunning, describes Wilkins's stock of books. The Harvard cataloguer assumed that the "Advertisement" was published together with the book, but it is mounted on a flyleaf autographed by that melancholy poet "Michael Wigglesworth Ejus

Liber 1700," the probable date of the binding, in original sprinkled sheep over scabbord. According to Dunton, Brunning was "a Compleat Bookseller . . . [who]'d promote a good Book whoever printed it,"[58] yet it seems unlikely that he would ever have advertised another bookseller. Wilkins probably inserted the flyer when he bound and sold the book to Wigglesworth. It describes a business chiefly devoted to providing books for the learned and gentry: "It has been thought proper to Certify unto all People, especially Ministers, Gentlemen, Physicians, Lawyers, and Students in any Sciences throughout this Country, That Mr. Richard Wilkins, who lives over against the West End of the Town-House in Boston has out of respect unto the Service & Honour of the Country taken care to furnish himself, with such a Variety of Books on all Subjects both Old & New, as is not to be found in any other part of Amercia [sic]; So that at the Shop of the said Wilkins, they that please, may be Supplyed with Various Treatises both of Polemical and Practical Divinity; & Commentaries upon the Scriptures; together with useful Treatises in Grammer, School-Books, Chyrurgery, Merchandize, Husbandry, Astronomy, Geometry, Law, Military Affayrs, and other Subjects; all at such Reasonable Rates, as have not heretofore been afforded in these parts of the World [italic reversed]." Wilkins's stock of polemical divinity, Biblical commentaries, medicine, and law, subjects normally confined to English printing, finds no counterpart in Perry's inventory; it is considerably broader than the stock of divinity that John Dunton advertised in his catalogue of 1684 and presumably imported to Boston in 1686.

At the other end of the economic spectrum from Wilkins, James Gray of Charlestown was a peddler who, according to his obituary (1705), "used to go up and down the Country selling of Books." The inventory of his estate consisted of eight bags of silver money (£591 1s. 2d.), a gold ring (£1), and "old clothes, books, & some small haberdashers ware" (£5). In addition, his executors sued to recover "£200 current silver money" from Edward Thomas, merchant, and Mary, widow and administratrix of David Jesse, goldsmith, in 1707.[59] Gray may have operated as a banker as well as a peddler. He is the only named representative of that occupation in our period, but it did not die with him, for Cotton Mather attacked it in 1711: "the Minds and Manners of many People about the Countrey are much corrupted, by foolish Songs and Ballads, which the Hawkers and Pedlars carry into all parts of the Countrey."[60] These foolish objects were probably imported, which Gray could well have afforded to do. His astonishing hoard of silver came from a cash business, whereas Perry and other booksellers on his level dealt for credit, and might be paid in "marchantable [i.e. salt] beefe," or pork, Indian corn, wampum, and other "commodity currency."[61]

At the bottom of the trade were bookbinders: Richard Wilkins, whose stock was dominated by English books, probably did less bookbinding than Michael Perry. The first person to be called a bookbinder is one John Sanders, a name, no more, recorded 1636–51; John Ratcliffe, possibly a Plymouth (England) bookseller who appears in a single English imprint (1662), and Edmund Ranger are the first binders whose work is identifiable today. Both, as we would expect, appear in imprints, which they commissioned in order to provide the raw material for their occupation, Ratcliffe's dated 1664–82, and Ranger's, 1673–79. Ratcliffe, in a petition of 1664, complained that he had removed to New England in hopes to bind Indian Bibles, and yet he had lost money by it since "in things belonging to my trade, I here pay 18s. for that which in England I could buy for four shillings, they being things not formerly much used in this country."[62] Ranger was more successful, opening a tavern in 1697, which he kept to his death in 1705. The occupation of bookbinding is otherwise only sporadically attested: William Nowell and Thomas Rand, bookbinders, petition to settle in Boston in 1672, Bartholomew Sprint in 1685, but there is no evidence that their petitions were granted. Rand, a cordwainer or shoemaker of Charlestown, may have done bookbinding on the side—as, one suspects, did other leatherworkers (tanners, curriers, and cordwainers).[63] His grandson, Thomas Rand, was working as a bookbinder in Boston from 1744 to 1756.

In seventeenth-century New England, there were few genuine booksellers outside of Boston. Primers, hornbooks, almanacs, catechisms and "other Small books" were generally available—from Eliza Cutler, for instance, the widow of a Charlestown merchant, in 1694; or from the merchants William Pyncheon of Springfield and Joseph Hawley of Northampton, who supplied the grammar school of Hadley, in the seventeenth century.[64] The merchants and ministers of Salem, Norwich, Brookfield, Farmington, and Windsor announced themselves in imprints of sermons and catechisms because there was no one else to distribute these books for them. Merchants like George Corwin (d. 1685) and Timothy Lindall (d. 1698) of Salem sold such staples as paper, inkhorns, psalters, Bibles, primers, and almanacs; we rarely find less generic books, such as those in the estate of the Salem merchant William Bowditch (d. 1681), which Harriet S. Tapley mistook for a private library. The estate of Col. Bartholomew Gedney (d. 1698) in Salem had "tools for a bookbinder," but his library consisted of a small stock of divinity, law, physic, history, and military matters, which were typically imported bound.[65]

The sale of anything more diverse than Bibles, primers, psalters, and almanacs (the Waldenbooks of the seventeenth century) followed wealth and

population density, the same factors associated with literacy. The Massachusetts General Court actually used these criteria to distribute the *Laws* of 1660
and allocated 275 copies for sale to Boston and the neighboring communities
of Dorchester, Roxbury, Watertown, Cambridge, and Charlestown.[66] These
townsfolk came to market in Boston "more or less every day," when they
crossed Roxbury Neck or took the Winnisimmet (Charlestown) ferry to sell
their produce. Salem, the other port of entry in Massachusetts, provided a
smaller center for such commerce to the north.[67] Boston lay on the periphery of London, which in turn operated on the periphery of Frankfurt and
Amsterdam in the heart of the European book trade.

4. Imports and Native Production

Some day, on that scorecard dear to American bibliographers, one would like
to enter the first American bookseller or printer to go bankrupt: possibly
Samuel Keimer in 1730? It was a risky business: a number, including Michael
Perry, certainly died insolvent, and one can point to others in the eighteenth
century who built a fortune by putting off their British creditors for uncon-
scionable periods—John Mein, Henry Knox, and Mathew Carey among
them. Big winners like Daniel Henchman were few, and the colonial trade in
general thought exceedingly small, putting most of their capital into steady
sellers. They financed their newspapers by subscription, and their hottest-
selling items—execution sermons and captivity narratives—were short and
issued in small editions. John Usher's edition of *Pilgrim's Progress* (1681) was
larger, but already by that date a sure steady seller. Daniel Henchman's secret
editions of the Bible and New Testament, traditionally dated in 1752, though
probably printed in 1731,[68] and Benjamin Franklin's *Pamela* (1742–43) and his
New Testament (1745) were certainly the earliest projects with a substantial
element of risk. When colonial booksellers gambled, in short, they tended to
gamble on London titles, and preferably on an imported parcel of twenty to
fifty copies than on a colonial reprint of 500.

The lapse of the Licensing Act in 1679 depressed the London book market, according to both John Dunton and Richard Chiswell: Dunton and
three other booksellers—Andrew Thorncomb, Job How, and Benjamin Harris—and the printer John Allen all came over in the 1680s to try their luck in
Boston, the first such exodus of the London trade; Robert Boulter and
Richard Chiswell, who stayed behind, were offering books to the colonists
at cut-rate discounts of from twenty-five to thirty-three percent off. The
number of London imprints soared, spurred on by the Popish Plot, and
Nonconformist voices were once more heard in print, but profits dropped,
as they would do again in 1695 after the final lapse of the Licensing Act,

when there was a second exodus, to the English provinces. Whatever its other virtues, freedom of the press does not pay: the margin of profit shrinks as the market grows more competitive.

The invoices of shipments sent between 1678 or 9 and April 1685 by Boulter and Chiswell to a single Boston merchant, John Usher, are the only direct evidence we have of this trans-Atlantic commerce in the seventeenth century.[69] Some of these were wholesale orders for ministers and other persons who do not appear in imprints; others Usher or his clerk Michael Perry retailed to the colony and the citizens of Boston. Booksellers like Samuel Phillips or Richard Wilkins were probably more important customers than the likes of Joseph Brunning, Nicholas Buttolph, or Benjamin Eliot, whose trade lay more in colonial imprints, which they commissioned, exchanged, and bound. Boulter sent books and stationery worth £445 11s. 6d. from 1679 to 1683, and Chiswell's shipments, from 1678 to 1685, were worth another £655 14s. 6d. John Dunton's Bostonian customers owed him some £500 by 1686, when he took a "ramble" to America to collect; he began business in 1681 and, assuming they had paid something on account, his sales must have at least equaled Chiswell's, who sent over £567 worth of books in roughly the same period.[70] In the years when these three booksellers' shipments overlapped (1681–82), they shipped an annual average of over £300 worth of books and stationery to Boston. Itemized invoices for this period do not survive, but Chiswell's invoices for 1683–85 record a total of 3,544 volumes worth about £295 and stationery worth about £35. One may conclude that between 3,500 and 4,000 volumes were annually exported to Boston in the 1680s, and that they sold out, since orders would not otherwise have continued.

For a comparable segment of colonial production, one may exclude the almanacs, session acts, and broadsides recorded in NAIP, which leaves only eighty-two titles printed in Boston and Cambridge from 1681 to 1689. Their edition sizes ranged from an Eliot Indian Bible (1680–85) of 2,000 copies, to catechisms and primers of perhaps 1,000 copies, down to 500 copies or less (all the rest), amounting to some 45,500 volumes in all. These almost certainly took longer to sell than imports, however. Samuel Sewall's purchases in the eighteenth century are one indication of their rate of sale: in 1728–29, the last year of his life, he distributed some 400 sermons, and there still survives a bill from Benjamin Eliot for purchases of more than fifteen and one half dozen copies of seven sermons, bound and/or gilt, worth £31 19s. 6d. One of these books had been printed twenty-eight years earlier, and clearly the edition was not yet exhausted; the median imprint date of his purchases fell around 1716.[71] To take another indicative example, at the end of Daniel

Travis's *Almanac* for 1711 [1710], there is a list of fifteen titles "Printed for, and are to be Sold by Nicholas Boone," the earliest of which was printed in 1700; a substantial number must still have remained "in print" to be worth advertising. Assuming an average edition-life of twelve years, and that sales over this period were steady, we can estimate that only 19,585 copies of the titles printed between 1681 and 1689 had actually sold by the end of that period, an average of 2,177 volumes a year. Local production would thus have amounted to no more than 60% of imports.

The 3,500 to 4,000 volumes imported annually at Boston in the 1680s were only part of the total for New England, moreover. From 1700 to 1713, British customs records show that an average of 68.81 hundredweight (or 7,607 lbs.) of books were exported annually to New England: the figures range from 19.5 cwt. (2184 lbs.) in 1705 to 116.5 cwt. (13,048 lbs.) in 1710. The conversion of these weights into books is necessarily conjectural, but we are probably safe in assuming that most of them were bound, and that the proportions of folios, quartos, and small formats was roughly the same as in Usher's invoices of 1683–85. A trial "shopping basket" of forty late seventeenth-century books made up in these proportions (1:3:36) weighed 41.5 lbs., averaging about a pound a volume.[72]

The six-fold variation between the smallest and the largest annual eighteenth-century figures should caution us not to rely too confidently on a few, probably favorable years in the 1680s: the figure for all of New England in 1705 was only half as large as the number of books annually imported for Boston alone in the 1680s. The customs dockets, moreover, record only the first destination, and some of these books may have been transshipped to other colonies. Nevertheless, it is quite unlikely that the average sale of local production ever exceeded that of imports during our period; indeed, when demand was strong, Boston booksellers relied more heavily on English than on local editions, even for colonial titles. The history of two such texts, the Bay Psalm Book, a steady seller, and Michael Wigglesworth's spectacular success, *The Day of Doom*, are instructive in this regard. In both cases, their editions divide between Boston and London, but for very different reasons.

The Cambridge press printed 1,700 copies of the Bay Psalm Book in quarto, 1640, followed by an unauthorized London reprint in 1647; Matthew Day printed 2,000 copies of a revised edition in octavo for Hezekiah Usher in 1651. The next colonial printings were an "eighth" edition for Samuel Phillips in Boston, 1695, and a "ninth" for Michael Perry in 1698. In between fall three London editions of the revised text printed for Richard Chiswell in London. John Usher imported a hundred copies of Chiswell's 1680 edition for Thomas Shepard, Jr., fifty of them unbound, in quires, and seventy bound copies on his own account. Besides these London editions, there were three surreptitious printings, ostensibly "for Hezekiah Usher of Boston," without date. These deceptive psalm books are often found bound with eighteenmo Bibles having an engraved imprint "Cambridge, 1648," but actually printed by Joachim Nosche in Amsterdam, ca. 1675 to ca. 1680.[73] The psalm books were certainly not printed in Boston, however, and if, as most authorities suppose, they were printed around the date of their Bibles, they were probably not printed for Hezekiah Usher, who had left business in 1663 and died in 1676. The Bibles may well have been a shipment "bound . . . in holland" that Usher's agent John Ive dispatched in 1675, half of which were spoiled "by sending them to Barbados first." In 1680, Chiswell wrote to say that "Bibles are very plenty and of divers sorts and very much cheaper than formerly of the true English prints," which may imply that he was not responsible for the previous shipment.[74]

The imprint of these psalm books was modeled on the 1651 Cambridge edition's, which the "eighth" and "ninth" Boston editions implicitly assume to be the first: Michael Perry, as John Usher's former clerk, should have been intimately familiar with the contraband trade of his master. Richard Chiswell told John Usher that the smallest number of the *New England Primer* worth printing in London was "Ten Gross"; the known editions of the Bay Psalm Book were only a third larger, and we may fairly take their size as a norm.[75] Eight editions of 2,000 copies each between 1651 and 1698 means that 16,000 copies sold over forty-seven years at roughly 340 copies a year. Better yet, the Bibles with which they were bound did not come with a complementary Book of Common Prayer, unlike most of those printed in England.

The psalm book was a steady seller, an exceptionally profitable one if, like Chiswell or the Ushers, you have the capital for 2,000 copies, but it sold in a very different way from *The Day of Doom*. Psalm books were quotidian and ubiquitous, carried by most merchants in New England; *The Day of Doom* had far fewer outlets, and even its author thought its sale miraculous: "It pleased the Lord to carry me through the difficulty of ye foreme[n]tioned works . . . & to give vent for my books & greater accepta[n]ce then I could have expected: so yt of 1800 there were scarce any unsold (or but few) at ye yeers end; so that I was a gainer by them, and not a loser . . . About 4 yeers after they were reprinted wth my consent, & I gave them the proofs [i.e. Biblical citations] & Margin[al] notes to affix."[76] It was the more miraculous since the first edition, of which only a fragment survives, was printed at the author's expense in Cambridge, 1662; the second (Cambridge, 1666?), surviving in three fragmentary copies, appeared at the expense of the printer or bookseller. Wigglesworth's early bibliographers posited two more lost

colonial editions, to account for the numbering of the "fifth edition" in
Boston, 1701, but the inference is no longer accepted.[77] It is surely easier to
suppose that the numbering reflects the appearance of three London editions
in 1666, 1673, and 1687, and the private character of the first edition. The
"first edition" for the London trade, in short, was 1662, but for Boston, 1666.
All of the English editions reprint the unrevised text and, to judge from the
provenance of their copies, sold mostly in England. Usher, at any rate,
imported none of them.

Did nearly 1,800 purchasers, then, as is generally believed, each end up
with a copy of *The Day of Doom* in only a year? It seems unlikely, even supposing that the copies were stitched, in paper wrappers—and there were
certainly not enough binders to issue them bound. Wigglesworth no doubt
had consigned his stock in varying quantities among his friends and the
Boston book trade, but he could hardly have known how many of these were
still on their hands at the end of the year. The trade, after all, declined to
enter this lucrative market for some four years, presumably because they still
had copies to sell. With the full apparatus of the state, Connecticut was
unable to dispose of a much smaller edition of its 1673 *Laws* in a like period,
and Cotton Mather and his associates were unable to give away more than
600 books a year in 1706. Either by pious benefactions, or by bargain and
sale, the distribution of *The Day of Doom* must have continued over at least
four years, before the edition was exhausted.

Nevertheless, an average sale of 450 copies a year is an astonishing
record, which even the Bay Psalm Book cannot match; it is nearly twice the
number of copies of the 1660 *Laws* that the General Court hoped to sell in
the Greater Boston area in a similar period. The aftermarket for the "trade"
edition must have been correspondingly smaller (500 copies?), and no more
were required for thirty-five years. In 1688, Judge Sewall presented his cousin
Stephen Greenleaf with "the Catechise, Day of Doom, &c. bound together
in a good Cover"; his language strongly suggests that Sewall had this tract
volume bound locally from sheets of the 1666 Cambridge edition, which was
therefore still "in print."[78] At that rate, the Bay Psalm Book's tortoise would
have caught up with our hare in only six years, if they had started selling
together. The numbering of the "fifth edition," moreover, acknowledges the
continuing popularity of the work in London, which a changed, more "English" Boston recognized and rewarded. The society that would later pour out
editions of *The Day of Doom* had outgrown the society that produced it;
indeed, the work would become a children's book, but it was written in a
very different spirit. Like *Gulliver's Travels* or *Robinson Crusoe, The Day of*

Doom ultimately moved into a new market niche, without which it might have remained a day's wonder.

The success of these exceptional titles sets an upper limit on the size of the Boston market, which could absorb 450 copies of a single title in a year, or some 3,500 volumes of an imported assortment, including parcels of from twenty to fifty copies of the more popular titles. Most seventeenth- and early eighteenth-century colonial editions were printed in small runs and sold off slowly—perhaps at the rate of only forty copies or so a year; only a few English titles achieved this rate, but the titles that were printed in the colonies were not very numerous either. The 600 sermons that Cotton Mather and his cronies handed out each year was about a ninth of his printers' annual production. The booksellers almost certainly realized a higher profit on colonial sheets than on English books, and at lower risk, since their printing was frequently subsidized. Colonial printing also reached a broader segment of the population than most English books, but the wonderful variety reported by Goddard, Morison, and Wolf was nearly all printed in Europe, as, indeed, was the Bible itself, before 1731.

5. The Ubiquity and Poverty of Print

If one had to characterize print culture in New England in brief, one might call it ubiquitous, but poor and shallow: "poor" because monotonous—only a few titles were widespread; "shallow" because few colonial titles were ever reprinted and most of its European editions were of recent date. The Harvard College Library catalogue of 1723 records the cumulated gifts and bequests of seventeenth-century ministers and magistrates. Despite some large English benefactions from Theophilus Gale and Sir John Maynard, no more than a fifth of the 3,516 volumes date from before 1600. Only 5.6 percent date from before 1560, and before 1501, we find only eight incunabula in ten volumes. All of these incunabula perished in a fire of 1764, and St. Augustine's *Opuscula plurima* (1491), which the Rev. Thomas Prince purchased in 1742, may be the first incunable with an authentic American provenance.[79]

Colonial libraries soon descended from these dizzy heights. The average minister's "study" might have a few hundred titles, some in the three learned languages of Latin, Greek, and Hebrew. The commonest description of a library in seventeenth-century Essex inventories, however, is just "a Bible and other books," the others being between five and ten volumes, when they are enumerated. When the editions can be identified, they are usually English, written by the authors venerated by an older generation, and a number reappear in later estates, as they are handed down in ever-shrinking parcels.[80]

There were probably colonial imprints as well, too little valued to be worth listing (and no inventory was required of estates of less than £5).

"Other books" were rather more prevalent and varied in urban Middlesex than in rural Essex,[81] yet we need not conclude that our Essex man felt especially poor or deprived. The Bible was print enough: indeed, Puritans honored the Reformation doctrine of *sola scriptura* to the point of arguing that Protestants should read little else. Together with the Bible, translations of Lewis Bayly's *Practice of Piety* (abridged), Richard Baxter's *Call to the Unconverted*, Thomas Shepard's *Sincere Convert*, and a few primers and catechisms sufficed for the Indians. What was sauce for the native goose was sauce for the European gander. Ann Hopkins, daughter of a Connecticut governor, "was fallne into a sadd infirmytye . . . by occasion of her givinge her selfe wholly to readinge & writinge," Winthrop noted (she showed Anabaptist symptoms); John Higginson recommended the "remarkable providence" of "godly Mr. Sharp" (as he later became) who, misled by "a strong inclination & eager affection to books" and a "stranger's" gift of an attractively unfamiliar title, found himself overcome by "a strange kind [of] Horror both of Body & minde" as he read. Thereafter he confined himself "to reading the Bible & other known good books of Divinity." Judge Sewall's bookplate cautioned, *Vita sine literis est Mortis Imago; At Vita sine Christo est Morte pejor*.[82] The Puritans honored learning and encouraged widespread literacy, but they feared unlicensed "bookishnes," even at the level of a deacon like Mr. Sharp.

Since the Bible served as a manual of law, literature, history, and warfare, as well as a primer for reading and, of course, religion, the sphere of "the Book" remained wide, but its content was remarkably uniform, and print was used as sparingly as iron in colonial hoes, ploughs, and shovels. Blank forms are among the commonest productions of the colonial press, as ubiquitous in their way as Bibles. "In examining the records of the colonial communities," remarks L. C. Wroth, "one is appalled by the amount of legal and official business that was transacted in this new country, but whoever else may have been the sufferer by this frequent lawing, it is certain that it was not the printer."[83] And he goes on to instance the first production of the Cambridge press, the *Freeman's Oath*. As with all such "firsts," there is a powerful implication that the press continued to pour out more editions of the same, but peculiarly, the Massachusetts presses never printed another edition. Later oaths (1676, 1678, 1692, etc.), which Winship describes as revised editions of the *Freeman's Oath*, and which Shipton and Mooney enter under Massachusetts (Colony), are in fact editions of the oaths of supremacy and abjuration required by English law.[84] Instead of reprinting the *Freeman's*

Oath separately, the magistrates appended it with other legal forms at the end of the colonial *Laws*, whence town clerks presumably promulgated it in manuscript. Even the oaths of supremacy and abjuration, moreover, were signed by groups, beginning at the foot of the document, and continuing on the back, as necessary. It is not clear whether each of the signers read the document individually, or whether it was read to them in a group before signing, but the latter seems more likely, if only to save time, paper, and print.[85]

As legalities comparable to these oaths, one might cite orders to the town constable to bring in a rate, which the town meeting will then subdivide among the constabulary, recording their individual responsibilities in manuscript. The earliest such printed warrant dates from 1679, and the treasurer of the colony would have required no more than thirty or forty copies a year, one for every township.[86] Printed orders to the constable to "warn" the inhabitants of the date for electing deputies to the Assembly or to pick jurors for the quarter sessions appear somewhat later in the Massachusetts archives. All of these orders differ from blanks that record transactions, such as recognizances, subpoenas, deeds, or letters of attorney, whose virtue lies in what Benjamin Franklin called their "correctness." The parties to the transaction want to be sure that they are following proper legal form, and print is their guarantee. Apart from bills of lading, whose earliest New England examples were probably printed in London, in my opinion, transactional forms date from the Dominion of New England, 1686–89. They reflect the heightened taxation, challenges to land titles, and insistence on "correct" English procedure introduced by Sir Edmund Andros. When the Andros regime fell, the parties resumed the use of manuscript subpoenas, only to return to printed forms when the 1692 Massachusetts Charter restored order.

The colonies were governed by a mixture of oral and written law. Written authorities included the Bible, English statutes (often mediated by some digest like Ferdinando Pulton's [1618] or Edmund Wingate's [1655], and continuously updated down to 1700), and colonial laws, in print or manuscript. The traditions of common law and colonial custom were oral. Conflicts between these various authorities were common enough. By the Charter of 1629, Massachusetts Bay was authorized to make laws that were not "contrary or repugnant" to those of England, but in Winthrop's view, the provision only applied to colonial statute law, not to local customs, and God's law, in the Bible, was usually of superior authority.[87] The Board of Trade and the Privy Council first seriously reviewed the colonial laws in the 1690s, however, and took a very different view of their legality.

The proportion of English to colonial law in the lawbook depended on how the colony had "received" English law, either at the moment of settlement, or later.[88] The sources of the 1648 Massachusetts *Laws and Liberties* were both English and colonial: Pulton's digest of the English statutes and the so-called "Body of Liberties" drawn up by the Ipswich poet and minister Nathaniel Ward, nineteen manuscript copies of which had been circulated to the towns for their approval in 1641. The early compilations of Connecticut, New Plymouth, and New Hampshire adopted many articles from the Massachusetts *Laws*, which were also, of course, New Hampshire laws down to 1679. This enactment did not exhaust the law in force in these jurisdictions, however: the 1648 *Laws* have often been called a "code," as though they covered the entire body of law, but they left most of civil law to custom. In the areas of tort, contract, and property, which English law settled through highly technical "forms of action," colonial courts proceeded by simple bill and a common sense of right and equity—much like the Court of Star Chamber, whose forthright avoidance of their "triques" and "quillets" scandalized the champions of so-called "common law."[89] The colonies usurped jurisdiction over pirates and privateers, so that their "code" was not only incomplete but *extra vires*, an abuse that was only removed after 1689.

Rhode Island's reception of English law was less formal and discriminating than that of the other New England colonies. Its four towns met in 1647 and drew up some ordinances in manuscript, one copy apiece; from time to time they enacted manuscript supplements, but when the Board of Trade demanded a "true copy" in 1698, the recorder was unable or unwilling to produce more than an "abstract" from the mass of paper. Lord Bellomont, governor at that time of New York, Massachusetts, and New Hampshire, tried to clarify the situation on the Board's behalf, but could only report "loose scripts of paper, not entered in any rolls or books; and oft times not to be found when inquiry is made for them at the office, that the people are at loss to know what is law among them."[90] The colony did not straighten out its records until 1704, when a careful compilation was drawn up for printing, but failed to find a printer; a still later compilation, in an edition of only eighty copies, finally issued from the press of John Allen in Boston, in 1719.

Were the Rhode Islanders therefore as "illiterate" and "ignorant and contemptible" as Bellomont obviously thought them?[91] In fact, the printed *Laws* of Massachusetts was not necessarily more, or more broadly, communicative than Rhode Island's manuscripts. In 1670, the deputies of the Massachusetts townships requested that the Body of Liberties be printed in a new edition of the *Laws and Liberties*; they were certain of its existence from the distribution of nineteen manuscript copies in 1641, yet evidently unaware that it had already been incorporated in two previous editions, and acknowledged as such in their title. Nor did print ensure a clearer relationship with metropolitan authority. In 1636, John Cotton had also drawn up a code at the request of the magistrates, which he called "Moses his Judicialls," but it was never adopted. Under the misleading title of *An Abstract or [sic] the Lavves of Nevv England, as they are Novv Established* (1641), however, it escaped into print in London, and though a 1655 reprint, entitled *An Abstract of Laws and Government . . . of Christ's Kingdome*, corrected the error, John Cotton's vision of New England as a Biblical commonwealth was a long time dying. The charters on which the whole structure rested, moreover, were never printed before 1689, for Massachusetts, and even 1718, for Connecticut, though election sermons often appealed to their invisible provisions.[92]

The colonies experimented with various commercial or official schemes for distributing their laws, with uneven success. The 600 copies of the 1648 Massachusetts *Laws* were "to be solde at the shop of Hezekiah Usher in Boston," but over a quarter of the impression was still on the hands of the colony treasurer, Richard Russell, in 1651, "unvendible" because of later revisions and additions.[93] The General Court sent out the 1660 *Laws* to the four county recorders, with instructions to apportion them to their towns pro rata, by tax rate. Since Watertown paid £41 5s. of a total rate of £616 4s. 6d., and received thirty-five copies, we may estimate that 525 copies were so distributed: about 203 copies to Suffolk County, 154 to Middlesex, 151 to Essex, and seventeen to Norfolk. Hampshire County, in western Massachusetts, was only formed in 1662, but its three townships and their court may have taken a handful more. With twenty copies apiece for Portsmouth and Dover, New Hampshire, fifty for the "eastern parts" (Maine), and sixty-six official copies designated for magistrates, deputies, and county recorders, an edition of 700 copies is accounted for.[94] This scheme also proved unsatisfactory, however, for in 1670, the Court declared that "there is a great want of law books . . . and very few of them that are extant are complete," and in 1672 it returned to the private sector, granting John Usher a seven-year privilege on the edition, to keep the value up; nevertheless, Usher still had 190 copies unsold in 1675. Connecticut resolved that every family should buy a copy of the 1673 *Laws*, but even with this mandate, the constables were unable to collect and 400 copies still remained unsold in 1677.[95]

Even when towns could afford to lodge a copy in the hands of each constable and selectman, the constables might not pass along their copies to their successors; Watertown bought a fresh supply for this reason in 1697, but it is also clear that the constables were able to carry out their duties without them. In 1642, Massachusetts appointed a broadside *Capital Laws*, extracted from Ward's "Body of Liberties," for the instruction of children: it was still "in print" in 1674, when Watertown duly ordered that "Each man heaue in his house a coppy," to be paid for out of the rates, as the law required.[96] Even this minimal, compendious summary, it seems, failed of its intended audience; the readers of the *Capital Laws* petered out with succeeding generations, and its provisions became obsolete.

None of this should be surprising: knowledge of the law at a personal or local level is still generally imperfect today, and New England had its proper share of Dogberries and Shallows. Most laymen encounter the law through blank forms, not by reading statutes and decisions. "Moses his Judicialls," though never enacted, was perhaps more realistic than the *Laws and Liberties* of Massachusetts, if only because the Bible was the only substantive body of law in which ordinary people were generally instructed. Otherwise, plaintiff and defendant crossed swords over a little quarter-sheet scrap of a subpoena, the only bit of printed law (when it was printed) that either of them would ever see.

Before the Glorious Revolution of 1688, the function of cumulated editions of the *Laws* was to establish the agreement of the magistrates and the deputies and to transmit it to the towns. The sessions acts, by which the cumulations were updated, were printed in editions too small for even this distribution, and probably served, like legislative bills, for internal use. The contents and arrangement of the law book strikingly resemble that of Michael Dalton's *Countrey Justice* (1618, etc.), a standard English handbook for justices of the peace: alphabetical by topic, with blank forms at the end, and for the most part concerned with criminal law. This format complicated revision of the law, since it obscured the historical context of the articles, but it better communicated their substance to a largely untrained magistracy and constabulary.[97]

After the Revolution of 1688, metropolitan authority brought about an "adjustment to empire," as Richard R. Johnson has called it, in the uses of print as in other matters. The colonial legislature now followed parliamentary procedure, where bills were read three times before being passed on to the governor and council for consent; and the validity of the law was subject to disallowance by the Board of Trade in London.[98] The laws themselves were arranged chronologically, by session and regnal year, just like the English sessions acts and Statutes at Large. Benjamin Harris and John Allen adorned the 1692 Massachusetts *Laws* with a cut of the royal arms which, unlike Richard Pierce's pitiful effort, was engraved in England. Print now served the imperial function of communicating between the colony and the mother country, whose delegation of authority to the colonies was explicitly proclaimed by the inclusion of the royal charter in the law book. Other New

England colonies followed suit: the first printing of the New Hampshire *Laws* responded to an order from the Board of Trade in 1698, not to a purely colonial initiative; and Massachusetts submitted a revised edition for the same purpose. Only Rhode Island resisted, sending an illegible manuscript "abstract" to gloss over its insubordination.

The "adjustment to empire" transformed even the meaning of colonial type faces. In England, the black-letter (or "english") face lingered on in a few books long after it had been generally superseded by roman: in laws, folio Bibles, and popular literature like ballads and chapbook romances. In particular, an exceptionally large size great primer (18 pt.) characterized the metropolitan printing of laws, whereas colonial laws had usually been printed in roman, english (14 pt.) or pica (12 pt.). The first New England printer to use black letter was Samuel Green, Jr., and he had little of it, since he was unable to set more than the initial words of paragraphs in blacks for his edition of the 1629 Massachusetts Bay Charter (1689), in pica. *A Vindication of Nevv-England* [1690?], ascribed to Increase Mather and Charles Morton, attacked the "Church of England" faction for their support of Andros, but the printer (Richard Pierce?) had no type of the proper size to express this invidious, "English" distinction. He therefore engraved "Church of England" in the characters proper to it on a woodblock. It seems an improbably laborious way of expressing his feelings for a mere pamphlet, especially since he was unlikely ever to use these words in the same way again.

The black-letter face had thus acquired a "foreign" connotation for the colonists. Time passed, however, the colonists took up wigs, drinking healths, celebrating Christmas, naming weekdays by their traditional, "pagan" names, and even acknowledging bishops and the Book of Common Prayer. English traditions and black letter became familiar. The publication of the law also took a new turn in 1704 with the *Boston News-Letter*, founded by the colony postmaster John Campbell. It was "published by authority," an explicit recognition of state property in "foreign intelligence,"[99] which Campbell had previously distributed to a select group in manuscript; and it regularly reprinted proclamations by the governor and council. It was printed down to 1707 by Bartholomew Green, and from 1707 to 1711 by John Allen.

In 1710, Francis Nicholson led an expedition against Port Royal in Nova Scotia, which capitulated without much of a fight. To celebrate the victory, John Campbell drew up an exceptionally expansive, twelve-page *Boston News-Letter* (Oct. 30/Nov. 6, 1710), containing Nicholson's journal of events and two of Governor Joseph Dudley's proclamations, for a fast and a day of thanksgiving. John Allen, the printer, had recently advertised his importation

of "all sorts of good new Letter" from London, and the generous format of
this victory issue gave him a brief chance to display his wares. The first
proclamation was in the traditional great primer "blacks" which, however, took
up so much space that the next proclamation, after opening with a paragraph
of great primer roman, gradually dwindled in ever less vocal paragraphs to
long primer (9 pt., or half the size). One can imagine Allen gloating "Just
like in England!" before cringing back to his true provincial status.

Puritan New England, Richard D. Brown observes, controlled information hierarchically.[100] Print shared this structure, and not simply as a consequence of government licensing. From the populated shelves of Harvard
College Library, down to the still numerous, but scantier collections of the
Winthrops and the Mathers, English printing dwindled to the "Bible and
other books" of rural Essex; colonial imprints descended from folio law-
books and church platforms to local catechisms, almanacs, and sermons in
small formats; literacy cadenced from writing to reading, from manuscript
to print, from Latin to English to Indian. All these hierarchical distinctions
in the sources, uses, scripts, languages, quantities, and distribution of print
mark out center and periphery, rulers and ruled, commercial and religious spheres. Because print was licensed and sanctioned, it was intimately
associated with power, as it could not be under a "free press" serving "the
diffusion of useful knowledge." The first step toward that distant nineteenth-
century goal was often the advent of a second press and printers of enterprise
like Marmaduke Johnson, Benjamin Harris, or John Allen. Proto-typogra-
phers have held center stage far too long in our histories of printing: the
Days, Greens, and Bradfords were neither Gutenbergs nor Caxtons, nor
were meant to be, and we can only distort their achievement by isolating it
from its English sources.

Notes

1. Sheila Lambert, "State Control of the Press in Theory and Practice: The Role
of the Stationers' Company Before 1640," in *Censorship and the Control of Print in
England and France, 1600–1910*, ed. Robin Myers and Michael Harris (Winchester,
UK: St. Paul's Bibliographies, 1992), 1–32; Michael Treadwell, "1695–1995: Some Tercentenary Thoughts on the Freedom of the Press," *HLB* n.s. 7 (1996): 3–19.

2. B. J. Mullin, "The Undated Editions of the Revised Bay Psalm Book," *PBSA*
95 (2001): 355–61, supports Amory's hypothesis regarding overseas printings.

3. Perry Miller, *The New England Mind: The Seventeenth Century* (1939; Cambridge, Mass.: Harvard University Press, 1982), ix; Miller's dismissal of book history
(pp. 91–92) seems connected with this summary. Among the historians who have
qualified this assertion of unanimity is, of course, Miller himself, in his sequel, sub-
titled *From Colony to Province* (1953).

4. Hugh Amory, "A Bible and Other Books: Enumerating the Copies in Seventeenth Century Essex County," in *Order and Connexion: Studies in Bibliography and Book History*, ed. R. C. Alston (Cambridge: D.S. Brewer, 1997), 17–37, reprinted in this collection.

5. Winship, *Cambridge Press*, 294; Ford, *Boston Book Market*, 116, 121, 139; Roger Thompson, *Sex in Middlesex: Popular Mores in a Massachusetts County, 1649–1699* (Amherst: University of Massachusetts Press, 1986).

6. Benjamin Lynde, Diaries, Nov. 4, 1687, Massachusetts Historical Society, Boston. On Quaker books, see *Mass. Records*, 4, pt. 1: 278.

7. Michael Treadwell, "1695–1995: Some Tercentenary Thoughts on the Freedoms of the Press."

8. Winship, *Cambridge Press*, 283, 317.

9. Ibid., 179; Bailyn, *Merchants*.

10. My count, differing somewhat from NAIP (which does not, of course, record lost editions), for reasons given in Appendix 1 [of *The Colonial Book in the Atlantic World*; this "Note on Statistics" is printed in full in this collection].

11. The Bay Psalm Book, the Eliot Indian Bible, and the various colonial Laws will usually be cited by uniform title in roman, not by their actual titles, e.g., *The Whole Book of Psalms* (or, *The Psalms, Hymns, and Spiritual Songs*), *Mamusse Wunnutupanatamwe*, etc.

12. William S. Reese, *The Printer's First Fruits: An Exhibition of American Imprints, 1640–1742* (Worcester, Mass.: American Antiquarian Society, 1989), no. 11; Sidney E. Berger, "Innovation and Diversity Among the Green Family of Printers," *Printing History* 12 (1990): 7.

13. Thomas Goddard Wright, *Literary Culture in Early New England, 1620–1730* (New Haven, Conn.: Yale University Press, 1920), 82.

14. Elizabeth C. Reilly, *A Dictionary of Colonial American Printers' Ornaments and Illustrations* (Worcester, Mass.: American Antiquarian Society, 1975), no. 849; that is the same ornament as Robert Steele, *A Bibliography of Royal Proclamations of the Tudor and Stuart Sovereigns*, 2 vols. (Oxford: Clarendon Press, 1910), "The Royal Arms as on Printed Proclamations" (2: 497–540): no. 22. The colonial printer cut out Charles's initials and replaced them with William's, in black-letter type.

15. William C. Kiessel, "The Green Family: A Dynasty of Printers," *NEHGR* 104 (1950): 81–93; Mass. Archives 58: 135 (State Archives, Columbia Point, Boston).

16. Thomas, *Hist. Printing*, 86–87.

17. See generally Winship, *Cambridge Press*; and for the later history of the press, William Kellaway, *The New England Company, 1649–1776: Missionary Society to the American Indians* (London: Longmans, 1961).

18. Winship, *Cambridge Press*, 266, 269.

19. Amory, *First Impressions*, 61–63, is an attempt to account for the use of this paper stock.

20. Bond and Amory, *Harvard Catalogues*, xxvii.

21. Bradford F. Swan, *Gregory Dexter of London and New England, 1610–1700* (Rochester, N.Y.: Leo Hart, 1949); Winship, *Cambridge Press*, 72.

22. Ibid., 30; Hugh Amory, *Steven Day's First Type* (Cambridge, Mass.: Houghton Library, 1989); Thomas, *Hist. Printing*, 54.

23. David Cressy, *Coming Over: Migration and Communication Between England and New England in the Seventeenth Century* (Cambridge: Cambridge University Press, 1987), chap. 1.

24. "Veremur enim (Proh Dolor!) ne si Prælum typographicum concidat, aut omnino nobis desit, et Characteres auferantur; imprimis, non modo Typographi Americam deserunt, aut Academia una cum Discipulis detrimentum in Studiorum progressu patietur, atq[ue] etiam Comitia, et ad Gradus suscipiendos opportunitas impedientur: Imo vero: Resp:, Leges-politicae in usum communem latæ, ad infandum Religionis Christianæ, et Ecclesiarum totius Politiæ Novæ-Angliæ tantum non damnum irreparabile, corruent et concident." *Some Correspondence Between the Governors and Treasurers of the New England Company in London and the Commissioners of the United Colonies in America* (London: Spottiswoode, 1896), 62, trans. 64–65.

25. *The Colonial Book in the Atlantic World*, ed. Hugh Amory and David D. Hall (New York: Cambridge University Press, 2000), chap. 4.

26. Morison, *Harv. Coll.*, 345; Amory, *First Impressions*, 41.

27. John Dunton, "Letters Written from New-England," ed. W. H. Whitmore, *Publications of the Prince Society* 4 (1867): 57; Winship, *Cambridge Press*, 226, 228.

28. Ibid., 320.

29. Cf. a bill from John Usher to Governor Bellingham, 1668, including items purchased from his father in 1662–63. Mass. Archives, 100: 158.

30. Samuel Abbot Green, *John Foster: The Earliest American Engraver and the First Boston Printer* (Boston: Massachusetts Historical Society, 1909); Sewall, *Diary*, "Sewall's Imprints," 2: 1108–11; order to pay Ratcliffe 9s. for government printing, 1675, Mass. Archives 100: 305; S. J. (ed.), "Letters of Chief Justice Sewall," *NEHGR* 9 (1855): 287–88.

31. Benjamin Harris, *Publick Occurrences* (Boston, 1690); William Kellaway, "Marmaduke Johnson and a Bill for Type," *HLB* 8 (1954): 224–27.

32. Duniway, *Freedom of the Press*, 60.

33. Ibid., 64.

34. Littlefield, *Boston Printers*, 2: 31–32, 47, 52.

35. Jeffries Papers, 1: 122, Massachusetts Historical Society, Boston; these engravings are Reilly, *Dictionary of Colonial Ornaments*, nos. 871, 931.

36. William H. Whitmore, *A Bibliographical Sketch of the Laws of the Massachusetts Colony from 1630 to 1686* (Boston: Rockwell and Churchill, 1890), 128–38; Jeffries papers, 1: 101.

37. Bartholomew Green's printing bill, Oct. 20, 1690, Mass. Archives, 58: 137; Winship, *Cambridge Press*, 328; Thomas's account of Green is based on the obituary in the *Boston News-Letter*, Jan. 4, 1733.

38. *DAB*, s.n. Green, Bartholomew.

39. Thomas, *Hist. Printing*, 90.

40. *Gospel Order Revived* ([New York], 1700).

41. Mather, *Diary*, 1: 472.

42. Thomas, *Hist. Printing*, 311.

43. Ibid., 296.

44. Rollo G. Silver, "Financing the Publication of Early New England Sermons," *SB* 11 (1958): 175–78.

45. Edmund S. Morgan, *The Puritan Family: Religion and Domestic Relations in*

Seventeenth-Century New England (1944; rev. ed., New York: Harper and Row, 1966), 173.

46. Michael Zuckerman, *Peaceable Kingdoms: New England Towns in the Eighteenth Century* (New York: Knopf, 1970).

47. Cotton Mather, *What Should Be Most of All Tho't Upon* (Boston, 1713), "To the Reader."

48. Wilberforce Eames, "Early New England Catechisms," *Procs. AAS* 12 (1898): 76–182. He lists a ghost of John Davenport's lost "shorter catechism" (Cambridge, 1650?) under Roxbury (by "Samuel Danforth"), and for Norris, see R. J. Roberts, "A New Cambridge, N.E., Imprint: The *Catechisme* of Edward Norris, 1649," *HLB* 13 (1959): 25–28.

49. Cotton Mather, *Work upon the Ark* (Boston, 1689), introd., sec. II.

50. On Pembroke's litigation, see Alicia C. Williams, "Plaintiff/Defendant Guide to Suffolk County (Mass.) Common Pleas," *Mayflower Descendant* 35 (1985): 153–54; 36 (1986): 50–51, 180; 40 (1990): 192–93; 41 (1991): 45, 197; 42 (1992): 166; on Wheeler, see Holmes, *Cotton Mather*, 1: 453 (= Evans 793, a lost title), 3: 973; and Evans 796.

51. Sewall, *Diary*, 1: 495; on this practice generally, see George Selement, *Keepers of the Vineyard: the Puritan Ministry and Collective Culture in Colonial New England* (Lanham, Md.: University Press of America, 1984), chap. 4.

52. Mather, *Diary*, 1: 548; 2: 135.

53. Ford, *Boston Book Market*, 108–20; George E. Bowman, "Governor Thomas Prence's Will and Inventory, and the Records of His Death," *Mayflower Descendant* 3 (1901): 203–16.

54. Ford, *Boston Book Market*, 86–87.

55. Hugh Amory, "Under the Exchange: The Unprofitable Business of Michael Perry, a Seventeenth-Century Boston Bookseller," *Procs. AAS* 103 (1993): 31–60, reprinted in this collection.

56. Richard R. Johnson, *Adjustment to Empire: The New England Colonies, 1675–1715* (New Brunswick, N.J.: Rutgers University Press, 1981), 355–56.

57. "The Mather Papers," 4 *Coll. MHS* 8 (1868): 493; H. R. Plomer et al., *A Dictionary of the Printers and Booksellers . . . in England, Scotland and Ireland from 1668 to 1725* (Oxford: Bibliographical Society [of London], 1922).

58. John Dunton, *The Life and Errors of John Dunton* (London, 1705), 127–28.

59. Suffolk County (Mass.) Common Pleas, Record Book (Oct. 7, 1707), p. 67 (State Archives, Columbia Point, Boston).

60. Mather, *Diary*, 2: 242; and cf. 283.

61. Winship, *Cambridge Press*, 293.

62. Ibid., 239.

63. Hannah D. French, "Bookbinding in the Colonial Period, 1636–1783," in *Bookbinding in America*, ed. Hellmut Lehmann-Haupt (Portland, Me.: Southworth-Anthoensen Press, 1941), 8–47.

64. Hall, *Worlds*, 48; Sylvester Judd, *History of Hadley* (Springfield, Mass.: H. R. Huntting & Co., 1905), 61. Eleazar Phillips was the first Massachusetts bookseller to appear in an imprint outside Boston (Charlestown, 1715).

65. Harriet S. Tapley, *Salem Imprints, 1768–1825* (Salem, Mass.: Essex Institute, 1927), 163–71.

66. Amory and Hall, *Colonial Book*, 58; and cf. Gloria L. Main, who uses books as

an "index of amenity" in "The Distribution of Consumer Goods in Colonial New England: A Subregional Approach," *Annual Proceedings of the Dublin Seminar for New England Folklife* 12 (1989): 165.

67. [Benjamin Colman], *Some Reasons and Arguments Offered to the Good People of Boston . . . for the Setting Up of Markets* (Boston, 1719); the regulations appointing market days on Thursday (1633/4) and on Tuesday, Thursday, and Saturday "and no other days" (1696) were apparently not enforced.

68. Cf. Draper's bill for "the &c.," 1731, reprinted in Rollo G. Silver, "Publishing in Boston, 1726–1757: The Accounts of Daniel Henchman," *Procs. AAS* 66 (1956): 32; discussed more extensively in Amory and Hall, *Colonial Book*, chap. 9.

69. Ford, *Boston Book Market*, "Lists no. I–V": 88–150.

70. Ibid., 21.

71. "Samuel Sewall," Shipton and Sibley, *Harvard Graduates* 2 (1881): 336; Littlefield, *Boston Booksellers*, facsimile. at 188: $4\frac{1}{2}$ doz. of Jonathan Mitchel's *Discourse of the Glory* (1721); $3\frac{1}{2}$ doz. of Increase Mather's *Several Sermons* (1715), 6 copies of his *Discourse concerning Faith and Fervency in Prayer* (1710), and 13 of his *Ichabod* (1702); 3 copies of Samuel Willard's *Truly Blessed Man* (1700); and $5\frac{3}{4}$ doz. of Samuel Lee's *Triumph of Mercy* (1718).

72. Giles Barber, "Books from the Old World and for the New: the British International Trade in Books in the Eighteenth Century," *Studies on Voltaire and the Eighteenth Century* 151 (1976): 185–224.

73. B. J. McMullin, "Joseph Athias and the Early History of Stereotyping," *Quærendo* 23 (1993): 184–207.

74. Ford, *Boston Book Market*, 8 n. 2, 85.

75. Ibid., 151.

76. Diary of Michael Wigglesworth, New England Historic Genealogical Society, Boston.

77. Matt B. Jones, "Notes for a Bibliography of Michael Wigglesworth's 'Day of Doom' and 'Meat out of the Eater,'" *Procs. AAS* 39 (1929): 77–84; the older theory that three colonial editions have been lost still survives in the *DAB* article on Wigglesworth.

78. Sewall, *Diary*, 1: 174.

79. These incunabula were four commentaries on Peter Lombard's *Sentences* by Pierre d'Ailly, St. Bonaventura, Robert of Holcot, and Guillaume d'Auxerre (Goff A-481, B-928, H-287, and G-718); the *Polychronicon* by Ranulf Higden and the *Nuremberg Chronicle* by Hartmann Schedel (Goff H-268 and S-367); William of Ockham's *Decisiones super Potestatem Summi Pontificis* and the *Epistolæ* of Pope Pius II (Goff O-7a and P-722). Undated editions of a *Hortus Sanitatis*, and the *Sermones* of "Wilh. Parisiensis," probably Guillaume d'Auvergne, may also have been incunabula, but it is impossible to be sure. The cataloguer misdated Johann Brentz, *Enarratio in Evangelia Dominicalia* "1500" for 1550 (Brentz was not born until 1499), and Pius II's *Epistolæ* "1487" for 1497; and Bonaventura's commentary, in two parts, was either bound in three volumes, or another work was shelved with it as part 3. [Other incunabula with a non-New England provenance are in the collections of the Library Company of Philadelphia.]

80. Amory, "Bible and Other Books."

81. Morison, *Intellectual Life*, 142.

82. *The Journal of John Winthrop 1630–1649*, ed. Richard S. Dunn, James Savage, and Laetitia Yeandle (Cambridge, Mass.: Harvard University Press, 1996), 570; "The Mather Papers," 285; Littlefield, *Boston Booksellers*, facsimile at 1:111.

83. Wroth, *Col. Printer*, 224.

84. Winship, *Cambridge Press*, 19.

85. Charles Evans, "Oaths of Allegiance in Colonial New England," *Proc. AAS* 31 (1921): 377–438; and cf. Sewall, *Diary*, 1: 319, for a multiple swearing-in.

86. Ford, *Mass. Broadsides*; the 1679 warrant is Bristol B50 (trimmed to the type area, but originally a half-sheet, probably with manuscript signatures, as in later such documents).

87. Winthrop, cit. Whitmore, *Bibliographical Sketch*, 7–8; Zechariah Chafee, Jr., ed., "Records of the Suffolk County Court, 1671–1680," *Pubs. CSM* 29–30 (1933): xxviii–xxxv.

88. Joseph H. Smith, "The English Criminal Law in Early America," in *The English Legal System: Carryover to the Colonies* (Los Angeles: William A. Clark Memorial Library, 1975), 3–60.

89. Thomas G. Barnes, "Law and Liberty (and Order) in Early Massachusetts," ibid., 61–89.

90. *The Records of the Colony of Rhode Island and Providence Plantations, in New England*, ed. John Russell Bartlett, 5 vols. (Providence: Greene & Bros., 1856–65), 3: 388.

91. Ibid., 387, 396.

92. Whitmore, *Bibliographical Sketch*, 122; Timothy H. Breen, *The Character of the Good Ruler: A Study of Puritan Political Ideas in New England, 1630–1730* (New Haven, Conn.: Yale University Press, 1970), 97–123.

93. Winship, *Cambridge Press*, 110.

94. *Mass. Records*, 4, pt. 1: 422; for the apportionment of the rate, ibid., 3: 28. *Watertown Records*, 6 vols. (Watertown, Mass., 1894–1939), 1: 68, 75.

95. Ford, *Boston Book Market*, 13; Albert C. Bates, *Connecticut Statute Laws: A Bibliographical List of Editions* ([Hartford, Conn.]: Acorn Club, 1900), 11.

96. *Watertown Records*, 1: 121; 2: 115.

97. To supply the place of the lawbook, the Dominion used Wingate's abridgment and Dalton: Jeffries papers, 1: 64, 71.

98. Johnson, *Adjustment to Empire*, 287, 293–94. Even the legislators found revision puzzling on occasion (*Mass. Records*, 4, pt. 2: 468–69).

99. Peter Fraser, *The Intelligence of the Secretaries of State & Their Monopoly of Licensed News, 1660–1688* (Cambridge: Cambridge University Press, 1956).

100. Richard D. Brown, *Knowledge Is Power: The Diffusion of Information in Early America, 1700–1865* (New York: Oxford University Press, 1989), chap. 1.

6. A Boston Society Library:
The Old South Church
and Thomas Prince

Published here for the first time, this essay describes the eighteenth-century anti-quarian and bibliophile Thomas Prince (1687–1758) and how he acquired the books that became the "New England Library." One purpose of the essay is to clarify the difference between that collection and others which have often been confused with it, the books that passed down within Prince's family or belonged to Boston Third (Old South) Church. To tell the story of Prince as collector, Hugh relied on physical evidence that is too readily ignored, the traces of prior own-ership in old books and the shelf marks made by successive caretakers and cata-loguers of the library. It is a charming tale, though Hugh also touched on certain moments of difficulty or unpleasantness, like the imperiling of the collection dur-ing the British occupation of Boston and the raids made upon it in the middle of the nineteenth century by bibliophiles in pursuit of copies of the Bay Psalm Book. Looking over his shoulder, as it were, we can share the pleasure he felt in deci-phering yet another set of marks in books, and making sense of them. Given as the seventy-third George Parker Winship Lecture at Houghton Library, Harvard University on November 8, 2000, entitled "An Eighteenth-Century Book Club: Thomas Prince and the Old South Church."

Manuscript in editor's possession. The illustrations that graced the lecture are not reproduced here.

Thomas Prince was born in Sandwich, New Plymouth, probably in 1686, and served as minister of Third or Old South Church, Boston, from 1718 until his death in 1758.[1] By his will, dated shortly before his death, he be-queathed the church a collection of books, maps, and manuscripts "either published in New England, or pertaining to its History, & Public Affairs," to be called "the New England Library" and kept in the "Steeple Chamber"[2] of the brick tower to the west of the main entrance of the new meetinghouse, familiar to us from the Freedom Trail today.[3] There Prince had pitched his study, and he anxiously noted its construction in two of his current acquisi-tions while it was being built in 1729.[4] The bookplate states that Prince began to form the library when he entered Harvard in 1703, and his will directs that it should remain a closed, non-circulating collection.

He also left his church "all my Books that are in Latin, Greek, & in the Oriental Languages, to be kept, and remain in their Public Library for ever." This second, "Public" or "South Church Library," according to its separate bookplate, goes back to 1718, when Prince began to serve as the church's pastor with his classmate Joseph Sewall. It is next attested to in 1726, when he approached Judge Sewall, Joseph's father, with a "Schêm for a Lending

Library." The Judge deemed it "inconvenient"—i.e., an inappropriate project for a church—and offered instead to contribute "forty shillings, or more, if need be" to buy Brian Walton's great polyglot Bible (1655–57) for the use of the two ministers.[5] "Several gentlemen of the congregation" accordingly purchased a copy that had recently come on the market from Increase Mather's library.[6] Shortly afterward, Prince approached Harvard's benefactors, Thomas Hollis and Samuel Holden, for further contributions, alleging that Harvard's orthodoxy was weakening.[7] Since this "declension" entailed greater tolerance for Hollis's fellow Baptists, the great man was understandably offended, but Holden sent four folio volumes of Richard Baxter's *Practical Works* (1707).

Both bookplates were printed in versions that allow for these donations by leaving a space for the donors' names.[8] Unlike such private book collectors as the Mathers, James Logan, or the Byrds of Westover, Prince collected for a community.[9] Given the constitution of a Congregational church, the closest model for his project is probably the social or proprietary library, first fully realized in the British colonies by Benjamin Franklin's Library Company in 1731. Franklin and his friends subsidized it by subscriptions, because Philadelphia was book-poor, but he had been a member of Old South Church, and we need not doubt his inspiration. Benjamin Franklin's father Josiah was one of the few who had contributed to both of Prince's libraries.

Prince kept meticulous records of his acquisitions, minuting the place, weekday, month, day, and year of receipt on the verso of the title-page, usually with a note of the price in a code that I am still unable to decipher.[10] Other annotations frequently cover the authorship, bibliography, and contents of the volume. As his notes on the construction of the new meetinghouse will already have suggested, these records constitute a ragged, discontinuous diary of his life, though their dispersal among some 1,500 volumes has meant that they have been little studied. Before analyzing their witness to Prince's life and collecting, however, I must discuss how two libraries belonging to the Old South Church gradually came to be viewed as a single private library formed by the Reverend Thomas Prince.

In 1761, three years after Prince's bequest, the Old South Church finally directed that a committee should prepare rules and orders for their Public Library, that cases "with Locks" should be provided for the New England Library, and that Oxenbridge Thacher, a Boston lawyer and bibliophile, should compile catalogues of the two collections.[11] Thacher died in 1765, apparently without having drawn up any catalogues, for the Church was obliged to renew its order five years later.[12] The first reader I have identified was the future president of Yale Ezra Stiles, who spent "all forenoon in [the] South Church Steeple transcribing &c. Mss." on July 20, 1770.[13] There may have been others, for in 1774, Jeremy Belknap, the historian of New Hampshire, found a "vast number" of the manuscripts from Prince's bequest "lying in a most shamefully chaotic state," but they were "put into some order" after his visit.[14] When John Adams consulted it in the same year, seeking information on Massachusetts's borders, the library was shelved on "the balcony"—presumably the structure running above the "galleries" where the children and servants sat during services.[15] Around this time, Benjamin Trumbull, the historian of Connecticut, used it to defend his colony's claim to part of Pennsylvania. The American Revolution supervened, and the godless British occupying forces gutted the meetinghouse for a riding school, retaining only the east gallery for spectators. Patriots whispered that they set up a grog shop and fired a stove with Prince's books and manuscripts,[16] but it seems likelier that the soldiers simply threw the books into the adjoining steeple chamber when they tore down the west gallery and balcony. When the Church again surveyed their property in 1811, at any rate, there they found "the Library in a very ruinous situation, the boxes were some broken to pieces, others uncovered and the books partly taken out and laying about the floor, trodden over and cover'd with dust."

The entire collection was then moved to the parsonage in Milk Street, a catalogue was prepared by a Mr. Lord, and 203 volumes were "new bound," for the substantial total cost of $340.81. The parson, Joshua Huntington, and the Society's secretary, Joseph Peirce, were also asked to "examine and see what Books . . . can be found, which may have been lent, that they may be replaced in our Library."[17] Five were eventually retrieved from the Boston Athenaeum, Jeremy Belknap, the late Deacon Samuel Salisbury (d. 1818), and the New Bedford Public Library; three more still repose in John Adams's library at the Boston Public.[18] A descendant of another deacon presented a tract volume to the American Antiquarian Society in 1815.[19] These are not, on the whole, evidence of very serious losses, I think.

Mr. Lord's catalogue does not survive, but he probably wrote a three-fold number in every volume, designating its case, shelf, and position on the shelf; evidence that the two collections were now intermingled in ten cases, on seven shelves, numbered from the folios at the foot to the smallest formats at the top. In 1814, the Church deposited 261 printed volumes and twelve manuscripts in the recently founded Massachusetts Historical Society, and Abiel Holmes, the Society's librarian, drew up a list of them.[20]

In 1843 the church again moved their library, to their chapel in Spring Lane, abandoning Lord's arrangement in the process;[21] a shelf-list by G. H. Whitman, with an appendix on the volumes deposited at the Historical Society, was published in 1847 under the misleading title of *A Catalogue of the*

Library of the Rev. Thomas Prince,[22] and, to those who cared to track down the widely scattered entries, inadvertently revealed that the church then owned no less than five copies of the Bay Psalm Book, the first book printed in British North America. Isaiah Thomas had known of only one copy in 1810, and a learned German visitor, Hermann Ludewig, had located only three in 1846, only a year before. Boston cognoscenti soon plied the church deacons with requests for their duplicates, and Edward Crowninshield, George Livermore, and Nathaniel Shurtleff bore away their prizes.[23] These depredations have been much criticized as betrayals of the terms of Prince's bequest, but in fact only one of these three copies had actually been in his possession: Richard Mather's copy, with the bookplate of the New England Library. The church unsuccessfully sued to recover it at the sale of Shurtleff's books in 1875, and it is now in the John Carter Brown Library.

The church withdrew their deposit from the Historical Society in 1859, and seven years later, when they vacated and sold the chapel before moving to their present Puginesque quarters in Copley Square,[24] they placed the entire collection in the Boston Public Library, where it remains today, numbering some 1,899 volumes and 3,444 titles. The catalogue celebrating this deposit again denominates it "the collection of books and manuscripts which formerly belonged to the Reverend Thomas Prince." In an attempt to justify this title and restore Prince's distinction between the New England Library and the rest of the collection, the Boston Public's librarian, Justin Winsor, returned a number of books with imprints dating after Prince's death,[25] and divided the remaining titles into an "American Part" and a "Foreign Part." The original distinction between the two libraries had been chronological, however, not political or geographical; for Prince, New England history was continuous with that of Great Britain and the Reformation,[26] so that the South Church Library was only an unspecialized supplement to a collection that served as a bibliography for his *Chronological History of New England* and closed in 1730.

The books that Winsor returned were therefore fully consonant with Prince's intentions in founding a "Public Library," while significant numbers of those he retained were not in Prince's bequests. Almost a fifth of the volumes now in the Boston Public were given by Prince's co-pastor Joseph Sewall, who had inherited most of them from his father Samuel, the famous diarist and judge who participated in the Salem witch trials.[27] A substantial body of English political pamphlets once crossed the desk of Jonathan Belcher, who receipted them during his tenure as governor of Massachusetts from 1730 to 1741; he added a run of Abel Boyer's *Political State of Great Britain* (1711–39), but the rest of his library, some 474 volumes, went to the

College of New Jersey (Princeton).[28] None of these books had "formerly belonged to the Reverend Thomas Prince."

Nor had Prince bequeathed all his books to the church. The remainder passed to his daughter and sole heir Sarah, wife of Lieutenant-Governor Moses Gill, together with 3,000 acres in Princeton, Massachusetts, where they built a lavish summer residence. Her private, pious meditations won Sarah the title of a woman of "great Merit in the Literary World";[29] John Singleton Copley's portrait balances the fashionable garb of a *grande dame* with the formidable gaze of an intellectual.[30] The house and her library eventually descended to Col. Moses Gill, the governor's nephew and executor, who dispersed the contents at a country sale in 1804, to satisfy a judgment for over $106,000 obtained by another nephew, Ward Nicholas Boylston.[31] Books from this source today are relatively numerous—Harvard alone has some twenty-five. All the titles I have seen fall within Prince's pastoral and scholarly interests, but others may well have ranged more widely.[32]

The titles of these two catalogues, then, neither do justice to the extent of Prince's personal library nor to the contributions of others to his church, nor, as I will now show, to a common book culture and inheritance in which all of them participated. Just as literary theorists have claimed that there are no authors, since writing is made of writing, so one might argue that there are no book collectors, whose efforts, however admirable, only shuffle about earlier assemblages of books until, like Prince's, they slumber undisturbed in a public institution. I turn, then, to Prince's life and the sources of his collections.

Prince was born in a relatively poor colony that only became part of Massachusetts in 1692, when the machinations of Increase Mather saved it from falling into the clutches of New York. The soil of the Old Colony is sandy and laced with swamps and bogs that today serve for growing cranberries or sheltering a rare breed of turtle when they are not filled in for shopping malls or gated estates. The cranky brood of the *Mayflower* had traditionally supported themselves by hunting whales and gathering clams, and in Prince's day by splitting shingles from the cedars that grew in their swamps and by ranching horses. In a burst of youthful irony, Prince described himself in one of his books as "Duke of Sandwich Earl of puncapog"—the latter being one of the more impoverished towns of "praying Indians."[33]

Prince's mother, Mercy Hinckley, daughter of the last governor of New Plymouth, taught him to read and gave him the Westminster Assembly's *Shorter Catechism* when he was eight, *The Marrow of Modern Divinity* when he was eleven, and, prophetically for his later scholarship, John Fox's *Time and the End of Time* when he was fifteen—which his brothers Enoch, Joseph, and Moses duly shared in turn. To these early, devotional acquisitions may be added two volumes inscribed by Prince's father Samuel. Prince's copy of Samuel Willard's *Remedy against Despair* (Boston, 1700; H. 25.28), appropriately enough, was the gift of Ruth Chipman, the midwife who delivered him. He later declared that the first history of New England "put into his hands" was *New-Englands Memoriall* by Nathaniel Morton (1669); he certainly read it as a child, but we do not know exactly when he acquired it, as the title page of his copy is wanting.[34] In 1697, when Prince was eleven, he was shipped off to a grammar school under Samuel Torrey in Weymouth, forty-five miles away; two years later, his father handed him over to be prepared for college by his grandfather, ex-Governor Thomas Hinckley, and after two more years he passed into the tutelage of his uncle Nathaniel Stone, minister of Harwich.[35] Hinckley gave his grandson at least four serious works of divinity, and Prince garnered in all his manuscripts after his grandfather's death in 1706.[36] The earliest symptoms of the future bibliophile were a hand-drawn label of "Thomas Prince, 1701," and a printed label dated 1704, after he had entered Harvard, aged seventeen.

After graduating from Harvard in 1707, he returned to Sandwich, where he taught school. Around this time, the minister of Sandwich, Rowland Cotton, or his wife, Elizabeth Saltonstall, gave the young scholar some thirty-seven titles in all: only one remotely concerns the history of New England, and the others are either editions of the classics or solid tomes of divinity and commentaries on the Bible. Mrs. Cotton's contribution derives either from her father Nathaniel Saltonstall, her brother Richard, or her grandfather, John Ward, first minister of Rowley, Massachusetts. After Mrs. Cotton's death in 1726, the rest of her husband's books were sold at auction, but so far as I can ascertain, Prince acquired no title from this sale until 1744, when he bought Cotton's copy of Polydore Vergil's *Historia Anglica* (1534).

Parson Cotton's opinion of the schoolmaster survives in a draft of a recommendation of him for the post of college librarian, vacated by John Gore in 1707:

He seems to be Indefatigably studious . . . but I perceive by some of his relatives that he is anxiously solicitous for further Accomplishments without which or at least without endeavors [for them?] I fear he will never be presuaded [!] to any publick busines of any sort but follow his plodding Everlastingly. . . . If Tom might Expire in the Library I suppose [it?] would be much to his satisfaction.[37]

The librarianship fell to Nathaniel Gookin, however,[38] and Tom left Massachusetts for the Congregational pulpits of Suffolk, England, where he preached from 1709 to 1717. His notes of acquisitions show him busily buying books at country sales. The largest single group of his purchases, some fifty-five titles, came from the library of the distinguished Sudbury minister Samuel Petto, sold on June 1, 1713. Petto had been a correspondent of Increase Mather and exchanged books with him,[39] but Prince's purchases were solidly European. In the course of a side trip to the Netherlands, he settled a correspondence in Rotterdam, from which he would receive Dutch catalogues and various titles down to the 1740s.

In his "plodding" pursuit of New England history, as Rowland Cotton called it, Prince rather neglected American printing before he was settled at Old South Church. A copy of William Hubbard's *Narrative of the Troubles with the Indians in New-England* (Boston, 1677; H. 11.24), which Prince bought in 1706 for 2s. 6d. from his classmate Joshua Moody, is unusual both for its early date of acquisition and because Prince paid hard cash.[40] Most of the American imprints in his collection were gifts, which implies that he did not systematically collect them. Prince's notes in the books themselves tell a more complex story, in short, than the bookplates on which our standard accounts of the collection have been largely founded.

His earliest important acquisitions of Americana were manuscripts: the Hinckley Papers in 1706, as I have already noted; the Cotton Papers from Rowland Cotton, soon afterwards; and by 1736, he claimed that he had so many manuscripts that he had "never yet had Leisure enough to read them."[41] Of these, the Mather library provided "the greatest and most valuable part," according to that unpopular Loyalist and historian of Massachusetts, Thomas Hutchinson.[42] Cotton Mather had been in financial difficulties since 1723, and sometime before his death in 1728 he bilked his creditors by conveying his library out of his estate.[43] It is sad to think how many honest tradesmen had postponed their demands out of respect for this elderly neurotic, but to be realistic, his 3,000-odd recondite tomes would never have realized anything like their full value on the Boston market, and the Mather Papers—and indeed Richard Mather's copy of the Bay Psalm Book—found a better home in the New England Library.

The property of these and some other manuscripts in Prince's possession, however, remains elusive. The Bradford Papers were lent to Prince in 1728, and he may never have owned them, though he inserted the New England Library bookplate in the manuscript of Bradford's *Of Plimmoth Plantation*.[44] In Prince's keeping were also two other manuscripts, neither to be published until a century later: William Hubbard's *General History of New England*, the property of Andrew Eliot, and volume three of John Winthrop's *History of New England*, which Prince had borrowed in 1754 and bequeathed to his church. The Winthrops had lost track of the other two volumes as well, which turned up in the hands of Jonathan Trumbull of Connecticut, from whom Jeremy Belknap took them into custody, before the entire manuscript was finally reunited at the Massachusetts Historical Society in 1814. Prince edited some of these sources in the 1730s and planned to edit Hubbard's *History*, which first saw print more than half a century after his death.[45]

In 1728, a few months before the completion of the new meetinghouse, Prince advertised for persons who had borrowed his books to return them, as he intended "to Dispose of his Library"—to set it in order, as we would say today, not, as some even at the time concluded, to sell it.[46] The first surviving fruit of this "disposition" is a manuscript list of Prince's "NEW-ENGLISH Books & Tracts," describing some 766 titles in about 500 volumes, arranged by imprint dates down to 1730.[47] The list was a prelude to his *Chronological History of New England*, announced in the same year, when Prince circulated requests for information and subscriptions.[48] The first volume eventually appeared in 1736, but broke off at 1630, a century before his proposed conclusion. The Great Awakening in the 1740s diverted his energies, and the second volume, entitled *The Annals of New England*, continued the story only three more years before his death. If Prince promised more than he could ultimately deliver, disappointing some subscribers, their very numbers—over 500—suggest more enthusiasm for the work than modern commentators have mustered. Shipton judges him "a far better historian than the Mathers, Hubbard, or Niles, but only in promise, not achievement," yet their achievements pale beside his promise. It energized the efforts of the Massachusetts Historical Society for more than a century after his death, without which, I imagine, we might never have heard of those village Gibbons, William Hubbard and Samuel Niles.[49] Cotton Mather's promise died with him, and that eminent historian of New England, James Savage, despised his achievement.

The lapse in the production of his history, however, did not cause Prince to neglect his library. In 1742, the books of John Norton of First Church, Boston, and of his nephew John of Hingham came on the market, following the death of the nephew's wife.[50] The uncle, an able Latinist but "bigoted, narrow-minded, and tyrannical" in his orthodoxy,[51] came over in 1635 and left a substantial library of 729 volumes at his death in 1663. His copy of St. Augustine's *Plurima opuscula*, printed in Venice in 1491, may be the first incunable north of the Rio Grande—one of three in the library, though Prince perhaps found their dates less fascinating than we do.[52] A rather more impressive rarity was the Norton run of *Mercurius Gallobelgicus*, a periodical compendium of notable events from 1588 to 1627; the only other publicly held sets in America today were bought in the twentieth century. In all, Prince acquired some thirty-five titles from the Norton sale, including a first edition of William Gilbert's epochal *De magnete* (1600).

Prince lost his only son, Thomas, Jr., in 1748. Young Tom's books descended to his sisters Sarah and Mercy, and they immediately presented one of the Latin volumes to their father.[53] This is probably the earliest date at which Prince might have contemplated his bequest of Latin, Greek, and oriental books to his church. In the same disastrous year, he acquired another batch of books from his younger brother Nathan, a brilliant mathematician and Harvard tutor. Nathan was a difficult, dissolute man who, disappointed of his hope for advancement at Harvard, converted to Anglicanism and died, aged fifty, on a mission for the Society for the Propagation of the Gospel to the Mosquito Indians of Honduras.[54] His brother duly consigned most of his "Collection of curious Mathematical, Philosophical, Historical, and Divinity BOOKS, chiefly in English" to John Gerrish of Boston for sale on December 15 and 22, 1748.[55] The auctioneer's manuscript catalogue describes 202 volumes, which sold for a total of £305 17s. 3d., including £22 5s. from duplicates consigned by Thomas Prince himself, and a few that had actually belonged to the SPG, part of his brother's equipment on his mission.[56] The somewhat tangled accounting for the profits of the sale, at any rate, took a while to straighten out, for Prince did not draw a bill on the auctioneer until October 14, 1751.

By that date, the New England Library alone had more than doubled, to 1,916 titles, a figure that only documents the growth of the pamphlets.[57] In the course of building his library, Prince had inevitably exchanged or sold off parts of it, improving his copies and discarding duplicates, but I can identify only nineteen such titles from his notes. These de-accessioned copies were surely not plated, and Prince may have defaced his notes of acquisition. He probably printed up the two bookplates in the 1750s, since he still had not completed plating his collections at his death.[58]

Unfortunately, I can only touch on the annotations that Prince entered in his books, but one unusually extended example of a diary entry merits attention. In his copy of George Fox's *Great Mystery of the Great Whore Unfolded* (London, 1659), Prince wrote as follows, but in Latin: "Milton, [Monday], October 18th, 1727, died, and [Friday], October 22nd, was buried Mr. P. Thacher; [Sunday], February 10th [1728], I preached at Milton; [Monday], February 11th, I turn over his library; [Monday], April 9th, I ride to Milton; [Tuesday], April 10th, I return to Boston"—carrying, no doubt, Thacher's copy of Fox and other treasures. Thacher had bequeathed his son,

Peter Jr., Prince's brother-in law, what Prince considered "the best and largest Collection of *Puritan Authors* that I have met with in *New-England*."[59] His library probably provided Prince's second copy of the Bay Psalm Book, receipted "Milton, [Monday] Apr. 9 - [Tuesday] 10. 1728"; yet other books in the Prince Collection have Thacher's inscription.

Most of Prince's annotations are too dryly bibliographical even for this audience, but sometimes he gets entertainingly personal. The anonymous *Short View of the Life and Reign of King Charles* (1658), by the Royalist hagiographer Peter Heylin, certainly pushed all his buttons. "This is a weak Performance of some highflying cavalier," he wrote on the front flyleaf, "full of slavery, superstition, & Persecution, utterly insensible of the Tyrannies & Oppressions under which the British Nations groaned." Pages of outraged adversaria follow, attacking Heylin's Stuart and Anglican biases.

Among the joys of the Prince Collection are volumes from the libraries of the Royalist soldier Sir Bevil Grenville, hero of ballads, the Puritan William Dowsing, whose goons destroyed the medieval stained-glass windows of Suffolk, and the merchant Robert Keayne, who founded Boston's first public library in 1656, apologizing for the small formats and vernacular contents of his benefaction.[60] The rings of Saturn were first described in Christiaan Huygens' *Systema Saturnium* (1659); Prince somehow acquired a copy addressed to the astronomer and alchemist Governor John Winthrop of Connecticut, many of whose books repose today in the New York Society Library and the Massachusetts Historical Society. Another was a volume from the library of the Puritan William Crashaw, father of the poet and Catholic Richard, stamped with William's initials and armorial device, a *digitus Dei*. Crashaw left most of his books to St. John's College, Cambridge.[61]

Many of the most interesting provenances appear in the gifts of Prince's co-pastor, Joseph Sewall, in part because Prince habitually defaced earlier marks of ownership on the title-page. A 1638 edition of Alexander Nowell's middle catechism, in Greek and Latin, belonged to John Bailey, later minister of First Church, Boston, in 1656;[62] then to Judge Sewall, who noted (in Latin) that he had "finished reading this very noble book" on August 7, 1697; the scribbles of some younger Sewalls indicate that they found it rather less imposing. What makes it exciting for us are the endpapers, which contain eight copies of a hornbook, still unseparated; since the catechism is in a contemporary binding, they were printed at some time between 1638 and 1656. This is among the earliest known specimens of the genre, and one of three survivals of copies in sheets.[63]

Leonard Hoar, later third president of Harvard, presented a specially bound copy of his *Index Biblicus* (London, 1669) to his "very valued freind and kinsman" John Hull, the Massachusetts mintmaster who coined the pine tree shilling. It is stamped with Hull's initials in gilt, bound in sheep with marbled endpapers, ruled in red, and inscribed in red by the author to Hull, from whom it descended to his son-in-law, Judge Sewall. Sewall himself distributed so many pious tracts and sermons that we can sometimes identify their private issues. Prince's copy of Samuel Lee's *Triumph of Mercy* (Boston, 1718) is bound in a sheepish imitation of the panelled calf then popular in London, and the Judge inscribed it to "Madam Elizabeth Sewall," his daughter-in-law; another copy, in the identical paneled sheep, inscribed to the wife of Prince's predecessor, Ebenezer Pemberton, is at Harvard. These are exceptionally elaborate colonial bindings.

A rather more romantic book, the Jesuit Christian Mayer's *Diarium meditationum* (Cologne, 1635), is inscribed by Sewall to the Jesuit missionary Sébastien Râle—known as Father Rally to the monolingual New Englanders and a major thorn in their side. The occasion for this gift was a conference at Arrowsic on the Kennebec River, to establish peace between Massachusetts and Father Râle's Abenaki Indians, who had been supporting their co-religionists in Québec.[64] The arrangements collapsed, and in 1723 a Massachusetts force raided the mission and murdered Father Râle; this volume and his manuscript dictionary of Abenaki, now in Houghton Library (Harvard), were part of their loot.

In 1659, the crypto-Catholic and Royalist Sir Kenelm Digby unexpectedly enriched the fledgling Puritan and Parliamentarian Harvard College Library with "as many books as were vallued at Sixty pound."[65] The only surviving evidence of any title in this donation, I believe, is a copy of Marsilio Ficino's edition of Plato (1590; H. 71.4F), bound in black calf stamped with Digby's arms in gilt; Prince bought it for 40s. in June 1740, noting that it was *supernumerarius*. If you wonder how so early a gift could ever have been considered a duplicate, the answer is that it had never been entered in the 1723 *Catalogus*,[66] so that Thomas Hollis and his cronies contributed a second copy, which was described in the Supplement of 1735, only to perish in the fire of 1764. Thaddeus Mason of Charlestown promptly replaced it with a third copy, misdated 1570 in the 1790 *Catalogue*. I wonder at the American vogue of this Genevan piracy of a Lyons reprint of a Venetian property.

The queen of the Prince Collection, however, is a finely bound copy of the Puritan Richard Greenham's folio *Workes* (1612), which once belonged to Rebecca Sherburne, wife of Henry, first minister of Portsmouth, New Hampshire, a "most famous, honored, and pious matron," Jonathan Mitchell gratefully noted in Latin, when she gave it to him on October 10th, 1650. "Matchless Mitchell," as his dazzled Cambridge congregation dubbed him, in turn presented the volume to his stepson Jonathan Shepard, who gave it to his "sister" Jen[nie], probably his cousin Jane, who was living with the Mitchells in 1658. His half-brother Thomas, later minister of Charlestown, has also left his childish signature in it. Thomas Prince bought it in November 1717.

I would like to close, however, with the books of Jeremiah Bumstead, a joiner, sometime Boston constable and tithingman, and a very pious and active member of Old South Church. Born in 1678, Jeremiah was still very much alive in 1748, when, aged 70, he married his third wife.[67] He printed a book label in 1700, and he must be the first Bostonian to print one who did not attend Harvard. His diary shows that he was skilled enough in books to be asked to appraise the library of Benjamin Franklin, the uncle of Boston's most famous son, and a major early literary influence on his nephew. In 1722, Bumstead financed an edition of Nathaniel Vincent's *Discourse on Forgiveness* from Uncle Benjamin's shorthand notes. Among the titles to which he subscribed were Samuel Willard's massive *Compleat Body of Divinity* (1726), Samuel Mather's *Life of Cotton Mather* (1729), and Prince's own *Chronological History*. Eleven titles published in Boston between 1685 and 1740, which Bumstead had acquired between 1700 and 1748, are now in the Prince Collection, for three of which Prince actually paid good money; two other Boston imprints, with the signatures of Susan Bumstead, Jeremiah's mother, and Bethiah Sherrar, his second wife, no doubt came from the same source.[68] Here is a relatively humble bibliophile, whose emulation of his betters was mediated through the community of the Old South Church.

"Social" the Prince Collection indubitably was; some have said "quasi-public," whiggishly casting it as a precursor of its present custodians;[69] though in no sense purely private, however, the library's "public" before 1866 was nominally restricted to the congregation of Old South Church—which might be either the hundred-odd pew-holders who made up the Society, or the 350 or so "visible saints" in full communion in the Church, or the entire congregation. By any measure, if we assume that women, servants, and children had limited access, the potential "public" probably did not exceed 150 persons.

Notes

1. The best biography of Prince is Clifford K. Shipton's, in Shipton and Sibley, *Harvard Graduates* 5 (1937): 341–68 (cited hereafter as Shipton for the biographical sketch of Prince, and Shipton and Sibley, *Harvard Graduates* otherwise), though marred by lack of sympathy for Prince's scholarship; the most recent account is by Kenneth Minkema, in *American National Biography*, ed. John A. Garraty and Mark Carnes (New York: Oxford University Press, 1999), 17: 881–82. For vital data, we

must still depend on Samuel G. Drake, "Some Memoirs of the Rev. Thomas Prince," *NEHGR* 5 (1851): 383, but for the year of birth (traditionally 1687), see *Vital Records of Sandwich, Mass.*, ed. Caroline Lewis Kardell and Russell A. Lovell, 3 vols. (Boston: New England Historic Genealogical Society, 1996), 1: 33.

2. The relevant provisions of the will are printed by Justin Winsor in *The Prince Library: A Catalogue of Books and Manuscripts which formerly belonged to the Reverend Thomas Prince and was by him bequeathed to the Old South Church* (Boston: A. Mudge and Son, 1870), ix (the fullest account of the library, cited hereafter as Winsor). Kevin J. Hayes, *Dictionary of Literary Biography* 134 (Detroit: Gale Research, 1994): 194–99, contributes valuable remarks on Prince's use of his collection. I am also indebted to an unpublished paper delivered to the Massachusetts Historical Society by the late John E. Alden.

3. The first meetinghouse had only a turret, so that the actual arrangement of the New England Library depended on the construction of this study. For the earlier building, see Mary Farwell Ayer, *The South Meeting-House, Boston (1669–1729)* (Boston: D. Clapp and Son, 1905), and Marian C. Donnelly, *The New England Meeting Houses of the Seventeenth Century* (Middletown, Conn.: Wesleyan University Press, 1968). For the second meetinghouse, see Hamilton A. Hill, *History of the Old South Church . . . 1669–1884*, 2 vols. (Boston: Houghton Mifflin, 1890), passim, and Michael Holleran, "The Old South: The Meetinghouse and the American Preservation Movement," *Old-Time New England* 76 (1998): 48–77.

4. Winsor, vii (but read H. 15.40 for H. 11.8).

5. *The Letterbook of Samuel Sewall*, 6 Colls. *MHS* 2 (1888): 208.

6. The set included Edmund Castell's companion folio *Lexicon Heptaglotton* (1659). Prince's note in the volumes dates the purchase 1724, but may be in error. The set had been Increase Mather's gift to his son Nathaniel, but Nathaniel died young; the sale was still proceeding in 1725, according to a note by Judge Sewall in Thomas Bradwardine, *De causa Dei, contra Pelagium* (1618; H. 61.7). Other books descended to Cotton Mather, who already owned a copy of the polyglot; see n. 43 below, for Cotton's finances at this period.

7. Thomas Hollis to Benjamin Colman, Jan. 9, 1726/7, *Pubs. CSM* 50 (1975): 594.

8. Notes by Prince in D. Clarkson, *Primitive Divinity* (1688; H. 59.69) and Robert Barclay's *Apology* (Newport, R.I., 1729; H. 21.1).

9. Carl J. Cannon, *American Book Collectors and Collecting from Colonial Times* (New York: H. W. Wilson, 1941), and the *Encyclopedia of Library and Information Science*, ed. Allen Kent et al., 47 vols. (New York: Dekker, 1968–1991), 24: 178, treat Prince's collection as a private library, however.

10. Occasional errors and the character of the handwriting suggest that these notes were retrospectively inserted in his earliest acquisitions.

11. Hill, *History*, 2: 64.

12. Hill, *History*, 2: 133.

13. *The Literary Diary of Ezra Stiles*, ed. F. B. Dexter, 3 vols. (New York: Scribner's, 1901), 1: 59.

14. Jeremy Belknap to Lt. Gov. John Wentworth, Mar. 15, 1774, 6 Colls. *MHS*, 4 (1891): 49; 1 *Colls. MHS* 1 (1792): 3.

15. Cf. John Adams to Elbridge Gerry, Oct. 17, 1779, *The Papers of John Adams*, ed. Robert J. Taylor et al., 11 vols. (Cambridge, Mass.: Harvard University Press,

1977–), 8: 208; Hill, *History*, 1: 453. The front (south) gallery had been divided into pews since 1742, ibid., 1: 532, 568.

16. Journal of Timothy Newell, Oct. 27, 1775, 4 *Colls. MHS* 1 (1852): 269; T[homas]. P[emberton]., "A Topographical and Historical Description of Boston, 1794," 1 *Colls. MHS* 3 (1794, repr. 1810): 258. Benjamin B. Wisner, *The History of the Old South Church in Boston* (Boston: Crocker & Brewster, 1830), 34, judiciously rejects this report.

17. Hill, *History*, 2: 373–74. "Mr. Lord" is probably Melvin Lord, clerk for the booksellers West and Richardson (*NEHGR* 31 [1877]: 250); not Eliezer Lord, as I conjectured in Amory, *First Impressions*, 24.

18. Cf. notes of the Society's librarian in Samuel Gorton, *Simplicities Defence* (1646; H. 13.4), the Royal Society's *Philosophical Transactions . . . Abridged* (1731–32; H. 34.5), and Nathaniel Ward, *Sermon before the House of Commons* (1647; H. 12.13–19), a tract volume; and see Robert Grove's *Gleanings* (1651; H. 20.12) and William Ames's *Bellarminus enervatus* (1629; H. 70a.25).

19. Cannon, *American Book Collectors*, 10–11; Shipton suggests that the congregation filched or trashed at least as much as the British soldiery, 360–61.

20. 2 *Colls. MHS* 7 (1818, repr. 1826): 179–85.

21. Cf. 1 *Procs. MHS*, 2 (1843): 250; for the Spring Lane Chapel, cf. Hill, *History*, 2: 404, 524.

22. A copy of Whitman's catalogue in the BPL is annotated with the shelves on which the volumes were placed (call no. T.R. 26.17 B).

23. For the complex history of these copies, see Amory, *First Impressions*, 24–27. In exchange, the library acquired Cotton Mather's *Coelestinus* (1723; H. 13.16) from Shurtleff; Thomas Prince's *Chronological History* (1736; H. 22.45) from Crowninshield; and Stephen Marshall's *The Churches Lamentation* (1644), bound with seventeen other contemporaneous tracts (H. 56.7–24) from Livermore.

24. Hill, *History*, 2: 524.

25. Leaving behind seventy-eight post-1758 imprints in the American part, and four in the Foreign part, however; Winsor, xii.

26. Thus, for example, he annotated his copy of Minsheu's *Ductor in Linguas* (1627; H. 81.2F), a polyglot dictionary containing the equivalent of eleven languages in nine, as follows: "I put this among the New England Books not only because it was made & printed in England before the Settlers of the Massachusett Colony came over; but also because it explains many Things wherewith they were well acquainted in England."

27. A typescript list of Judge Sewall's books in the Prince Collection, prepared by Stewart Stokes, is available in the Boston Public Library. Some of these volumes have the signatures of Joseph Sewall's in-laws, the Walleys, and of his grandfather John Hull.

28. Shipton and Sibley, *Harvard Graduates* 4 (1933): 448.

29. *Boston Evening-Post*, 12 Aug. 1771. "Her natural inclination, led her to books, and her many private papers discover a good acquaintance with them"; John Hunt, *A Sermon Occasioned by the Death of Mrs. Sarah Gill* (Boston, 1771), 41.

30. The portrait is reproduced in Jules Prown, *John Singleton Copley* (Cambridge, Mass.: Harvard University Press, 1966).

31. See generally Francis E. Blake, *History of the Town of Princeton*, 2 vols. (Princeton, Mass., 1915), 1: 19–21, 278–80; 2: 114–15. For the date of the sale, see the note by

George Sheldon on a volume from the library of Mercy and Sarah Prince, *NEHGR* 37 (1883): 85, inscribed "Eliphaz Coplands Book Bought at the Vandue 1804." Two more titles at the Houghton Library (call nos. *EC7.St425.C732w & *52–2284) and two at the Massachusetts Historical Society have notes of "Ward Cotton Bôt from Gill's Library 1804." Sarah gave or lent a group of personal papers to her cousin Jane, wife of Chandler Robbins (1738–1799), most of which their grandson presented to the MHS; a diary from this fonds, which Shipton knew only from excerpts printed in the *North American Review*, is now in the Houghton Library (acc. no. *96M–40). On a visit to Gill's descendants in 1835, the American Antiquarian Society librarian found the cupboard bare; *The Diary of Christopher Columbus Baldwin . . . 1829–1835* (Worcester, Mass.: American Antiquarian Society, 1901), 348.

32. Thus, in a Logbook & Journal of 1709–10 (MHS), Prince copied extracts from Thomas Shadwell's *Squire of Alsatia*, Tom Brown's *Collection of Miscellany Poems*, Richard Leigh's *Poems upon Several Occasions. A Collection of Poems for and against Henry Sacheverell*, and Delariviere Manly's scandalous *New Atalantis*.

33. John Shower, *Some Account of the Life of Henry Gearing* (1704; H. 24.59). Cf. Daniel T. Huntoon, *History of the Town of Canton* (Cambridge, Mass.: J. Wilson & Son, 1893), chap. 2, "Punkapoag Plantation."

34. Shipton (p. 341) says "he learned to read from Morton's *Memoriall*, and at the age of ten read carefully and annotated *The Marrow of Modern Divinity*, which his confident mother had placed in his hands." Prince's acquaintance with Morton's history probably came after he had already learned to write, judging from notes of "Thorn" (p. 30) and "Commend not man befor his face / bhind [sic] his back do not disgrace" (pp. 188, 192) in the same childish hand; other adversaria are in his mature hand, and, since they cite Bradford's Mss., were certainly written later than 1728. The "annotations" in the *Marrow* consist of marginal lines, and corrections of two obvious errata (pp. 235, 240); all of uncertain authorship, none warranting much maternal confidence.

35. John E. Van de Wetering, "Thomas Prince: Puritan Polemicist" (Ph.D. dissertation, University of Washington, 1959), 28; notes of acquisitions dated Harwich, 1701–2; Prince later said he had attended four grammar schools in all, Shipton, 341.

36. Winsor, vi; *The Hinckley Papers*, 4 *Colls. MHS* 5 (1861): 131.

37. Misc. Mss. (MHS), Jan. 31, 1708/9.

38. Alfred C. Potter and Charles K. Bolton, "The Librarians of Harvard College," *Bibliographical Contributions* / Library of Harvard University 4 (1897): 13.

39. *The Mather Papers*, 4 *Colls. MHS* 8 (1868): 341–50.

40. The notes on p. 116 make its provenance clear, though Prince's later note on the verso of the t.-p. says he acquired it in 1704. It was later submitted to a Commission for settling the eastern boundary of Rhode Island, but the Commission rejected it as "improper and insufficient Evidce" (ms. note of the clerk, Mathew Robinson, dated 23 June 1741).

41. In his *Chronological History*, he dated the formation of the New England Library from reading "Mr. Chamberlain's Account of the Cottonian Library"—"all Manuscripts," Chamberlayne declared. This fired Prince with an ambition "of laying hold of every Book, Pamphlet, and Paper, both in Print and Manuscript which are either written by Persons who lived here, or that have any Tendency to enlighten our History." Thomas Prince, *A Chronological History of New England* (Boston, 1736), Preface; Edward Chamberlayne, *Angliae Notitia* (1702).

42. Cf. Thomas Hutchinson, *A History of the Colony and Province of the Massachusetts Bay*, ed. L. S. Mayo, 3 vols. (Cambridge, Mass.: Harvard University Press, 1936), 1: xxvii–viii.

43. Mather, *Diary*, 2: 703, 708, 739, and 745; Kenneth Silverman, *The Life and Times of Cotton Mather* (New York: Harper and Row, 1984), 395–96, 428, and, for the litigation, 366, 381, 383, 397.

44. The best account of the Bradford Papers is in Samuel Eliot Morison's introduction to Bradford's *Of Plymouth Plantation* (New York: Knopf, 1952). The ms. of his *History* surfaced in the possession of the Bishop of London in 1855, and is now in the Massachusetts State Library.

45. 2 *Colls. MHS* 5–6 (1815), continuously paged; for other mss. that Prince used, see 2 *Procs. MHS* 17 (1889): 300.

46. So most modern authorities, beginning with Drake's *Memoirs* (1851); but cf. *OED*, s.v. "dispose," 8, and Winsor, xii. The advertisement of Prince's loans appeared in the *New-England Weekly Journal*, Oct. 28, 1728, and it was first misinterpreted by Judge Sewall (Sewall, *Diary*, 2: 1064).

47. The gift of Col. Moses Gill to the MHS in 1815. Prince's *Chronological History of New England* (1736) was planned to end with "the *Arrival* of Governor BELCHER [the dedicatee], in 1730" (t.-p.), the centennial of the founding of Boston. Some entries in the catalogue for octavos in 1731–32 are crossed out, and a sole entry for Franklin's *Experiments & Observations on Electricity* (1751) appears under quartos, 1731–. Winsor (p. xii) hence concludes that the list was not written before 1750, but the entry for Franklin looks like a late addition; and though some titles in the list were acquired in 1742, the catalogue must be a fair copy of a working list, probably drafted before the publication of the *Chronological History*, when Prince boasted that his collection contained "*above a Thousand* Books, Pamphlets, and Papers . . . in Print."

48. *Boston News-Letter*, May 23/30 1728; his earliest surviving circular, dated Feb. 20 1728/9 (Shipton and Mooney, *National Index*, # 39928), which could not be located for the Evans microprint series, is bound in the Paine copy of Prince's *Chronological History* (1736) at the MHS.

49. Shipton, 355; John Van de Wetering, "Thomas Prince's *Chronological History*," *WMQ* 3rd ser. 18 (1961): 550, 552; Michael Krause, *The Writing of American History* (Norman: University of Oklahoma Press, 1953), 47–49. For Prince's influence, see Louis L. Tucker, *Clio's Consort: Jeremy Belknap and the Founding of the Massachusetts Historical Society* (Boston: The Society, 1990); and on the frequent slur on Prince's "medieval" chronology, see Donald J. Wilcox, *The Measure of Time* (Chicago: University of Chicago Press, 1987), 195–203. It is about as "medieval" as the Greenwich meridian.

50. For the Norton family, see [George Lincoln], *History of the Town of Hingham, Mass.*, 3 vols. (Hingham, Mass., 1893), vol. 3.

51. James Truslow Adams, in DAB.

52. Edwin Wolf, 2nd, "Great American Book Collectors to 1800," *Gazette of the Grolier Club*, n.s., 16 (1971); Frederick R. Goff, *Incunabula in American Libraries: A Third Census* (New York: Kraus International Pubs., 1964), ix, credits the information to John E. Alden.

53. Alessandro d'Alessandri, *Genialium dierum libri sex* (1539; H. 72.2); it had been the gift of Cotton Mather to Thomas, Jr.

54. Shipton and Sibley, *Harvard Graduates* 6 (1942): 268–79.

55. Prince kept only three printed books from Nathan's library: John Callender's *Historical Discourse on . . . Rhode Island* (1739; H. 27.30); H. Hickman, *Apologia pro ministris in Anglia non-conformistis* (1664; H. 58.31); and W. Schickard, *Rota Hebraea* (1639; H. 501.18). Nathan's manuscript list of Harvard desiderata, entitled "The Lives, Characters & Works of all ye Authors in those Arts & Sciences wch I Intend to Gain an Insight into," with the New England Library plate but formerly in the library of the Bishop of London, is now in the Houghton Library.

56. *Boston Weekly News-Letter*, Dec. 8, 1748; Charles Deane, 1 *Procs. MHS* 17 (1879): 172–74; Shipton, 359. The list was drawn up by Prince himself, with notes of the prices and buyers in the hand of Gerrish.

57. Winsor, xii.

58. A copy of Richard Rogers's classic *Seaven Treatises* (1603; H. 60a.21F), acquired by the Boston Public in 1899, was inscribed by Prince to his wife in 1747. It is listed in Prince's Ms. catalogue of "NEW-ENGLISH Books & Tracts" at the Massachusetts Historical Society (above, n. 46), but it does not have the New England Library bookplate, which suggests that these bookplates postdate 1747. Nor do the Gill books carry either bookplate.

59. *Christian History* 2 (1745): 78.

60. These are Jean Gerson, *Opera*, vol. 2 (1496; H. 20a.4F); William Perkins, *Workes*, 3 vols. (1612–13; H. 61.4F); and Charles I, *Collection of all remonstrances . . . between the Kings Majesty, and Parliament* (1643; H. 78.5). See Michael J. Canavan, "The Old Boston Public Library, 1656–1747," *Pubs. CSM* 12 (1908): 116–33.

61. P. J. Wallis, "The Library of William Crashawe," *Transactions of the Cambridge Bibliographical Society* 2 (1954–58): 213–28. Prince's volume contains the *Tractatus VII* of the Jesuit historian Juan de Mariana (Cologne, 1609), bound with *Epideigma, sive Specimen historiae . . . civitatis Vbiorum* (Cologne, 1608), by the learned Stephan Brölmann.

62. For the various titles, versions, and editions of Nowell's "tribe" of catechisms, see Ian Green, *The Christian's ABC* (Oxford: Clarendon Press, 1996), 189–93.

63. Andrew W. Tuer, *History of the Horn-Book*, 2 vols. (New York: Scribner's, 1896), 2: 134.

64. Sewall, *Diary*, 1: 1126 (allowing the correction of an illegible reading).

65. *Harvard College Records*, pt. 1, *Pubs. CSM* 15 (1925): 200.

66. This and the 1790 *Catalogue*, referred to, below, were reproduced in Bond and Amory, *Harvard Catalogues*.

67. On Bumstead, see S. F. Haven, ed., "Diary of Jeremiah Bumstead of Boston, 1722–1727," *NEHGR* 15 (1861): 193–204, 305–15 (now at the AAS); Hazel P. Brook, "The Bumstead Family," typescript at the New England Historic Genealogical Society (1962); and R. W. G. Vail, "Seventeenth Century American Book Labels," *Procs. AAS* 43 (1933): 314, who, however, wrongly identifies the collector with a glazier who died in 1747; for his occupation see the Thwing Index (MHS).

68. Add Thomas Hooker's *Comment upon Christ's Last Prayer* (1656), with Bumstead's label, in the Massachusetts Historical Society; and *The Marrow of Modern Divinity* pts. 1–2 (1658; H. 86.149), with his signature dated 1713, in the BPL, but *not* in the Prince Collection.

69. Jesse H. Shera, *Foundations of the Public Library* (Chicago: University of Chicago Press, 1949), 52.

7. A Note on Statistics, or, What Do Our Imprint Bibliographies Mean by "Book"?

As *The Colonial Book in the Atlantic World* was being prepared, the question arose of how best to indicate the quantitative aspects of the book trade in the seventeenth and eighteenth centuries. We had at our disposal a recently created machine-readable catalogue, the North American Imprint Projects (NAIP, for short) located at the American Antiquarian Society. And we had the services of Russell Martin, a staff member at AAS whom we were able to employ for our purposes. But from Amory's point of view this question could not be answered until we had recognized the strengths and limitations of our data sets on which we were relying, chiefly NAIP but also its ancestors. Drawing on his immense experience as a rare book cataloguer, Amory knew that "our [imprint] bibliographies do not form a coherent series," the reason being that each employed "different measures and various categories of the book."[1] The purpose of the "Note on Statistics" he wrote for *The Colonial Book in the Atlantic World* was to describe these measures and categories and to warn historians not to rely on such lists for quantitative information about book production. Aside from their inconsistency, what were the flaws of these imprint bibliographies? Here and in a companion essay, "Pseudodoxia Bibliographica, or When is a Book not a Book? When it's a Record," he pointed out that such lists omitted much of what they should have included (e.g., serials, in the case of NAIP) and misidentified much of what they did include (e.g., in how they dealt with shared printing). Nor did a mere listing of titles indicate the actual scale of the printer's business. For this to be properly assessed, we would need to know edition sizes (how many copies were printed) and the sheet count for each printed item (that is, how much paper was used). Otherwise, we were comparing apples and oranges, according a single sheet broadside the same significance as a several-hundred-page book. As he pointed out elsewhere ("Pseudodoxia," 6–7), "the 6,371 colonial government publications might easily have been comprised in from 200 to 250 folio volumes." Hence it was "meaningless" to compare the ostensibly greater production of the Boston press with that of Oxford or Cambridge University in the first decade of the eighteenth century, when Boston was printing broadsides and Cambridge three-volume folio works of scholarship. For the American story, moreover, bibliographies organized according to geography told us almost nothing about the trade in imported books or the hybridities of books printed overseas for the American market.

Amory urged us not to include any statistical charts derived from NAIP in *The Colonial Book in the Atlantic World*, an argument he lost. Instead, he wanted to rely on sheet counts. Given the impossibility of doing so for the entirety of colonial printing, he settled on doing a sheet count of Boston production in 1765 (table 9.2 in *The Colonial Book*) and a second of Williamsburg, Virginia, production in 1760–61 (Table 7.1); related information for Philadelphia printing was included in James Green's chapter on the book trade in the middle colonies.

Anyone wanting to know the significance of this information should turn to the relevant pages of *The Colonial Book*. Meanwhile, Russell Martin was mining the NAIP data base for sets of data that, as Hugh came to acknowledge, alerted us to comparative dimensions of the trade and, in broad terms, to changes over time. These tables and charts can be found in Appendices 1 and 2 of that volume.

The moral of the essay that follows has not been heeded by literary, cultural, and social historians in the past and is not likely to be heeded in the future. Assertions as to the importance of this or that book or writer (e.g., that one-day wonder George Whitefield) abound, assertions that are often made without any awareness of the pertinent (and easily available) bibliographical information, as Hugh pointed out in the two review essays I cite in the introduction. All such quantitative claims should be taken with a large grain of salt; and anyone tempted to make them should heed Amory's analysis of the imprint bibliographies on which such assertions rest.

SOURCE: manuscript, American Antiquarian Society; a much abbreviated version was printed as Appendix 1 in Amory and Hall, eds., *The Colonial Book in the Atlantic World* (2000).

The statistics in this essay derive from the North American Imprints Program (NAIP), an on-line machine-readable database maintained by the American Antiquarian Society. Historically, NAIP may be regarded as a revision of the *American Bibliography* of Charles Evans (1903–55) and its supplement by Roger P. Bristol (1970), both of them cumulated and corrected in the *National Index of American Imprints* (1969) by Shipton and Mooney. All of these, in different ways, are national retrospective listings of American imprints down to 1800.

An imprint is a text that, in its fullest possible form, gives the date of publication and the names and locations of the printer(s), distributor(s), and/or publisher(s) of the book. Not all books have imprints, and in a surprisingly large number of cases, the imprint is incomplete or slightly incorrect. The missing or correct information must then be supplied from other sources, principally advertisements and/or the identification of the book's ornaments and type. Some books, especially the politically, morally, and socially incorrect, may have false or fictitious imprints. Like any discourse, imprints have a rhetorical dimension, though they are often taken as primary, objective "facts."

Since no one library holds copies of all the books ever printed, even from a single city, the usual tool for the systematic assembly and study of imprints is a union catalogue or database: the most general such catalogue in print (for books printed before 1956 in the United States and Canada) is the *National Union Catalogue*, and the largest such on-line catalogue is probably OCLC (Online Computer Library Center, which maintains the online catalogue known as Worldcat). The union catalogues described above are much more specialized. To some extent, each of them descends from, corrects, and supplements its predecessor(s), but in various ways each of them also describes a different set of books. The printed catalogues (Evans, Bristol, and Shipton and Mooney) are fixed and therefore authoritative; the online catalogue (NAIP) is subject to change without record and is therefore primarily a tool for distributing information. In general, NAIP is fuller, more accurate, and much more accessible than any of its precursors: as of June 16, 1997, it contained about 2,866 entries "not in Evans or Bristol," of which 1,162 were printed after 1790.[2]

Library catalogues form the basic sources for all these reference tools, and printed ephemera and engraved prints are therefore weakly represented in them. Ephemera are generally better preserved in manuscript archives where, however, they are accessible only by the class of their associated material. Prints are usually archived in museums, which also have large collections of illustrated books that are not recorded in these lists and, in any case, may be described on wholly different principles. As in any union catalogue, these lists were created by matching records of books, not by a direct comparison of the physical objects themselves. Our statistics therefore depend both on the collecting policies and the cataloguing of the contributing institutions, for the most part libraries and historical societies.

The scope and cataloguing policies of all four reference works are different, and the number of books they describe never exactly corresponds to the number of their entries. Evans designed his numbers as a measure of each year's printed production, so that he distributed multivolume sets, newspapers, and periodicals into their different years. He included entries for lost editions and for advertisements that he suspected, sometimes mistakenly, were for American imprints. He generally ignored variant imprints, a fertile source of additions in Bristol. As numbers, his are probably the most consistent index of annual printed production, but they are seriously incomplete.

Shipton and Mooney designed their "index" as a guide to the Readex microprint edition of *Early American Imprints*; as such, it could not include any lost editions, and it excluded the *Colonial Newspapers* that formed another Readex microprint series. In addition, however, the editors generally excluded any items that were printed in Europe, even when the imprints announced that they were for sale in America, and even when the sheets were reissued with cancel title-pages bearing American imprints, an exclusion that ran counter to the policies not only of Evans but also of its sister short-title catalogues covering British publications down to 1700, by Donald G. Wing and Pollard and Redgrave. Confusingly, too, Shipton extended the concept of a bibliographical "ghost" to mean not just an entry that was included or misplaced in a bibliography by reason of a misdescription, but also to cover a possibly correct description of a lost edition, and even an undeniably correct description of a surviving item that Shipton's purist view of "American imprints" had banished from that category. These reservations do not seriously qualify the importance of the *Early American Imprints*, much less Shipton and Mooney's magnificently patient corrections of Evans's descriptions; nevertheless, their concept of an "American imprint" must be resisted. The more reliable Shipton and Mooney are as guides to American technology, the less comprehensive they become as guides to American history and culture.

NAIP includes British printing that was issued or reissued in the colonies, as well as false colonial imprints like that perennial European canard "Philadelphia," but it excludes lost editions, however well attested, and periodicals and newspapers, apart from almanacs and keepsakes. It records multivolume sets of books and the separately printed, but continuously paged and signed, issues of state and federal legislative journals as single units of publication, yet it breaks up the separately printed, but continuously paged and signed, colonial session laws into their individual units of production. These decisions accord with well-established cataloguing policies, but they forbid considering the resulting numbers of entries as a consistent index of either production or of publication.

Single units of production (e.g., editions) as well as single units of publication (e.g., works in parts), moreover, may be multiply recorded in NAIP. Users of the *Early American Imprints* ought to be aware that the same edition may well appear under different imprints, either printed for a variety of booksellers in the same year or at different dates. Such bibliographical variants are known as "issues": although they were printed together, they were published and will be catalogued separately. Cataloguers, moreover, will often "analyze" a part of a work, especially one with a separate title-page, as a separate imprint. The first edition of the Eliot Indian Bible (1661–63), for example, contains the New Testament, first published in a temporary binding of limp parchment in 1661; the Old Testament and the general title-pages, published in 1663; and the Metrical Psalms ("VVame ket8homae uket8homoaongash David"), undated but printed in 1663 or 4. The three parts are almost invariably found bound together in full calf, as their English originals also were: separate copies of the New Testament (one at the Houghton Library, Harvard University in its original binding) are not technically imperfect, but they hardly represent the final intentions of the editor and his translators, and there seems to be no good reason why the three parts should not be catalogued together, in parallel to the records for scores of

other Bibles, as the "Bible. Massachusett. 1661–63." On the contrary, depending on whether the English or the Indian title-page ("Mamusse wun-
neetupanatamwe Up-Biblum God") survives, or even depending on which
title-page was bound first, the "Indian" Bible may be catalogued under either
title and/or analyzed under both; and two analytics for the New Testament
or the Metrical Psalms will be added, generating a possible five "imprints"
for a single item. Every effort has been made to eliminate such "analytics"
from the following statistics, but the problem of variant issues remains.[3]

The numbers of lost editions, I believe, have often been exaggerated by
compounding books, whose losses may be reliably estimated, with job printing, whose rate of survival is quite unknowable. Thus Lawrence C. Wroth,
generalizing from the Franklin-Hall ledgers for 1760–65, estimates that only
one out of 4.7 pieces that they printed survives today (*Col. Printer*, 216), a
conclusion that is widely and authoritatively repeated. The researches of
C. William Miller have now reduced the ratio to only one in three, but fundamentally, the whole way of posing the inquiry is mistaken. A disproportion-
ate number of the *desaparecidos* are ephemeral "job printing" that Miller quite
rightly relegates to an appendix. There we find some 280 entries for 1760–65,
representing "only a portion of such work" that Franklin and Hall printed,
since they often failed to record it at all. In the main sequence of his bibliography, Miller lists 128 entries for the same period: of these, eighteen
entries are for items such as tickets and currency that, however lucrative for
the firm, may also be considered "job printing." Of the remaining 110 items,
only four, all folio half-sheets, no longer survive.[4] Even if we add an estimated four editions of 2,000 copies each of the *New England Primer* and one
or two editions of Thomas Dilworth's *New Guide to the English Tongue*,
which Franklin may have printed but did not enter in the ledger, one might
estimate that some ninety percent of the titles he printed survive in at least
one copy today. By comparison, only seven percent of Cotton Mather's
exceptionally well-recorded production has wholly perished. Ninety-one
percent of American newspapers printed from 1690 to 1820 survive in at least
a single issue; eighty-two percent survive in more than one issue: not a bad
record for material that was frequently thrown away or recycled in out-
houses, and which was printed in tiny editions of 250–500 copies.

That there was a vast sea of printing in addition to this production of
books is undeniable, but we can never estimate its extent until we can match
the record with the survivors. It is essentially impossible to date job printing
outside of the context of a manuscript archive, and we can rarely assign it
to a printer because most eighteenth-century colonial printers used the
same types (by 1760, generally Caslon). Thus it is often the case that more

ephemera survive than we can positively identify in our records. Not that "survival" is very meaningful, when a single lottery ticket out of 14,000 is our evidence. Printed seventy to a demy sheet in a composite run of 200 sheets, the result counts as seventy "editions" of 200 copies each, conformably to the rules of entry in NAIP, an absurdity that is better avoided by not counting such items at all.

NAIP indeed was never intended to provide reliable and useful statistics of printing or publication; like any union catalogue, it was designed as a tool for locating copies and answering questions about their contents. Nevertheless, it forms the basis for most of the following statistical tables, as the fullest and most accurate account available to us and the one that would yield numbers at the cheapest cost. For the historical interpretation of these numbers, one should stress that they ignore imports, the most significant sector of the American market; newspapers, the largest single component of American production; and lost books, however reliably attested. The units in which these statistics are expressed, moreover, are of records, not of books: NAIP inherits Bristol's haphazard account of blank forms and other job printing, multiplies entries for the same book in variant imprints, and collapses multivolume titles into a single record. Finally, there is no way to extract any accurate measure of the number of sheets printed in colonial times from NAIP without a painstaking reexamination of every individual record and often of the books themselves. In these various respects, there is no ascertainable relationship between the numbers and the books or their production.

To control the misleading implications of these statistics, which possibly would have been better omitted altogether, we have tried to supplement them with brief *sondages*, impressionistic summaries of anecdotal evidence, and hand-counts from other bibliographies, principally Clarence Brigham's standard account of American newspapers. It is relatively simple to compensate for the absence of newspapers and periodicals, but there is no easy way to correct the other distortions. If one eliminated broadsides, in an effort to reduce job printing, one would also eliminate many items that most people would consider "books," including the *Declaration of Independence*. The identification of lost editions and variant imprints must be done item by item, and the incorporation of lost editions in the database would violate its rules of construction. In short, *A History of the Book in America* requires a database formed on very different principles from NAIP, for objectives on which there is still no general agreement.

Beyond such considerations of scope and consistency of record, the significance of an "entry" is problematic, since our statistics equate a half-sheet broadside with a thousand-page folio like Samuel Willard's *Compleat Body of Divinity* (1726) and ignore the size of an edition, which may range from fifty copies of a flyer to 10,000 for an almanac or primer. Brigham provides no systematic account of the size of the individual issues and their not infrequent supplements. To begin to control these elements would require consistent, accurate information on the format and collation of these thousands of items that is not, or not yet, available. As G. Thomas Tanselle has observed, in an attempt to construct statistics from Evans and Bristol, the data may give some "suggestive" measure of relationships, but their absolute value is of little worth ("Some Statistics on American Printing, 1764–1783," in Bernard Bailyn and John B. Hench, eds., *The Press & the American Revolution* [Worcester, Mass.: American Antiquarian Society, 1980], 321).

Even in assessing relationships, moreover, everything depends on our unit of measurement. Professor Tanselle, reckoning in entries, concludes that 15.9 percent of the 1765 Massachusetts product was printed for the government; reckoned in sheets, however, it was only 6.5%. Mary Ann Yodelis, in another effort to measure print production during the colonial period, used the number of pages as an index of the importance of an entry ("Who Paid the Piper?" in *Journalism Monographs* 38 [1975]). On this basis, she argued that religious printing was economically more important than government printing in 1765–75, despite assertions to the contrary by Rollo Silver and others; and that the Loyalists were therefore on target in attacking the "black regiment" of clergymen who criticized the colonial administration. Unfortunately for this argument, printers charged by the sheet, not by the page. Most government printing was in folio (4 pp. to a sheet) or in half-sheets (1–2 pp.), whereas religious printing was occasionally in quarto (8 pp.) but usually in octavo (16 pp.) or smaller; the ratio in sheets between the two categories of material is thus about four times the ratio in pages. Government printing in 1765 totaled 29.5 percent of religious printing (including the psalter) reckoned in sheets, but only 11.5 percent, as Yodelis reckoned it in pages.

In general, sheets are the only appropriate and accurate unit of measurement of production. An exact count of sheets, and indeed any cogent estimate of edition sizes, goes far beyond our project, however, and involves developing criteria for estimating the average sizes of editions from the extremely fragmentary records available to us: government records, still incompletely utilized by bibliographers; printer's ledgers and bills, available for only a few firms in Boston, Philadelphia, Williamsburg, and Worcester; and the occasional reports of authors, of whom Cotton Mather is the most important, or of booksellers like Jeremy Condy in Boston and William Hunter in Williamsburg.

Finally, one must offer a word of warning about the localization and dating of anonymous imprints. This is tedious and difficult work that can rarely be undertaken by library cataloguers, who must often assign imprints by conjecture, using the subject or authorship of the piece as "evidence," or referring to some authority that was often based on nothing better. Funeral elegies, for example, are often dated from the death of the subject, and localized by his or her burial place. The first systematic basis for such work was provided by Elizabeth C. Reilly's *Dictionary of Colonial American Printers' Ornaments* (Worcester, Mass.: American Antiquarian Society, 1975), but it has been too little used. John Bidwell, however, has shown what can be done with it ("Some Caslon Ornaments in Some American Books," *Printing History* no. 4 [1980]: 21–5); the dating of the states of frequently reused items like the Royal Arms in particular would be a useful desideratum.

Our fullest database, then, will not yet provide data as comprehensive, consistent, and relevant as one might hope for. Imprints tell us comparatively little about the geographical distribution of texts or about the people responsible for it anywhere in North America, and the assignment of anonymous imprints (adespota) is still very subjective. Charles Evans's *American Bibliography*, in some respects, is more complete and useful than its latest successor, on which we rely here, but one cannot consider any of them as more than a compilation of library records, which is exactly what a union catalogue is designed to be. In effect, a union catalogue tells us more about twentieth-century library economics and administration than about printing and publication, aspects of the book that can only be recuperated from a study of the copies themselves, their structure, binding, rebinding, and history of ownership. No union catalogue, even including the on-line Incunabula Short-Title Catalogue (ISTC), comes even close to this ideal.

Notes

1. "Pseudodoxia Bibliographica, or When Is a Book Not a Book? When It's a Record," in *The Scholar & the Database*, ed. Lotte Hellinga (London: Consortium of European Research Libraries, 2001), 1.

2. [As of January 6, 2004, the figures are 2,977 and 1,216 respectively, information provided by Alan Degutis, Head of Cataloguing (American Antiquarian Society)].

3. C. William Miller, *Benjamin Franklin's Philadelphia Printing, 1728-1766: A Descriptive Bibliography* (Philadelphia: American Philosophical Society, 1974).

4. [Alan Degutis wrote to me on January 6, 2004: "I fully agree with Hugh that it was a mistake to create analytic records for parts of a work. That practice was an unfortunate carryover from the practice followed in the AAS Imprints Catalogue (card catalogue). We've ceased to do that, and have begun the work of purging analytic records from NAIP."]

Index

Adams, John, 148
Ainsworth, Henry, 42, 55 n. 29
Allen, John, 90, 114, 117–19, 128, 138–40
almanacs, 83, 88, 89, 109, 113, 116–18, 121–22, 125, 127; formats of, 39, market for, 39, 54 n. 17; Perry's stock of, 87
Amsterdam, 128, 131; Bibles printed in for colonial trade, 24, 70, 72, 86; supposed source of type, 36
Andros, Edmund, 105, 117, 125, 135, 139
Artillery Company (of Boston), 81, 84, 91, 112
Axtell, James, 11, 12, 14

Bailey, John, 91, 125
Bailyn, Bernard, 39, 71
Barker, Christopher, 22
Barthes, Roland, 12
Bay Psalm Book, 69, 72, 105, 109, 112, 149, 152; false imprints of, 24, 112, 131; fonts of, 36; as icon for collectors, 40–44; printing of, 35–40, 45–48; Richard Mather's copy of, 41; sales of, 54 n. 21, 130–31; variations in text, 44–45. *See also* Bible
Belknap, Jeremy, 148, 153
Bible, 69, 88–89, 134; bound with Book of Common Prayer, 58, 68–95, 107, 131; declining supply of in New England, 58, 70–71; Eliot Indian, 11, 79 n. 45, 109, 113, 129, 166–67; formats of, 19–21, 24, 58, 65–67; Geneva version, 62, 68; German version, 58; pirated editions, 22–24, 68, 131; ownership of in probate inventories, 58–79; women and, 67, 69
bibliography. *See* New Bibliography
Bidwell, John, 170
black letter printing, 139–40
blank forms, 87, 109, 134–35
"Body of Liberties," 48, 105, 137, 138
book collecting, 146–62. *See also* Bay Psalm Book
Book of Common Prayer, 87; bound with Bibles, 58, 68–69, 107; imported copies, 95
Book of Martyrs (Foxe), 88
book ownership, 58–79, 90, 133–34; in

Essex County, 146–62. *See also* probate inventories
book selling, 80–104, 120–28; booksellers' stock, 124–26
bookbinding, 27, 83–84, 91–82, 127
Boone, Nicholas, 85, 92, 123, 124, 130
Boston press, 108, 115–19
Boston Society Library, 146–62
Botein, Stephen, 65, 81–82, 89
Boulter, Robert, 128
Bowers, Fredson, 12, 29
Bradford, William (of New York), 118, 124
Bradley, James W., 14
Bradshaw, Henry, 12
Brigham, Clarence, 168
Bristol, Roger, 168–69
Brown, John, Rev., 64–65
Brown, Richard D., 150
Brunning, Joseph, 123, 125, 126, 129
Bruyning, Mercy, 24
Bumstead, Jeremiah, 157
Buttolph, Nicholas, 81, 85, 90, 120–21, 129

Campbell, Duncan, 120
Campbell, John, 120, 139
Cambridge press, 34–57, 105, 111, 115–18; production compared with Boston press, 108–9; genres of, 109; sources of type for, 36, 38. *See also* Bay Psalm Book
catechism, 109, 116, 122, 127. *See also* Perry, Michael
censorship, 105, 107, 108, 118–19
Chauncy, Charles, 59, 113
Chiswell, Richard, 72, 85, 86, 128–31
church membership, 79 n. 46, 81, 100 n. 2
colonial book trade, differentiated from provincial, 7–8
commencement, Harvard, and printing, 111, 113, 117
Condy, Jeremy, 84, 101 n. 16, 169
congers, 80, 82, 89. *See also* Stationers Company; Usher invoices
Cotton, John, 42, 44, 60, 64, 136, 152
Crowninshield, Edward, 34, 41

Darnton, Robert, 3, 76 n. 2
Day, Matthew, 48, 111, 130. *See also* Bay
 Psalm Book; Cambridge press
Day of Doom, 5, 105, sales of, 130–33
Day, Stephen, 35–40, 46–49. *See also*
 Cambridge press
Dexter, Gregory, 49, 112
Dominion of New England, 116–17, 123, 135
Dow, George F., 61
Dunlop, John, 64, 66
Dunster, Henry, 33 n. 12, 34–35, 40, 42, 44,
 48, 111–12
Dunton, John, 81, 115, 123, 124, 126, 129

Eames, Wilberforce, 55
edition size, 86, 102 n. 27. *See also* Bay Psalm
 Book; laws
Eliot, Benjamin, 81, 85, 91, 124, 129
Eliot, John, 49, 107, 113, 115, 121; translation
 of Bible, 11, 16, 113–14
Emerson, Ralph Waldo, 11
Essex County, Massachusetts, and books in
 probate inventories, 5, 58–79, 137
ethnobibliography: defined, 12; used to
 decipher meaning, 24–30
Evans, Charles, 4, 7, 59, 72, 164–66, 169–70

Fleet, Thomas, 114
Ford, Worthington C., 81
Foster, John, 64–65, 115
Foster, Stephen, 81, 88–89
Franklin, Benjamin, 128, 135, 147, 167
Freeman's Oath, 46, 134

Gill, Obadiah, 122
Glover, Elizabeth, 35
Glover, Jose, 35, 49, 111–12
Grabo, Norman, 44, 45
Gray, James, 87, 126
Green, Bartholomew, 90, 110, 117–20, 139
Green, Samuel, Jr., 110, 112, 116–17, 139
Green, Sergeant Samuel, 35, 40, 108, 110–13,
 115, 117
Green, Timothy, 108, 119, 124
Greg, W. W., 2, 12–13, 28, 30, 34
Gutjahr, Paul, 4

Hall, David D., 61, 89, 167
Haraszti, Zoltán, 34
Harris, Benjamin, 109, 116–17, 123–25, 128,
 138, 140
Harvard, John, 59

Harvard College, 35, 49; library, 59, 60, 61,
 133. *See also* Cambridge press
Hebrew fonts, 36, 38, 118
Henchman, Daniel, 85, 128
Higginson, John, 134
Hill, Christopher, 69
Hinckley, Thomas, 151
Hinman, Charlton, 30
history of the book, 2, 3, 60
Hoar, Leonard, 38, 155
Hoggart, Richard, 28
Hollis, Thomas, 147, 156
Hopkins, Ann, 134
hornbooks, 127, 155

imported books, 5; compared with domestic
 production, 105–6, 128–30, 132
imprint, 105; definition of, 164; falsifications
 of, 58; methods of recording, 163–70
incunabula, 133, 144 n. 79, 153
Indian College, 35, 117

James Printer, 28, 33 n. 15, 114
Jennings, Francis, 11
Jesuits, 17, 28
Johnson, Marmaduke, 35, 113–17, 140

Keayne, Robert, 120, 155
Kellaway, William, 105
King Philip's War, 114
Knight, Sarah Kemble, 16, 33 n. 11
Knox, Henry, 83

Lambert, Sheila, 105
Laud, Archbishop William, 43, 68
laws: printed for various colonies, 85, 105,
 108, 117, 128, 135–39; distribution of, 39,
 90, 128, 132, 137–38
Lechford, Thomas, 107
Lévi-Strauss, Claude, 11, 14–15
libraries. *See* book ownership
Licensing Act of 1662, 109, 128; in relation to
 monopolies, 107–8
Littlefield, George E., 16, 40, 116
lost editions, 167
Lyon, Richard, 44

Main, Gloria, 64, 143 n. 66
Mann, Charles W., 22
Maori, 2, 11, 14, 28
Martin, Russell, 163–64
Mashantucket. *See* Pequot